Powhatan Bouldin

Home Reminiscences of John Randolph

Powhatan Bouldin

Home Reminiscences of John Randolph

ISBN/EAN: 9783744677844

Printed in Europe, USA, Canada, Australia, Japan

Cover: Foto ©Thomas Meinert / pixelio.de

More available books at **www.hansebooks.com**

SOME REMINISCENCES
OF
JOHN RANDOLPH,
OF
ROANOKE.
BY
POWHATAN BOULDIN.

PUBLISHED BY THE AUTHOR.

CLEMMITT & JONES, PRINTERS.

Entered according to Act of Congress, in the year 1877,

BY POWHATAN BOULDIN,

In the Office of the Librarian of Congress, at Washington.

PREFACE.

THE inquisitive reader perhaps has some curiosity to know how this book came to be written.

About fifteen years ago, I resided in Charlotte, my native county, and my business called me to the homes of nearly all the old citizens. Around the social circle they often spoke of JOHN RANDOLPH—never seeming to tire of the theme. So interesting were they, that I determined to write down their recollections, intending, at some future day, to arrange them for a book. I had the reminiscences of my father, the Hon. James W. Bouldin, to begin with. To his were soon added those of William H. Elliott, Esq., who generously came forward with a most valuable contribution. The manuscripts of these two old citizens of Charlotte, Mr. Randolph's own county, formed the nucleus around which many others were gathered. So that, in the course of time, I found myself in the possession of a fund of choice *ana*, which had never been published. The recollections of a large number of Mr. Randolph's old neighbors and acquaintances, which have been woven into these pages, insure a good picture, and give a pleasing variety to the work.

Since my task was begun, many of my contributors have departed this life; and it is fortunate that their testimony *de bene esse* was taken; otherwise the world might never have known what sort of man John Randolph of Roanoke really was. The original manuscripts which go in part to make up this volume, constitute a precious bundle, which I shall preserve with "miser care," as memorials of dear friends of the olden time.

Great pains has been taken to gather *fresh* materials; but, while gathering fresh materials, I have brought the works of others into requisition. Frequent quotations have been made from Sawyer, Garland, Baldwin, Benton and Sparks. If possibly a valuable book has been written, it is owing to the highly interesting and original contributions which have been kindly furnished me, and to the choice extracts from other sources. I claim no credit save that which attaches to the laborious bee, gathering its precious freight, here a little and there a little, from every blooming flower.

I am glad to be able to furnish the reader with a good likeness of Mr. Randolph. The engraving is taken from a portrait presented by a citizen of Philadelphia to the State of Virginia, which several old persons, who were acquainted with Mr. Randolph, have assured me is an excellent likeness.

It affords me great pleasure to express my thanks to several friends, who have, in various ways, and in a special manner, aided me in my undertaking: namely, Dr. H. C. Alexander, of the Union Theological Seminary; Judge F. N. Watkins, of Prince Edward county, and Messrs. R. A. Brock and John Booker, of Richmond, Va.

And now, gentle reader, hoping that you may be pleased, I place the result of my labors before you; and to all to whom I am, in any way, indebted for assistance, I hereby tender my heartfelt thanks.

POWHATAN BOULDIN.

DANVILLE, VIRGINIA,
January, 1878.

ERRATA:

Page 3: For *Parks*, read *Sparks*.
    80: For *jesture*, read *gesture*.
 139: For *Parks*, read *Sparks*.
 157: For *timid*, read *kind*.

CONTENTS.

CHAPTER I.
                                                PAGE.

Outline of Mr. Randolph's Life, ... 1

CHAPTER II.

His Personal Appearance — His Eyes — Voice — Incidents by Hon. James W. Bouldin and William H. Elliott, Esq., . . . 10

CHAPTER III.

At Home — House — Diet — Horses — Dogs — English Prejudices — Conversations — Recollections of Wm. B. Green, Esq. — "Unfortunate Temper of the Man" — Interesting Scene in Court by Judge Wood Bouldin, ... 20

CHAPTER IV.

Devotion to Old Things — Good Fortune — Electioneering among the People — His Church — Visit to a Young Lady — Could have written Childe Harold, ... 35

CHAPTER V.

Speeches on the Hustings — His Style of Speaking — Sketches by Hon. James W. Bouldin — Extract from "Schoolboy Reminiscences," by W. H. Elliott — Sketch by James M. Whittle — Recollections by Dr. C. II. Jordan and Hon. Thomas S. Flournoy — His Great Speech at Halifax Court-house against calling a State Convention, ... 47

CHAPTER I.

AN OUTLINE OF MR. RANDOLPH'S LIFE.

JOHN RANDOLPH was the most remarkable character that this country has ever produced; indeed, it is doubted whether there ever lived in *any* country a man so brilliant and at the same time so eccentric. A great deal has been written concerning him, and yet the public curiosity has been by no means satisfied. We purpose to add our contribution, which is composed in a great measure of the recollections of his old constituents and neighbors. But, before entering upon our proper task of *home* reminiscences, let us give an outline of our subject, reserving future chapters for the completion of the picture.

John Randolph—of Roanoke, as he styled himself—was born at Cawsons, near the mouth of the Appomattox river, on the 3d of June, 1773. His father, John Randolph, Sen'r, died in 1775, and his mother, whose maiden name was Frances Bland, married St. George Tucker, Esq. By her first marriage she had three children, Richard Randolph, Theoderick Bland Randolph and John Randolph. From the second union were born Henry St. George Tucker, Beverly Tucker and Mrs. Judge Coalter. The family residence was at Matoax, near Petersburg, Va., until Arnold's invasion, when Mrs. Tucker and her young children were forced to flee from that part of the country to Bizarre near Farmville. John Randolph was only two years of age when his father died, and fifteen at the time of his mother's second marriage. His mother was a highly accomplished woman, as beautiful in person as she was amiable in disposition, and withal a woman of great piety. Often in manhood he was wont to remark that his mother was the only human being who knew him. Through life he held her memory in the deepest veneration; indeed, he idolized her.

At the age of nine, he was sent to school in Orange county, Va.; at fourteen to Princeton, and the year following, to Columbia College, N. Y. When his father-in-law, Judge Tucker, was appointed professor of law at Williamsburg, Mr. Randolph was placed in the grammar school, and afterwards advanced to some of the higher classes. He seems not to have been well pleased with his teachers, that is to say, he complained of their partiality and incompetency, and expressed a very great contempt for college honors. Having never pursued a regular course of studies, he never graduated. Before leaving Williamsburg, he attended a course of lectures on law; he afterwards went to Philadelphia to complete his studies for that profession, entering the office of his uncle, Edmund Randolph, who was then attorney general.

While at college, he had an affair of honor with a fellow-student, Robert B. Taylor, of Norfolk, an account of which is given by Mr. Lemuel Sawyer, Mr. Randolph's first biographer. He states that the two young students "had taken opposite sides in politics, and were both fiery spirits and full of Virginia pride of chivalry. Their quarrel arose in a debating society to which they both belonged, from that most fertile cause, politics. For some personalities of an unpalatable nature, Mr. Taylor challenged him. They met in a field near the town, and the first fire was exchanged without effect. While preparing for the second, Mr. Randolph promised to hit him next time, which he did, dangerously wounding him in the hip, and he carried the ball in him to the day of his death. They were reconciled on the spot, and Mr. Randolph always spoke of him in the highest terms of admiration, as well of his high sense of honor as his superior talents."

Though Mr. Randolph did not pursue a regular course at college, in the solitudes of Roanoke he, no doubt, continued his study of the classics, and spent many of his leisure hours in miscellaneous reading. He had a choice selection of books, and it was remarkable how many notes in his own hand were on the margin of most of the volumes in his library. He was a fine Latin and English scholar, had a large acquaintance with history and was perhaps the best geographer of his day. Mr. Parks, author of "The Memories of Fifty Years," says: "He knew more, and knew it more accurately, than any other man of his country, except, perhaps, that wonderful man, William Lowndes."

Mr. Randolph was passionately fond of the sports of the field, and after he left college much of his time was spent in visiting his friends in different parts of the country with his dog and gun. He kept up a regular correspondence, however, with his schoolmates; indeed, letter writing seems to have been a source of gratification to him all his life. We doubt if any other man ever wrote as many letters.

Among his early companions was one by the name of John Thompson—a wild, dissipated, but brilliant young man. A warm and lasting friendship sprang up between them. Mr. Randolph invited him to his house, treated him as a brother, and used every effort to effect his reformation, but without success. His letters to him are filled with the tenderest feeling, the soundest advice and the largest charity for his faults. Joseph Bryan, of Georgia, who afterwards became a member of Congress, was another of his youthful friends. When Mr. Bryan had the misfortune to lose his wife, Mr. Randolph took charge of the two infant children. John Randolph Bryan, his namesake, in the course of time, married his niece.

Mr. Randolph's brother, Richard, married Judith, daughter of Thomas Mann Randolph, of Tuckahoe; her sister, Ann Cary, a woman of rare genius and personal accomplishments, married Gouverneur Morris. The hero of our narrative never married; but, in early youth, he formed a deep attachment to a young lady, whose name was Maria Ward—the daughter of his mother's friend. For many years they were engaged to be married, but for some cause the engagement was suddenly broken off. It is stated that the distinguished lover left the presence of his idol very much incensed, and that, when he came to his horse, which was tied to the limb of a tree near the front gate, he cut the reins loose with his knife and rode off in great haste. For a time, Mr. Randolph and Miss Ward were not on speaking terms, and they seldom met after their engagement was broken off. Miss Ward is described as having been a lovely and fascinating woman—the greatest belle of her day in the state. She married Peyton Randolph, son of Edmund Randolph, who was secretary of state under General Washington.

It is related of Mrs. Randolph that, when Gen. Lafayette visited Richmond, he was so charmed with her engaging manners and agreeable conversation, that he proposed to adopt her as his daughter, and, as she was in delicate health at the time, he invited her to visit him in France. She died, however, before he left this country for his home across the sea. John Randolph survived her several years, and it is believed that both retained, to the end of their lives, a melancholy interest in each other. He used to call her his "angel," and in one of his letters, written after her death, he uses this remarkable expression: "I loved, aye, and was loved again, not wisely, but too well."

Mr. Randolph had not only the advantage of a classical education, but the most refined and elegant society, having grown up with Peyton Randolph, George Mason and Thomas Jefferson. He had, besides, the opportunity of hearing the glowing speeches of Patrick Henry—an inestimable privilege to a young man of his aspiring genius. The glories and triumphs of Henry's eloquence was one of the favorite themes of his fascinating conversations. He was the constant attendant on the sittings of the first Congress. In one of his speeches to his constituents, he said: "I was at Federal Hall and I saw Washington, but could not hear him take the oath to support the Federal constitution. The constitution was in its chrysalis state. I saw what Washington did not see; but two other men in Virginia saw it— George Mason and Patrick Henry—*the poison under its wings.*"

It so happened that the first act which brought Mr. Randolph into public notice, was his answer to the last speech of the great orator of the revolution, he then being a candidate for Congress and only twenty-six years of age. And here we must be permitted to remark, that we have not language to express our admiration for his moral courage in undertaking such a task.

Then it was that the bright star of his genius rose, and thus early did he strike the key note of his political life. On the occasion alluded to, he spoke in opposition to the alien and sedition law. His family were Whigs, opposed to the adoption of the Federal constitution, and it is not surprising, after it had been adopted, that he should have advocated a strict construction of it.

Mr. Randolph was elected to Congress, and Patrick Henry to the Legislature, the latter having been drawn from his retirement by the earnest solicitation of Gen'l Washington, who greatly needed his services to save the falling fortunes of the Federal party. From that time to the day of his death, Mr. Randolph was the able, fearless, unceasing advocate of State Rights. He, at once, took position by the side of such men as W. B. Giles, W. H. Crawford, and Littleton Waller Tazewell; having risen to eminence more suddenly than any young man of his day.

As soon as he entered Congress, he commenced his war of opposition, for which he was by nature preëminently qualified. He opposed the bill for increasing the army in view of our difficulties with France; the great Yazoo fraud, the embargo during Mr. Jefferson's administration, and the entire system of restrictive commerce; the war with England during the administration of Mr. Madison, and all offensive war; the bill to aid the Greeks in their efforts to throw off the Turkish yoke; the Panama mission, and all foreign alliances or affiliations. He made war upon the national bank, tariff, internal improvement by the general government, the Missouri compromise—in short, every measure which, in his opinion, was calculated, in the slightest degree, to enlarge the powers of the general government, or infringe upon the rights of the states.

In answer to the taunts made by his political opponents, that he never proposed any measure, but was always pulling down other men's work, he replied, that he regarded it "the brightest feather in his cap." In a speech he delivered at Halifax Court-house, a few years before his death, he stated that "his whole aim had been to prevent, not to promote, legislation."

There was a wide difference between Mr. Clay's policy and the policy of Mr. Randolph. The contrast is well marked by Mr. Baldwin in his "Party Leaders," who says:

"Clay thought the general government a vast and mighty agency, which, made vital by the will of a free and energetic people, could accomplish, by its affirmative action, signal blessings to his country and the world. He desired to build up a mighty nation, whose power should be felt and acknowledged throughout the world. The American system was, through a national bank, to afford a national currency, and to facilitate the transactions of commerce; internal improvements were to be the ties of a close commercial union and personal correspondence between the different sections and to bind the States together with bands of iron; the tariff was to make us independent of foreign nations for the munitions of war and the comforts of life, and to build up vast storehouses of wealth for the country; the navigation laws were to foster an independent marine; the Panama mission to place us at the head of the continent, controlling and drawing its trade, and governing its policy; the public lands were to give to the States the means of improving their communications and educating their people; and a navy and army were to protect our commerce on the ocean, and command the respect of foreign powers. He boasted that he was an AMERICAN CITIZEN, and was proud of the title, knowing no North, no South, no East, no West. Randolph, on the other hand, claimed to be a Virginian, owing his primary and only allegiance to that venerable commonwealth, acknowledging the Federal government but as a limited agency, which she, with others, had established, for a few simple purposes. His doctrine was that that government should be watched with jealousy; that it had an inherent proclivity to enlarge powers, originally too strong; which enlargement would lead to the greatest possible evil, *consolidation.*"

It was in the year 1810 that he changed his residence from Bizarre, in Prince Edward county, to Roanoke on the Staunton, in Charlotte, in which county he owned a large landed estate and hundreds of negro slaves. For years he lived in a log house, in the midst of a dense forest. The yard was unenclosed, the trees were unpruned, nor was there a flower or green shrub to relieve the wild aspect of the abode of this descendant of Pocahontas.

From the time that Mr. Randolph was first elected to Congress, in 1798, until his death, in 1833, with the exception of a few years, he was in the public service, once as senator of the United States, but mostly as a member of the House of Representatives. When he declined a reelection to Congress, intending to retire from public life, at the solicitation of his friends and admirers, he was induced to run for a seat in the Virginia Convention of 1829, and was elected. His speeches before that body, as able as any body ever assembled on affairs of State, are said to have been the most interesting, if not the most effective, that were made. His object was to save, as much as possible, the old constitution, under which he had grown up, and "which was the representative of all in the past that was glorious and honorable of the land of his fathers." He opposed all changes; and where he found that changes would be made, he endeavored to make them as slight as possible.

A few years before his death, he committed the great blunder of his political life, in accepting a mission to Russia. He visited Europe three times. When his eyes first met the shores of Old England, he exclaimed: "Thank God! that I have lived to behold the land of Shakespeare, of Milton, and of my forefathers!"

Mr. Randolph never enjoyed an hour of good health, being a sufferer from bodily disease all his days. The death of his mother, his devotion to whom we have already noticed, was a crushing blow to him; but a still heavier blow was the marriage to another of the object of his early affection. "Long years afterwards," says Mr. Garland, "when the body was locked in the fitful embrace of a feverish sleep, and the soul wandering in dreams, that once loved name has been heard to escape from his lips, in a tone that evinced how deeply the love of the being who bore it had been engraved on the inmost sanctuary of his heart." He was greatly affected by the untimely loss of his brothers and other relatives and friends.

Having attracted, as no other man in this country ever did, the eyes of the world for thirty-five years, he breathed his last in the city of Philadelphia, on the 24th day of June, 1833, and was buried at Roanoke under a tall pine selected by himself, with no marble or monument to mark the spot where rest the remains of the great Virginia orator, satirist, and statesman.

CHAPTER II.

His Personal Appearance — His Eyes — Voice — Incidents by Hon. James W. Bouldin and William H. Elliott, Esq.

MR. RANDOLPH was perhaps the most impressive man that ever lived; and much of what he said and did could be gathered from the recollections of others, even at this late day. And not only is this the case, but his image is still alive in the minds of all who had the good fortune to see him—his tall and slender frame, his long, bony fingers, his dark eyes, his withered and beardless face, upon which there were so many wrinkles, his graceful bow, his lofty bearing.

The most remarkable feature about him was his eyes. They were brilliant beyond all comparison, and ever vigilant. When he first entered an assembly of people, they were the eyes of the eagle in search of his prey, darting about from place to place to see upon whom to light; when his person was assailed, they flashed fire, and proclaimed a torrent of rage within.

And he had a voice which was distinguished among ten thousand. One might live a hundred years and not hear such a sound as proceeded from his lungs; and the wonder was, why the sweet tone of a woman was so harmoniously blended with that of a man. He could be heard as far as any speaker, we presume; and it is curious that the individual sitting immediately under him would experience no inconvenience. His very whisper could be distinguished above the ordinary tone of other men. His voice was so singularly clear, distinct and melodious, that it was a positive pleasure to hear him articulate anything. The Hon. James W. Bouldin, whose "Recollections" are before us in the original manuscript, says:

"I once stayed all night with Mr. Randolph at Roanoke, and for some reason which I do not remember I slept in the same room with him. Having gone to bed, Mr. Randolph, at a late hour of the night, roused me by setting his books to rights and singing:

'Fresh and strong the breeze is blowing,
As your bark at anchor rides.'

"I thought his *singing* as far surpassed *other men's* singing as his *speaking* surpassed *other men's* speaking."

Mr. Randolph was fond of music and had a talent for it; but so prodigal was nature with him, that he could afford to let this gift lie dormant, from which others realize fame and fortune. He was perhaps ashamed to work in mines of silver and gold when diamonds were in his reach.

The moment one laid eyes on Mr. Randolph he felt conscious of seeing a great man. Under great mental excitement his appearance was unusually striking. On one occasion, when he was about to make a speech at Charlotte Court-house, says the same gentleman from whose manuscript we quoted above:

"As he saw the people gather around the stand, his eye began to kindle, his color to rise; and as he became more and more animated, his eyes sparkled brighter and brighter; and his cheeks grew rosy, the wrinkles on his face seemed to disappear with the sallowness and languor, and he became almost transfigured."

This was the case with Patrick Henry on great occasions; but the appearance of Mr. Randolph was remarkable on all occasions. "Patrick Henry's countenance, which," Mr. Baldwin in his Party Leaders remarks, "under the excitement of speech was almost articulate with the emotions that thrilled his soul, was almost dull in repose; and Mr. Clay had nothing but a lofty brow and bright eye to redeem his face from uncommon plainness."

There was nothing plain or common about the features of Mr. Randolph. When he made his appearance he not only caused the schoolboy to drop his paddle, while the ball passed unheeded by, but the pious member of the church forgot to say his prayers, and the grave senator turned his eyes from the affairs of state and fixed them on him. Other men were great, but it required some unusual occasion to bring them out. The slumbering fire must be roused upon the field of battle, or never waked to action. The latent energies must be stimulated by stirring scenes, or sleep forever. Even the immortal Clay was sometimes vapid and dull; Mr. Randolph never. His lamp was always burning. In him, the *vivida vis animi* was always resplendent. His feelings were intense, and all his faculties morbidly active. Hence, whatever he said or did, was done in the most impressive manner. His words and actions were so many vivid pictures which fixed themselves indelibly upon the minds of others. Owing to this cause, his conversations upon subjects the most trivial, possessed a charm which few could create, upon subjects the most important.

It is a remarkable fact, that we scarcely ever heard a person tell an anecdote, or repeat a saying of Mr. Randolph's, without attempting to imitate his inimitable style, and making at the same time a most signal failure. Each seemed to feel it a duty he owed to the author, to convey, if possible, some idea of his peerless manner. This, they deemed altogether necessary to forming a proper estimate of the man. And as they were forced to acknowledge, that they were wholly inadequate to the task, we fancied we saw upon their countenances, mingled with a feeling of dissatisfaction at their own want of powers of imitation, evident traces of regret, that such looks and tones could never be transmitted to others; that, of the magical powers which rendered him immortal, posterity could form no just conception.

It is not wonderful, therefore, that so many of his sayings are remembered to this day. We are confident that, while the manner cannot be conveyed, more·of the matter of what Mr. Randolph said, could be accurately reported from the memories of others, than of any man who ever lived in America. And the interest which he excited in his congressional district was wholly unrivalled. Wherever he stopped, those who had seen him all their lives, would stare and gaze at him, as if he had been some show, or as if they had never seen him before, or anything like him.

It is said that every great man has a glance which no one can imitate. A learned physiologist goes farther and states, that "every man of decided character reveals it in his eyes." We have already expressed the opinion that the most remarkable feature about Mr. Randolph was his eyes. The following incident, touching upon this point, taken from the written *memoranda* of Mr. Bouldin, will no doubt be read with interest: He says—

"Soon after I first knew Mr. Randolph,.I had occasion to visit Winchester, Virginia. On my way there I stopped at Gordonsville, and was reclining on the porch bench, being very tired, when a man rode up just from Norfolk. He immediately began on politics, and told of a rencounter which, he said, had recently taken place between Mr. Randolph and a Mr. L., at Prince Edward Court-house, a few days before, in which Mr. Randolph was so completely vanquished that everybody deserted him; but, while his young competitor was speaking, such was the attention paid to him, that you might have heard a pin fall.

"I observed that the tavern keeper looked very incredulous, and though he did not contradict or cross-examine much, he was evidently slow to believe the story. He had found out from my servant where I was from, and as soon as he had an opportunity, he asked me, when alone, how much of the story was true?

"I told him that if he would say *Charlotte* instead of Prince Edward, and *M.*, a man in the prime of life, instead of L., a young man, and then say *Randolph* instead of M., it was *all* true. For that Mr. Randolph and L. had no rencounter at that time; but, after several rounds, late in the evening, M. was left alone, except one man whom he held by the coat lapelle, talking to him on the same stage. This is literally true.

"M., a lawyer of about forty years of age, was considered a man of talents; though he was always objected to for loquacity.

"The landlord then explained his incredulity. He could not believe that any audience would desert Mr. Randolph, although he had not seen him since he was quite a youth.

"He said: About '98, he and several of his neighbors were Federalists. They held a social club at his house: dinner was being prepared and the gentlemen assembling, when two striplings came up walking and called for dinner. The club being assembled in a private apartment, the boys called him off frequently to attend to them; and seeing that they were genteel and intelligent, he asked permission to invite them to participate in the proceedings. They said very little and were modest all the time.

"After dinner, the company, with a cooler of wine, retired to a shade back of the house, and commenced talking politics very heartily. All made speeches in turn, and at last the landlord. When he had finished, one of the boys rose on his feet before him. He did not know which side he would advocate; but, as he was not accustomed to public speaking, he feared the young gentleman had risen against him. He raised his eyes slowly from the feet of those boys to the eyes of the one on foot and before him. He said, the moment he saw it, he was sure the d—l was in it; and he placed his eyes again on the ground, and there let them remain until the shower was over.

"Shortly afterwards, the company dispersed, and he found that the boy who stood before him was John Randolph, and the other John Thompson, on a stroll, he believed, on foot, over the mountains. He remarked that such a storm had never fallen on his head, as did on that occasion; and although he had not heard him or seen him afterwards; yet he had heard of him, and could scarcely have believed his own eyes, if he had seen a youth get the better of him, or an audience desert him to the extent described by the stranger from Norfolk."

Apropos of the same subject—we mean Mr. Randolph's eyes, we will make an extract from the "School-boy Reminiscences of John Randolph of Roanoke," by the late William H. Elliott, of Charlotte county, Virginia. They were written many years ago for the press; but the author, as soon as he was acquainted with the fact that we were gathering materials for the present volume, generously donated them to us, and we promise the reader to make frequent use of his valuable manuscript. Mr. Elliott is a man of decided genius, whose prose is only equalled by his beautiful lines in verse.

"The Rev. Dr. R.," says Mr. Elliott, "taught a classical school in the county of Charlotte, about fifteen miles from Roanoke, the residence of Mr. Randolph. Here I must observe, by the way, that this Dr. R. was one of the ripest scholars and one of the most conscientious and thorough instructors of youth that ever engaged in that arduous and responsible vocation.

"Among the pupils of this school was the writer and Theoderick Tudor Randolph, a nephew of him of Roanoke. The school was divided into two classes, one of which pronounced orations every alternate Friday evening. One class was named the Henrian, after the deceased orator of Red Hill; the other, the Randolphian, after the then living Randolph. The speeches were wholly at second hand — short extracts committed to memory from some British or American orator. On speaking evenings it was usual for the family, and company, if there was any, to gather into the schoolroom to witness the performance. It so happened on one Friday evening that there were some visitors, and Mr. Randolph among them. To speak before a commonplace crowd was a thing we had gotten quite accustomed to, and could go through with without having the nerves; but to speak before Mr. Randolph was insupportable, intolerable, annihilating. The class in a body implored Dr. R. to excuse them from speaking on this occasion;—but no, speak we must. The very reason we wished to be excused was his reason for ruling us up to it.

"The company was introduced, occupying one side of the room, and the orators arranged on a bench on the opposite side. The writer, who was the youngest, and perhaps the most timid of the oratorical corps, had to break the ice.

The Doctor looked towards our quarter, as much as to say, 'Go on.' I chose not to take the hint, because I had not finished screwing my courage up to the speaking point.— Dr. R. in the meantime filling up the awkward interval with some commonplace remarks to Mr. Randolph. But, all suspense must end somehow or other. At length our dominee looked towards us with a stern expression—'time for exercises to commence.' It was time to move now, live or die. I rose, advanced a step or two on the floor, and made my bow, without venturing to look directly at him. I saw that Mr. Randolph returned my bow, though no one else did. I regarded all the rest of the company as only so many saplings in the woods. It may well be supposed that I commenced in a very tremulous manner; for I imagined he was stabbing me through and through with his perforating dirk-like gaze. After twisting and wriggling about for some minutes like a worm in the focus of a sun-glass, I ventured to raise my eyes to him, and to my inexpressible comfort and encouragement, I found that he had un-Randolphed himself, *pro tem*. That is to say, by quenching his eyes, looking down on the floor, and assuming a listless, uncriticising air, he had diluted himself in the crowd around him.

"All this, I have since thought, was done to lessen, if possible, the embarrassment of the speakers; for he saw intuitively that his presence was oppressive. But, at that time, when I saw him look so humble, I fancied I was getting the better of him. While I had him down, I poured it upon him; my enthusiasm rose, and I fairly deluged him with a cataract of Fox's eloquence. When I concluded, he seemed to come partially to life; looked up with a pleased expression, as much as to say, 'That does pretty well.'

"At the conclusion of the whole affair, he arose and collectively complimented the young gentlemen on their creditable performance; but thinking, no doubt, he had witnessed a storm in a puddle, or a tempest in a teapot."

That voice and that eye will long be remembered. The former is fresh in the memory of those from whose ears almost all other sounds have died away, and his "perforating dirk-like gaze" will be distinctly recalled, when the features of the most familiar friends have long been buried in oblivion. Even now there are those who shrink from it; and although Mr. Randolph has been dead for more than forty years, there are doubtless some who writhe under the torture of his long, bony finger, which they fancy still pointing at them. There are words, long buried in forgetfulness, which if whispered in the ears of his victims, would cause them to startle as from a ghost of the spectred night. There are wounds inflicted by him, still bleeding; feelings harrowed up, which time cannot cure, wounded pride still drooping under the effects of his ridicule and scorn. Years after he had ceased to breathe, men would scarcely speak their minds, because his image was before them. So vivid was the mental picture that it overpowered their bodily senses, and it was with difficulty that they could realize the fact that it was John Randolph of Roanoke they had put into the grave and covered over with the sod.

His influence is still felt. The hoary heads of fraud and corruption, when the name of John Randolph is mentioned, are cursed with many a retrospection. From him they may have received their first rebuke. His terrible image is associated perhaps with their earliest and bitterest recollections. And there remain upon the stage of life, some of his old acquaintances, who dwell with pleasure and pride upon the advantage which they derived from his valuable example. For, while they may be forced to own that he had many faults; still they recognize in him all that is most noble and manly in sentiment, in personal character and accomplishments; and by those who even deny his claims to statesmanship and utterly repudiate the controlling principle of his political life, he is held as a model of an orator, equal to any which the Republic has produced.

CHAPTER III.

At Home—House—Diet—Horses—Dogs—English Prejudices—Conversations—Recollections of Wm. B. Green, Esq.—" Unfortunate Temper of the Man "—Interesting Scene in Court by Judge Wood Bouldin.

IN relating the anecdotes and incidents which we have in relation to our subject, we shall not aim at the order in which they actually occurred; when we attempt any arrangement at all, it will be with the view of illustrating more fully some particular trait of Mr. Randolph's character. But even though our incidents should be out of time, we are consoled by the remark of Mr. Sawyer, who states that "any facts, circumstances, or anecdotes relating to John Randolph are interesting and appropriate wheresoever placed." Mr. William H. Elliott, to whom the reader has already been introduced, once said to the writer, that "a few pages of *Randolphiana* would leaven a whole library." It might have been stated in the beginning, that far the greater portion of the matters and things which we shall publish is original—that is, they have never been in print before. We deem it proper, also, to inform the reader that the individuals who have furnished us information, reside or resided (for some of them have since passed away) in the county of Charlotte.

It was in Charlotte that Mr. Randolph lived from youth to old age. At his solitary residence at Roanoke he consumed days and nights in acquiring the knowledge of books by which he astonished the world. It was in Charlotte and the other counties of his congressional district, that he practiced the lessons which he learned of men, with such consummate skill. From the people of his adopted county, therefore, may be obtained a picture of the man. They can tell what sort of neighbor, friend and master he was. From them we may best obtain a description of his personal conduct and manners. It would be unwise to go to a distance to obtain a near view of our subject. Were we writing the *public life* of Mr. Randolph, we confess we should apply to the great men of the nation for information, but as we desire to learn his *private character*, we prefer a conversation with his plainest neighbor of intelligence to one with Thomas H. Benton himself. The great men saw him principally in public and on the stage; his neighbors peeped at him behind the curtain; and while we shall make some comments as we proceed with our narrative, we have undertaken to furnish the reader with materials to enable him to form his own opinions.

Mr. Bouldin, in his "Recollections," gives an interesting account of a visit he paid Mr. Randolph at his home at Roanoke. We give it to the reader in his own words, as follows:

> While I was a single man, and quite young, Mr. Randolph passed my residence, on his way from Prince Edward to his plantation in Charlotte, where he afterwards resided, and where he was buried. He said he would be lonesome, and asked me to go with him and stay a few days. No white persons were then residing there. I went with him, and stayed a week. It was during the war. At that time he drank but little—I think only wine. His manners were, during this visit, gentle and kind, as they always were when he was quite sober.
>
> It was not hunting season, and therefore we had no hunting; but our horses were saddled every morning, and we rode out in the plantation, or not, as we liked—together or separate, as fancy led. He rode most frequently along the roads in the woods which surrounded his house.
>
> He was minutely attentive to all of his household affairs, and his neatness and economy were praiseworthy and remarkable. His diet, though

simple, was excellent. His dwelling was at that time a single-story wood building, with two good rooms down stairs, and the roof had also two. He had no unnecessary furniture, but what he had was of the neatest kind, and generally of the best materials. His breakfast was coffee, butter and honey, with cold bacon ham, of the best quality, dressed in the most palatable and neatest style. If he retired to his room, I did not venture to knock at his door; and if I retired to mine, he would not call on me until I came out.

His conversation during this visit was varied. His remarks on one occasion were remarkable from their identity almost with a conversation between Bonaparte and Dr. O'Meara, many years afterwards.

He said: "Sooner or later Bonaparte would be put down, and that Great Britain would be the principal means of doing it; but, when she did it, she would require remuneration for her extra services and expenses, and that she would get it."

I asked him what kind of remuneration she would get.

He said: "Various kinds. She would require of Spain that she should have the exclusive trade with South America, for perhaps eighty years, by which time she would teach the people of that country how to rear all the raw material for her manufactories that she got from us—their soil and climate were better than ours for that purpose." He said that "Spain would grant it, and that we would lose the market for ours."

I think Bonaparte told Dr. O'Meara that, for not doing this thing, Lord Castlereagh ought to have been hanged. And when I saw what Bonaparte said, I was struck with the coincidence of opinion. Though Randolph hated Bonaparte, there was a remarkable similarity, both in expression and opinions, between them.

Mr. Bouldin, in his "Recollections," mentions two facts, which, he says, "If they were generally known, have not generally been borne in mind by those who have spoken of him and his character and peculiarities." The first of these facts we purpose now to give the reader, reserving the second for future use. Says Mr. Bouldin:

When Mr. Randolph took possession of his property, on his attaining twenty-one years of age, it was mortgaged for fully as much as it was worth. The estate consisted, I believe, of land and slaves only—perhaps some few town lots. By the time, or about the time, he went to Russia he paid off the last of this debt and interest, having in the meantime purchased nearly as much more property, and, I believe, paid for it. It has often been said by him and others, and was generally reported, that his estate was mortgaged for nearly or quite as much as it was worth; but I speak on the authority of the late John Wickham, of Richmond, Virginia, who told me that he had the collection of most or all of these debts, and that, without giving very long credits, the property, if sold, would not have paid them. As to Mr. Wickham, his character is so generally known, that it needs not anything that I could say to give his words or his judgment credit. Gratitude, however, for unexpected kindness, as gently and warmly bestowed as if I had either merited or had a right to demand it, impels me to pay some tribute to his memory. I say, *unexpected* kindness, for I was from rumor impressed firmly with the belief that he was cold and selfish. I was surprised, therefore, to find him warm and generous. I say, *if I had merited it*, because no man merits the kindness of another who suffers such impressions to take hold on him from mere rumor, or from the prejudices of others. A more manly, noble, kind-hearted man I never knew; a more social, cordial, jovial fireside companion I never saw. As to his talents, few, if any, in this country, have surpassed him at the bar or as a practical farmer.

Mr. Randolph, having no other resources but the proceeds of his crops, and the sale of a few horses of his own raising, and a portion of his slaves at first, paid his mortgage debt and purchased much other property. Need any comment be made as to his practical skill and judgment in business?

Shortly after Mr. Randolph came to the county of Charlotte to reside, Miss Francenia Bouldin paid a visit to Roanoke. Judge Beverley Tucker, his half brother, had resided there for some time previous, as master of ceremonies. It is scarcely necessary to state that Miss Bouldin remembered some things that transpired on that occasion. We envy not the intellectual treasures of the individual who came out of such company having received no lasting impression.

Mr. Randolph's conversation is represented as having

been highly entertaining, though it was rather on the "teaching order." Miss Bouldin thought he would have been still more agreeable, if he had not been in a perpetual strain. He seemed to be in a stretch during the whole time. She felt as if she would like for him to unbend himself occasionally.

From a walk in the garden, the ladies came in with some heads of rye, which they were examining.

"Ladies," said he, "I wish you better employment."

Mr. Tucker was caressing his pointer. "Sir," said Mr. Randolph, "You must never play with the thing you wish to command."

When dinner was announced, Mr. Randolph was not present. Mr. Tucker took the foot, as usual, and they were all seated at the table when Mr. Randolph made his appearance. Mr. Tucker rose, saying, "We did as you told us, sir;" and resumed his seat.

While they were at the table, Mr. Peter Randolph came in. Mr. John Randolph then seemed somewhat freer in his conversation.

"Peter," he remarked, "you see I have not forgotten how to drink old Madeira."

"It would be very strange," replied Mr. Peter Randolph, "if one so well versed in the practice should forget it."

Mr. Randolph was always at work for or against the feelings of others. This trait is illustrated by a curious little manœuvre which we hardly expected of this great personage.

During the same visit of Miss Francenia Bouldin, to which we have alluded, the Rev. Dr. John Holt Rice came to Roanoke. At meals, Mr. Tucker had invariably occupied the foot of the table until Saturday, which was the day of Mr. Rice's arrival,—then Mr. Randolph took the foot. He did not return thanks himself, nor did he invite the reverend gentleman, his guest, to do so, and it was generally understood that he had no other object in view but to prevent grace being said by the minister.

Why he should desire to prevent a blessing being asked on this occasion may be a matter of conflicting speculation; but, in the opinion of Miss Bouldin, he merely wished to make Dr. Rice feel himself checked and handled. He really had no spite against the religious ceremony, but, inasmuch as Dr. Rice occupied a conspicuous place in the community—was in fact one of the most talented men in the county—he wanted him to understand he did not mean to be under him, and he chose to take this singular way of showing it.

The following is from the manuscript of Mr. W. B. Green, a resident of Charlotte county, who was well acquainted with Mr. Randolph. His recollections were written in the year 1866, at our special request—not without reluctance, however, because, as he said, much that he was compelled to state is personal to himself. They are not the less valuable and interesting to the reader, however, who doubtless will be glad to learn something of the inner life of a most eccentric genius from such an authentic source. He says:

> Mr. Randolph was a frequent visitor at the house of Captain William M. Watkins. He was fond of horses, dogs and guns; and whenever he made a visit he brought some of his dogs with him, and they were suffered to poke their noses into everything and to go where they pleased, from kitchen to parlor. They were a great annoyance to ladies and housekeepers. This, however, was obliged to be quietly submitted to, as any unkind treatment to his dogs would have been regarded as an insult to himself.
>
> Very early in life, and before I knew him, he had imported English stallions and blooded mares, and at all times had a large number on hand. He occasionally put horses on the turf; but he was generally unsuccessful.

Speaking of horses, I may be permitted to mention an occurrence which took place at an early period, and which may be considered characteristic. It was court day and in the afternoon he offered for sale at public auction one of his best stallions. If I am not mistaken, it was Roanoke, by the celebrated horse Old Sir Archie, and out of Lady Bunsbury. For a considerable time after the horse was put up there was no bid made; but, at length, Hugh Wyllie, Esq., the owner of the celebrated race horse Marske, bid fifty pounds. Mr. Randolph was very indignant at so small a bid; and turning fiercely on Mr. Wyllie, looking him full in the face, said: "Do you, Sir, bid fifty pounds for a horse that pushed Marske up to the throat-latch?" There was a dead silence; no one spoke a word. The horse was led off the yard.

While I am on horses I will mention another incident equally characteristic.

You have doubtless heard of the great match race between Eclipse and Henry—the North against the South. Mr. Randolph attended the race. Just as the horses were about to start, a stranger stepped up to Mr. Randolph and offered to bet five hundred dollars on Eclipse. "Done," said Randolph. "Colonel Thompson will hold the stakes," replied the stranger. "Who will hold Colonel Thompson?" said Mr. Randolph.

Randolph saw the trap, and gobbled up Colonel, Thompson's friend without mercy.

After Mr. Randolph's death his fine stud of blooded horses were sold by auction at high prices; many of them were purchased by gentlemen who resided out of the State.

Mr. Green continues:

Although I had occasionally seen Mr. Randolph when I resided at the Court-house, I did not make his acquaintance until after my removal to Captain Watkins's, which was in September, 1807. Here I had an opportunity of frequently meeting him, both in public and in a private family. He was a frequent visitor at the house of Captain Watkins, where I then boarded and where I continued to board for many years after.

Notwithstanding the fact that I at a later period incurred the displeasure of Mr. Randolph, I must acknowledge that during the early part of our acquaintance he was polite and kind.

Not long after I went to live at Captain Watkins's, I had a severe spell of bilious fever which confined me to my room for six weeks or more. I was very low. During my illness Mr. Randolph paid me a visit. His suggestions in relation to diet and his encouraging conversation and sympathy were very grateful to my feelings.

When I first knew him he was about thirty-five or thirty-six years of age. He was then a Republican, and hated Federalism with a perfect hatred. But, notwithstanding this, he was always regarded, in heart and in sentiment, an Englishman to the core. In his earlier speeches he was guilty of what might be considered as bad taste at the present day, namely, too frequently quoting and making allusions to English authors—Milton, Shakspeare, Tillotson, Sherlock, Burke, and so on. The coincidence of manner and thought between the speeches of Mr. Randolph and the writings of Lawrence Sterne has always appeared to my mind so striking that I have not been able to resist the belief that he had, without making the acknowledgment, appropriated the manner and thought of that great writer. But however this may have been, I am free to acknowledge that, in my poor judgment, Mr. Randolph was by far the greatest and most interesting speaker I have ever heard or ever expect to hear.

About this time our difficulties with England had greatly increased—war became probable; the administration resorted to measures of restriction upon commerce, such as embargo and non-intercourse laws. On these measures Mr. Randolph took strong grounds against the administration. The consequence was, that at the next congressional election he was opposed by John W. Eppes, who was the son-in-law of Thomas Jefferson. In due time the election came on. Mr. Eppes brought with him from Washington what was called a *cart-load* of *authorities*, laid the books on the stile in front of the court-house—large tomes and documents, such as had never been seen by the natives. This was about fifty-five years ago. There was an immense crowd present. Natives and foreigners from all the surrounding and adjoining counties came to hear Mr. Randolph speak and to see the son-in-law of Thomas Jefferson.

Eppes led off from the stile, knee-deep in books and documents. He was rather a dull speaker—read too much, and fatigued the people. Mr. Randolph in reply remarked that "the gentleman is a very good *reader*." His wit and humor soon caused interruption by some of the injudicious and impulsive friends of Mr. Eppes; Colonel Gideon Spencer was the first who interrupted him. High words ensued; the excitement was beyond anything I ever witnessed; the crowd seemed to apprehend a collision of parties. Some friend of Mr. Randolph hallooed out, "Stand firm and keep cool," or something to that effect; then we have the reply of Mr. Randolph which has been so often repeated that it has become stale, "I am as cool as the centre seed of a cucumber."

Mr. Randolph remained on the court-yard for some time after the speaking was over. The excitement was even greater than before. Mr. Randolph at that time had an overseer by the name of P., a large, rough, raw-boned man, head and shoulders above the crowd. This man P., with a large horseman's whip in his hand, held in a threatening attitude, followed Mr. Randolph through the crowd, which was waving to and fro, insisting that Mr. Randolph would be attacked and that he should be protected; while Randolph, on his part, directed P. to keep quiet. The day, however, passed without disturbance.

In due time the congressional election came on, and I voted for Eppes. Mr. Randolph was defeated. He had proclaimed, not only in Congress, but elsewhere, "that he was descended from a race who never forgot or forgave an injury."* He certainly did not often forgive. I must remark, however, that the vote given for Eppes was not my only offence. On the revision of the State Constitution, I voted for James Bruce, the elder, instead of Randolph. In 1828 I was a member of the Anti-Jackson Convention, and used my best efforts for the election of J. Q. Adams. Mr. Randolph, in writing to his friends in Washington, stated that we were all for Jackson; the result of the election in Charlotte showed that he was mistaken, although the majority was large.

In addition to this, I had the misfortune, at a later time, to come in contact with Mr. Randolph in matters of business, the settlement of which might not have been satisfactory to him. I will mention two of the cases. There was a very unpleasant, I might say angry, controversy between Mr. Randolph and Robert Carrington on the subject of roads and right of

---

*The following is copied from a memorandum in Mr. Randolph's own words:

"Pocahontas (whose true name was Matoaca), baptized by the name of Rebecca, married John Rolfe, Esq., and left an only son, Thomas, whose only daughter married Robert Bolling, of Bolling Hall, West Riding, of York, who left a son, John Bolling, one of whose daughters married Richard Randolph, of Curles, whose youngest son, John Randolph, of Roanoke, married Frances Bland. Your humble servant is one of the only surviving issue of that marriage, and sixth in descent from Pocahontas."

way. Under an order of the County Court of Charlotte the late Dennis E. Morgan, Captain Fowlkes, and myself, were directed to view the road and report to Court. The case was a plain one, admitting of no sort of doubt whatever. The commissioners went upon the road, and found pasted up on a gate-post a large sheet of foolscap paper, giving notice that all persons whose names were written thereon were permitted to pass through the plantation and use the road as formerly. The paper was filled from top to bottom with names, male and female; and it was read over and closely examined, to see if anyone in the neighborhood, either male or female, who had used the road, or who might probably wish to do so, had been omitted; and it was found from this examination that Robert Carrington's name only was omitted. The land through which this road passed was not a part of his homestead, but a small tract then recently purchased of Dr. Bouldin. The report of the commissioners, in substance, was, that the land through which the road ran was exceedingly poor and of but little value; that the road had been in constant use, as a mill and neighborhood road, for about fifty years; and that it had been interdicted to Robert Carrington only.

I will mention another case, somewhat similar to the one above. Under a decree of the county court, Joseph M. Daniel, myself and others (names not now recollected), were ordered to make sale of a tract of land adjoining the lands of Mr. Randolph, which belonged to the heirs of a Mr. Lipscomb. The land was sold at public auction, and Mr. Randolph was the purchaser. As soon as the land was knocked off, Mr. Randolph, somewhat excited, stepped up to me hastily with his long strides and said, "Mr. Green, you cannot call this *real estate.*" And then said, "My attorney or agent, Mr. Leigh, will have a deed written and will pay you the money at next court." I told him that would be entirely satisfactory. Whether the land could be called *real estate* or not, it sold for at least double its value. But, when I saw Mr. Leigh (now Judge Leigh) he requested me to delay making a report, saying that Mr. Randolph entertained doubts as to whether the title would be good under the circumstances, the land having sold for more than three hundred dollars for each child or legatee. I felt quite confident, however, that Mr. Leigh entertained no such doubt, but was simply acting under instructions. I felt bound, in accordance with the decree of the court, to report the sale of the land, and did so immediately—stating that Mr. Randolph having left the county, and Mr. Leigh having declined to pay the purchase money, no deed had been made. On this transaction I may remark, that the land had been appraised according to law, and all the necessary forms gone through before the sale, and consequently the objection made on account of title was a mere pretext for delay. The explanation is simply this: There was an old man in the neighborhood whom Mr. Randolph called "the old turkey and 'coon hunter," who had greatly annoyed him by hunting on his plantation. This man, B., was the only bidder against Randolph. The land was exceedingly poor, and, to Mr. Randolph, worthless. It was purchased solely for the purpose of keeping out a disagreeable neighbor. Knowing that he had made a bad bargain, and having no use for the land, he determined to carry the matter into court. The court, however, decided against him, and ordered the money to be paid, which was accordingly done. I mention these transactions to show the unfortunate temper of the man.

I have now mentioned in detail everything that I can recollect that in the slightest degree was calculated to provoke or irritate Mr. Randolph. And what does it all amount to? Simply this: That on two occasions, I had voted for other gentlemen rather than for him; that in 1828, I voted for Adams rather than for Jackson, and had also, in two business transactions, made reports to the County court which might be considered adverse to him. This was all.

It was, I think, shortly after the election of the State Convention, when I voted for James Bruce and General Carrington and others, that Mr. Randolph approached my old friend and partner, Captain Watkins, for the purpose of breaking up the mercantile business so long carried on by us, and conducted by myself. He opened the subject by sending a note to the Captain to borrow a few nails, saying that he "did not wish to have anything to do with Mr. Green;" and subsequently, in conversation with Captain Watkins, he remarked that he thought it strange that Captain Watkins would continue business with a man who had always differed in politics with him.

Mr. Randolph regarded a difference of opinion a sufficient cause for severing business connections. The Captain was of a different opinion.

These facts were derived from Captain Watkins himself.

But, notwithstanding all that I have related, I, at no time of my life, suffered myself to indulge in bitter and relentless feelings towards Mr.

Randolph, being always disposed to make due allowances for the unfortunate temperament of the man. And moreover, I have the pleasure to know that some time before his death, his intolerant and vindictive feelings towards me had become considerably modified.

Mr. Randolph once ordered all his negroes to pull fodder on the Sabbath. The grand jury were considering the question of presenting him. The Hon. Judge Wood Bouldin, late judge of the Virginia Supreme Court of Appeals, who was an eye-witness to the scene in court, furnished us with the following interesting sketch of what transpired, which, while it portrays the character of our subject, illustrates the firmness and devotion to duty of one of the purest judges that our State has produced—we refer to the late William Leigh, of Halifax.

The scene described occurred in the circuit court for the county of Charlotte. Judge Bouldin writes:

I was present in court at the time, and heard what passed.

The grand jury had called up the subject in their room, and the late John Marshall, who happened to be a guest of Mr. Randoiph, and heard the order given to the slaves, was summoned to prove the offence. He positively refused to answer, because, as he alleged, he was Mr. Randolph's guest, and what took place under such circumstances, in his presence, was deemed sacred among gentlemen; and voluntarily to divulge it would be an act of dishonor, and in gross violation of the decencies and proprieties of social intercourse. The grand jury said they could not be governed by such a consideration in the discharge of their legal duty. Mr. Marshall still refusing to answer, the jury, through their foreman, appealed to the court (Judge Leigh). The judge, without a moment's hesitation, announced that a guest, however unpleasant his situation might be, could claim no such privilege as that asserted by Mr. Marshall, and ordered him to answer.

Mr. Marshall returned to the jury room, and about that time Mr. Randolph, in his English coach—a very clumsy vehicle, by the way—drawn by four blooded horses, drove rapidly into the village, and stopped immediately in front of the court-house. He came directly into the court-room, and took his seat in front of the bar, between that and the jury bench, and almost immediately in front of the judge. As he took his seat, Mr. Marshall, who had just come down from the jury room, approached him. Mr. Randolph, in one of his peculiar half-whispers, which penetrated every portion of the court-room, and which was heard as plainly as if spoken in the loudest tone, said to him: "I understand I am to be presented, sir, and I have come to make my own defence." Mr. Marshall immediately replied that the matter had been dropped by the jury, and he would hear no more of it.

Mr. Marshall, when sent back to the jury with orders to answer, had referred to the Revised Code of 1819, the then law of the court, and ascertained that the act of each slave was a separate offence, and the penalty only $1.67, being below the jurisdiction of the circuit court. The grand jury being satisfied on reference to the statute that they had no jurisdiction of the offence, abandoned the investigation, and thus the presentment was not made.

The foreman of that jury, if my memory is not at fault, was Mr. E. W. Henry, and he is still alive—the last of the sons of Patrick Henry.

In order to let Mr. Marshall know the line of argument he intended to pursue, Mr. Randolph remarked privately to him: "The Bible justified a man in pulling his ox out of the mire on the Sabbath. How do they know which is the Sabbath? The Jews keep the seventh day and we keep the first. Besides, if I hadn't pulled my fodder when I did, I should have been pulling the damned oxen out of the mire every Sabbath through the year."

After this, we are told, some of the preachers in the county thought it necessary to prove to their congregations that they were keeping the right day.

For the following incident we are indebted to Miss Mary Bouldin. It is related to show in what terror Mr. Randolph was held by the negroes of the neighborhood:

Mr. Randolph was on his way to one of his quarters, intending, it is thought, to surprise the overseer. Such a step was in keeping with his character.

He went by way of Judge Thomas T. Bouldin's, who happened not to be at home. Seeing a negro in the yard, he hailed him. The negro paid no attention, not having heard him, or not recognizing his voice. He called again, inquiring if there was any way through to his plantation. Hambleton (for that was the name of the negro) informed him there was no way through without pulling down fences; that if he pulled them down he must put them up. "And there is Jack Randolph," said he, "on the other side, who allows nobody to pass through his plantation."

"I'll have you to know that I am Jack Randolph myself, sir, and that I neither pull down fences nor put them up. If your master were at home, you would not talk to me after that style."

Hambleton by this time became alarmed. He was one of those persons who could never be awed; but he was scared outright; affrighted nearly to death. He meditated flight, but he was afraid Mr. Randolph would shoot him. At last he mustered up courage to go up to him; and by way of apology he told him he mistook him for an overseer.

"Sir," replied Mr. Randolph, "you knew better."

Hambleton went with him to pull down the fences. When they arrived at a small stream, presenting some difficulty, he offered to take hold of Mr. Randolph's horse.

"No man takes hold of my steed when I am on him," replied Mr. Randolph.

It was thought that nothing could have been more grateful to the feelings of Mr. Randolph than to have been told, in the way he was, that "there's Jack Randolph on the other side, who allows nobody to pass through his plantation."

He liked to have the assurance that all the negroes in the neighborhood were dreadfully afraid of him. To have heard this scene described by Hambleton himself, we are told, was highly interesting. From time to time, for several years, he was required by the neighbors to repeat it over and over, and they never ceased to be amused.

CHAPTER IV.

Devotion to Old Things—Good Fortune—Electioneering among the People—His Church—Visit to a Young Lady—Could have written Childe Harold.

THERE are those now living in the county who remember to have seen, on one occasion, a coach and four coming dashing into the village of Charlotte Courthouse, with a driver on one of the wheel horses and another upon one of the leaders. They came whipping with might and main, and in the height of their rapid career, the table of a poor old woman, upon which was displayed her choice stock of cakes, was overturned. Thereupon a shrill voice issued from the window, cursing and damning the driver for going at such a rate.

The driver responded: "Why, master, you told us to drive fast."

There are no coaches and four in the county of Charlotte now. Mr. Randolph was about the last man that travelled in that style. His clumsy coach was imported from England, as was almost his entire stock of furniture and books. He was the last man that kept a park.

There is a reason for these changes; nor does it consist in the want of means. There are men now residing in the county as able to keep parks and drive four horses as Mr. Randolph was. The reason is that aristocratic feelings, such as inhabited the breasts of our forefathers of colonial times, have been extinguished. The gentleman who, in our day, should venture to keep a park and drive four horses, would be pronounced an aristocrat, and would hazard his election to any office within the gift of the people. "Aristocrat" is an awful cry to be raised against a politician.

The revolution which caused the adoption of the constitution of Mason, as it is styled, produced a great change in the manners, customs and sentiments of our people. And the laws so earnestly advocated by Thomas Jefferson produced a great change from what we were under the old constitution. Mr. Randolph was the last man in the State, of prominent abilities, who made open war upon the prevailing opinions, who threw himself right across the current and attempted to arrest its progress. He was unsuccessful, of course. A single individual had as well undertake to dike in the Mississippi, as to check a great popular movement. By skillful management he may, to some extent, guide it; but never arrest it.

Mr. Randolph's prejudices were too strong to be moulded by the prevailing opinions. Indeed, he would have been a much happier man, in all probability, if he had lived in England.

The old habits and customs had passed away; the law of inheritance and entail had been repealed; there were no rich barons living in splendor, as in days gone by; when the father died the inheritance was equally divided among all the children; the poor and the rich intermarried and mingled freely together; the religious forms had undergone an entire change; the Church of England, which Mr. Randolph never could renounce, with all its pomp and ceremony, had gone down with the monarchical form of government, and the mind, taken from its ancient channel, sought out divers new modes of worship.

All these changes were deprecated by Mr. Randolph; nor could he ever tolerate them. His government did not suit him; his people did not suit him; hence, an everlasting strife with the surrounding elements.

We are reminded just here of a little incident related to us by an old lady who was personally acquainted with Mr. Randolph. She said:

"On one occasion, when he was on a visit to Judge Thomas T. Bouldin, speaking of his devotion to old things, he remarked: 'Now, if one of these ladies were to sing us an old song, and a young fellow were to come along, singing, as he came, one of his own composition, and were to say it was better, we would not believe him.'"

The old lady who related to us this incident remarked, that she could see in her mind the fellow singing along as he came, exactly as he described him, and that the scene was as fresh in her memory as if it had occurred yesterday.

Other men might describe a scene, and it would make no more impression than an advertisement in a newspaper; but, when Mr. Randolph drew the picture, it was as vividly impressed upon the imagination as if one had seen it with his own eyes.

During his canvass with Eppes, when he was hard pressed, Hon. James W. Bouldin states that he courted the support of the Presbyterian church. "He spoke in high and just praise of Dr. Hoge, a Presbyterian minister and president of Hampden Sidney college; no doubt sincerely, but more frequently perhaps and more openly than he would have done had he not been a candidate and hard pressed." He frequently talked about Dr. Hoge and his church, we are informed by another gentleman, in such a manner that any one who did not know him might think he had a notion of joining that denomination; but he invariably wound up by stating emphatically, that "having been born in the Church of England, he did not mean to renounce it."

He was too aristocratic in his feelings to unite with the Presbyterians, although there was no minister of his church in the county, and although he considered the Presbyterians the most learned of any of the other religious sects. He was attached to the old church and all the associations which clustered around it. He had no idea of substituting new forms and ceremonies, or rather doing away with all forms and ceremonies. He could not tolerate the unrestrained liberty of the camp meeting.

The train of thought which we have been following brings to mind a little incident which happened in Mr. Randolph's neighborhood.

But we must first introduce to the reader an old citizen of the county of Charlotte, upon whom we have drawn largely for opinions and facts concerning our subject. We refer to the late Miss Mary Bouldin, an old maiden lady, who lived to nearly a hundred years of age. She was one of the few persons we had the pleasure of meeting, when we were gathering up the materials for this volume, who could take in Mr. Randolph's whole career. This sensible old lady, whose mind was stored with an accurate knowledge of the men and things of her day, told us a great deal about Mr. Randolph. She might have told us what roused the generous feelings of resentment in his youthful breast, which first brought into notice his high and manly courage—the time when he stood upon the court green and bid defiance to those who, he charged, had cast a foul aspersion on the character of his brother. And she could tell the first time his transcendent genius was waked into life. She remembered some things that were said when Patrick Henry made his last speech on earth at Charlotte Court-house, and when Mr. Randolph, a mere stripling, had the boldness to answer him—the time when the crowd, filled with the eloquence of Henry, and indignant that any one should attempt to answer him, were suddenly arrested and brought back to the stand by the music of a strange voice which was to enchant them for many long years to come.

O! that was a glorious scene. And Charlotte Courthouse is classic ground, and deserves to live in "songs of distant days." It was there that one sun set in all its glory, and another of equal splendor rose exactly on the same spot.

Miss Mary Bouldin watched with no ordinary curiosity the long and brilliant career of that courageous youth, and no one could be in her company, when the conversation happened to turn upon him, without being edified and highly entertained.

Such was our good fortune one day, when the spirited old lady was reminded by something that was said of a rencounter which she herself once had with Mr. Randolph.

Many years ago, she informed us, she passed through Mr. Randolph's plantation over into Halifax county to attend religious service at the Episcopal church. On her return she stopped at Mr. Carrington's to dine. Pretty soon Mr. Randolph came in. But although, as we are informed by others, she possessed at that time considerable personal attractions, his was not the pursuit of the lover. No, "beauty had no charms" for him. But he had doubtless been brooding over his troubles in the solitudes of Roanoke ("quiet, to quick bosoms, is a hell"). He perhaps was suffering, from the want of mental stimulus, all the horrors of *ennui*—"that dreadful scourge and enemy to human repose." His chief pleasure, no doubt, consisted in the exercise of his mental faculties, and he was then in pursuit of talents which he knew would afford him some sport. He was aware, moreover, that the lady in question would not surrender without a fight.

The two were seated in the parlor alone. She said she saw the moment she laid her eyes upon him that he had some mischief in view, and she determined at a glance to match him.

The subject of her going over into Halifax to the Episcopal church was introduced. Mr. Randolph made a thousand insinuations, to the effect that his fair companion ought to have stayed at home and attended the "Methodist meeting-house" in her neighborhood. He put it in every possible shape. After a while he said something about the folly of talking about having an Episcopal church in this country. In England, he maintained, they could have such a church, but not here. It did not accord with the spirit of our institutions; and he was proceeding in that disparaging strain, when the tables were suddenly turned upon him by his fair companion.

"I suppose then, Mr. Randolph, you are a Methodist," said she, in her emphatic style.

He was highly incensed, but said not a word in reply. Yet, the muscles of his face seemed to contract to the size of his fist. Indeed, she thought his face at that time very much resembled a man's fist.

The reader will better understand how much nerve it required to make the above retort upon Mr. Randolph when he gets through this volume. We should like to have witnessed an intellectual battle between them; for, if he was of the oak, she was not of the willow.

Though Mr. Randolph was proud as Lucifer, and though the institutions of his country were repugnant to his feelings, and though he was of all men the least disposed to yield his prejudices; still, on some occasions he let himself down from his lofty state. No one can remain in any country for any considerable time, without having his habits to some extent modified by public opinion. The spirit of the age is obliged to have its effect, not only in changing the habits, but moulding the minds of individuals.

Mr. Randolph once remarked, that "if electioneering were allowed in heaven, it would corrupt the angels." If forcing a little civility towards the common people, for whom he really had scarcely any sympathy, be corruption, why then it must be admitted that he was slightly corrupted. He was never so civil as on the eve of an election. It was the Saturday before the Charlotte election, as we shall learn from the "Recollections" of Hon. James W. Bouldin, that he conversed freely and familiarly with the people on various subjects, and evinced a great desire to make himself agreeable and acceptable.

But, judging from one little circumstance, which was related to us by a reverend gentleman, whose mind was stored with some lively recollections of his peculiar countryman, we should say he had no civility to waste upon those who were of no use to him.

Riding from Prince Edward court he overtook a gentleman on horseback.

"How do you do, Mr. L.?" said Mr. Randolph, in the politest manner imaginable.

Having exchanged salutations, he informed the gentleman that he was a candidate again for Congress, and asked him outright for his vote.

Mr. L. regretted that by the laws of the land he was not entitled to vote.

"Good morning, Mr. L.," replied Mr. Randolph abruptly, and rode off.

Some men place themselves in the middle of a stream, to be wafted smoothly down by a popular gale, but Mr. Randolph would attempt to go right across, and the present end in view must be the object of his chief ambition, to induce him for a moment to humor the current. To ask an humble voter for his support was galling to his nature; but he must do it, or else remain in obscurity. And that he could not endure, for there was "a fire and motion of his soul" which would not suffer him to dwell in the solitudes of Roanoke. His unquiet spirit longed for high adventure.

In many respects Mr. Randolph was one of the most fortunate of men. Nature lavished upon her unhappy child all the noblest qualities of the head. She seems to have thought it but just, when she put into one side of the scale all that could depress the soul, to put into the other all that elevates the mind. She made him miserable; but she also made him glorious. More fortunate than Byron, who, says Macaulay, was born to all that men covet and admire, he was sprung from a house ancient and noble, but not degraded by crimes and follies. The parent, to whom was entrusted the office of moulding his youthful nature, did not pass from paroxysms of rage to paroxysms of fondness, at one time stifling him with caresses, at another time insulting his misfortunes. But she was a kind and gentle mother, and one who, while perhaps a little too indulgent, understood thoroughly the nature of her child.

Mr. Randolph was blessed in another respect. Often men spend years in employments for which they have neither taste nor talents. The prime of life is frequently wasted before they are aware of being endowed with a peculiar genius. Then perhaps it bursts upon them, as it were by accident, like a flood of light, and a new world is opened before them, filled with new life, new aspirations,.

new hopes. Mr. Randolph engaged at once in those pursuits best suited to his nature. It has been said that one of the causes of his unhappiness was, that "he saw other men of less talent rising far above him in place and position." We know not to what office he aspired. He must have indeed been hard to please, if being placed in a position, from youth to age, where he could attract the eyes of a continent to the splendor of his genius, was not sufficient for him.

We have a county pride (the writer was born and raised in Charlotte), a State pride, and a national pride in Mr. Randolph, but we do not regret that he was not made President of the United States. If, by nothing else, he was disqualified for that office by his misanthropy. Whatever pearls there may be in the head, if poison be in the heart, the man is unfit. One of his biographers might say he ought never to have occupied the presidential chair, "because he wanted the profound views of a great statesman.". His views, we submit, were profound upon every subject he touched. That is not what was the matter. His *affections* were too contracted. His views were indeed profound, but he wished to turn them to the advantage of his own State only. His mind was expanded, but he could never expand his soul, so as to include the entire nation. It is natural and well for one to desire the prosperity and glory of his own State; but if his feelings be as intensely Virginian, as Mr. Randolph's, his ambition should be limited to the highest position which that State can confer. And here we take occasion to remark, that the only act which mars the beauty of Mr. Randolph's political life was his acceptance of a foreign mission.

We repeat he was not qualified for a high executive office, nor do we imagine that he was much disappointed at not being made President of the United States.

In his young days he obtained a license to practice law;

but we are quite confident he could never have succeeded at the bar. It would have been impossible for him to have endured the necessary application to business. The field of politics afforded him the best opportunity of displaying his brilliant parts. The halls of Congress and the hustings permitted him to show to the world that he was not only a statesman but an orator of the first magnitude. Public life, moreover, suited his moody and restless temperament. He was not obliged to speak when the spirit did not move, nor to exert his body when he did not feel disposed.

In view of this state of things we cannot blame Mr. Randolph much for deviating even from his own high standard of political integrity, and for doing to the extent that he did, what he owned would corrupt the angels in heaven.

The feeling described by the poet in the following lines was never experienced by John Randolph:

"O, who can tell how hard it is to climb
The steep where fame's proud temple shines afar."

He was doomed to great mental anguish from many causes, and to much bodily suffering; but the pangs of the want of appreciation he never knew. The world at once acknowledged his preëminent abilities; and he looked as if he felt that the eyes of the world were upon him. At an age when most politicians have scarcely taken the first step upon the ladder he had ascended the summit. He was not compelled to climb slowly, step by step, but by a single leap mounted to the top. He was called before the public as it were by accident, and, as he says himself, elected by "sheer accident." In this instance opportunity conspired with his tastes and talents to develop the resources of his great mind. And he not only was following the natural bent of his genius, but his constituents had taken the advice of

Patrick Henry, and commenced with him in time. And if, when they elected him to Congress, the clerk before administering the oath of office inquired what was his age, they were not the least chagrined, for they felt entirely confident that the boy in years was a man in mature reflection.

We intimated that we knew not in what other profession Mr. Randolph could have distinguished himself. We forgot that Mr. Baldwin says he is the only man he ever heard of who could have written Childe Harold. There are indeed passages in that poem which breathe the same spirit of misanthropy and despair which pervade all the private letters of Mr. Randolph. Such as the following:

"I can no longer imagine any state of things under which I should not be wretched." "I am sick of both (men and measures) and only wish to find some resting place where I may die in peace." "What a fate ours would have been, if we had been condemned to immortality here." "Whichever way I look around me I see no cheering object. All is dark and comfortless and hopeless." "Language cannot express the thousandth part of the misery I feel." "They have dried up (his resources) one by one, and I am left in the desert alone."

Such are a few extracts from the voluminous correspondence of Mr. Randolph with his most intimate friends. They are filled with gloomy sentiments like those we have quoted. But we cannot impose any more upon the reader; the heart sickens at the repetition of such unmitigated woe.

How much these expressions of Mr. Randolph remind us of Lord Byron, when he sings of—

> "The dull satiety which all destroys—
> And root from out the soul the deadly weed which cloys."

Again:

"We wither from our youth, we gasp away—
Sick—sick; unfound the boon, unslaked the thirst."

And again:

"I have not loved the world, nor the world loved me;
I have not flattered its rank breath, nor bowed
To its idolatries a patient knee,—
Nor coin'd my cheeks to smiles,—nor cried aloud
In worship of an echo; in the crowd
They could not deem me one of such; I stood
Among them, but not of them."

We agree with Mr. Baldwin that Mr. Randolph could have written Childe Harold; but we are glad he did not turn his attention to poetry. If the muses had taken up their abode at Roanoke, a strain of bitterness and despair would have issued from its native wilds compared with which the song "To Inez" would be gay and happy.

CHAPTER V.

Speeches on the Hustings—His Style of Speaking—Sketches by Hon. James W. Bouldin—Extract from "Schoolboy Reminiscences," by W. H. Elliott—Sketch by James M. Whittle—Recollections by Dr. C. H. Jordan and Hon. Thomas S. Flournoy—His Great Speech at Halifax Court-house against calling a State Convention.

SINCE our plan is to entertain the reader with home reminiscences, we shall not dwell upon the great speeches made by Mr. Randolph in Congress. The world has been made acquainted with them by such authors as Thomas H. Benton and Hugh A. Garland. We shall devote our space mainly to the speeches he made to his constituents, of which very little has been said by those who have undertaken to describe his wonderful powers of elocution.

The Hon. James W. Bouldin was a close observer, had a very accurate memory, and heard many of Mr. Randolph's speeches on the hustings.

The first time I saw Mr. Randolph (says Mr. Bouldin) was at Prince Edward court, in October 1808 or '9. He was then at his zenith. For the first time since his first election, which was closely contested with Powhatan Bolling, some opposition began to discover itself to him in the district. It was said he was to speak, and I rode twenty miles to hear him. I remember well his appearance. When I saw him he was approaching the court-house, walking very slowly, and alone—a tall, spare, straight man, very neatly dressed in summer apparel—shoes, nankeen gaiters and pantaloons, white vest, drab cloth coat of very fine quality, and white beaver hat. Though he had no shape, but that he was forked, and had very long arms, all the way of the same size, with long bony fingers, with gloves on, still he had a most graceful appearance. His bow, notwithstanding it was slight, bending his body very little, and rather leaning his head back than forward, was winning to those to whom it was addressed, and seemed to carry with it marked attention and respect. His eyes were hazel, of the darkest hue, and had the appearance of being entirely black, unless you were very near him. They opened round, and when open nearly hid the lids, the dark long lashes only showing. Their brilliancy surpassed any I have ever seen. His appearance was remarkable and commanding, and would attract the attention of any one. His manner, though stately, possessed a charm to those to whom he wished to make himself agreeable, but had something terrible in it to those to whom he felt a dislike. To mere strangers it was simply lofty and graceful.

I said the first time I saw Mr. Randolph was at Prince Edward court, in October 1808 or 1809. I saw him once before when I was at school. He was riding by on horseback. I had the paddle raised to strike a ball while playing a game of cat. So remarkable was his appearance that I failed to strike while gazing at him. I had no idea who he was, or that he was a distinguished man.

Very soon after Mr. Randolph made his appearance, the people began to gather around the steps of the railing, where those who addressed them generally stood. Much curiosity was discovered to hear him, and I suppose of various kinds. Politicians, I imagine, wished to hear what he had to say on public affairs, and others for other reasons. My anxiety was to hear a great orator speak. He made but a short address; but I was much gratified. He was the first very great man I had ever heard deliver a public speech.

I remember his commencement. It was thus: "After, an absence, fellow-citizens, of nearly six months, I have returned to the bosom of my constituents to be—chastised."

We have printed this sentence exactly as it was delivered. Mr. Randolph made a pause wherever we have placed the comma or the dash. The writer has heard Mr. Bouldin repeat this little sentence a hundred times, as nearly as possible after the manner of Mr. Randolph. The reader will ask, why so much importance is attached to this apparently trifling matter? We answer: It was not the idea, but the *manner,* which impressed these words upon the mind. Strange, that thousands of expressions of other men, and events of momentous consequences, had been forgotten, while this sentence was as fresh in the old man's memory as if it had just fallen from the lips of the eloquent speaker.

I remember little else now of what he said literally. He was defending himself against charges made of his having deserted the Republican party.

As to his manner, its fascination was felt by all who ever heard him, and those who have not, can be little edified by any attempt to describe it.

During his canvass with Mr. Eppes, a Mr. Dabbs, a minister of the Baptist Association, took a very active part in the canvass in favor of Eppes, and introduced him to many of his brethren and others, he being personally an entire stranger in the district. Eppes went with him to many places where Dabbs had appointments to preach. Randolph went to very few places of worship during the canvass. He sometimes went to hear Mr. Hoge, a Presbyterian minister, and president of Hampden Sidney College—a man of great talents and piety, and though he had an impediment in his speech, was decidedly the most eloquent man I ever knew, except Mr. Randolph himself.

Mr. Randolph evidently courted the support of the Presbyterian church. He spoke in high and just praise of Mr. Hoge, and I have no doubt sincerely, but doubtless more frequently and openly than he would have done had he not been a candidate, and hard pressed.

On one occasion, at Sandy Creek, when it was rumored that Mr. Eppes and Mr. Dabbs would be there, Mr. Hugh Wyllie, a Scotchman, and a great friend of Mr. Randolph, wrote him a note, informing him that such was the expectation, and inviting him down. Mr. Randolph replied, in a very courteous note in pencil, that he should be glad to attend worship, but he could not violate the Sabbath by profanely attending the house of God for electioneering purposes.

This note was circulated through the congregation, and read with approbation by most of them.

He attended many musters and public gatherings during his two canvasses with Eppes, in the first of which he was beaten, and in the second successful.

I went with him on one occasion to a muster near where I was born. He did not address the people; nearly all at that place were opposed to him. He took me aside, and asked me whether he had best address them. I told him I thought not. He talked however freely and familiarly with the people on various subjects. He had much to say to a certain lady who was present—very intelligent, but I thought a little hysterical. He was polite and respectful to her, as he was always to ladies, while in their presence. I never saw him show so plainly his desire to make himself agreeable and acceptable as on this occasion.

It was Saturday night before the Charlotte election, which was the first in the district, the elections being then held on the different court days through the district.

He went with me to Charlotte court, where I lived, and stayed in the room with me until Monday. He kept in his room on Sunday, except going to the tavern to dinner. Sunday night he slept very little, and looked badly in the morning—drank very little then, but freely at the muster. In the morning when I went to breakfast he did not go, but asked me to send him a bottle of wine with his breakfast:

He was very fond of good coffee, and had it strong and excellent at home, but he would hardly drink it bad.* He preferred bad wine, if he could get neither good. He made his breakfast principally on wine, and drank the most of the bottle, yet it did not intoxicate him.

Shortly after breakfast he dressed himself with great neatness and care. He looked very languid and pale, as he always did, when he was quite sober and not excited.

There was great expectation from the orators, especially from Mr. Randolph. My door was immediately in view of the rostrum, where he always stood to speak. The people began to draw around this place, to be sure of a stand near it, very early in the morning.

While he was walking backward and forward, his eyes flashing with more and more brilliancy, as the crowd became larger and larger, he exclaimed: "The subject is so large I do not know where to lay hold on it first."

---

* On one occasion he was at breakfast, when a cup was set at his plate. "Servant," said he, "If this be coffee, give me tea, and if it be tea, give me coffee."

It was still early; but said I, "Sir, you see the crowd is gathered around the stand, and if you do not begin, Eppes will begin first, and read until sunset, and you will be wearied to death before you get a chance to say a word." He immediately made his way through the crowd, which was at this time large and dense, and commenced his address. I was much engaged at the time, and did not go out until he had nearly gotten through.

I do not know how Mr. Eppes appeared elsewhere, and in comparison with others; but compared with Mr. Randoph and on the hustings I thought him dull and heavy. He was self-possessed, and much of a gentleman, but I thought greatly inferior to Randolph in eloquence and ability.

Probably Mr. Randolph's greatest efforts at speaking were made during the canvass with Mr. Eppes, in which he was beaten. I heard many of them, including the one at Prince Edward court, in the Fall preceding the election. He was told by a friend that this was considered to be the best speech he ever made. He replied, that it was the only time he ever felt conscious of being eloquent while speaking. He remarked that he felt the truth of what Mark Anthony said—"Passion, thou art catching"— that he felt the electricity passing from him to the crowd, and from the crowd back to him.

I remember but one expression, literally, during that speech. Speaking of Bonaparte's strides to universal dominion, he said: "He stood with one foot upon European and the other upon American shores. It is said that Moloch smiled at the blood of human sacrifice running at the foot of the altar; this great arch enemy of mankind is now grinning and smiling at American blood, flowing in support of his inordinate ambition."

He spoke for an hour, perhaps, and when he concluded, I found myself musing and walking without any aim or object; and looking around, found the crowd gradually dispersing in the same mood. The Rev. Moses Hoge was sitting in a chair opposite the speaker, and remained till I observed him, still with his mouth open, and looking steadfastly in the same direction. Parson Lyle was standing by him. Said Mr. Hoge to Lyle, "I never heard the like before, and I never expect to hear the like again."

It was at the next succeeding Charlotte court that he made the reply to Colonel S. that has sometimes been alluded to in print.

Mr. Eppes had lately moved into the district, and Mr. Randolph charged him with having been imported, like a stallion, for the purpose of being run against him. He said the district had no necessity to import one; they had good stock of their own. If the people did not like his services, they could elect one from their own stock. "Where are your Daniels, your Bouldins, your Carringtons,"—and was proceeding with the enumeration, but made a pause as was much his custom (he spoke very slowly and distinctly). Said Colonel S., "There are other families in the district as respectable as those you have mentioned." "Certainly," replied Mr. Randolph, "None more so than the S.'s, but you are an exception."

Mr. Eppes read many documents at Prince Edward and more at Charlotte court. When Mr. Randolph rose to reply, he said: "It is true I am not asleep, but I must confess I am somewhat drowsy. The gentleman may not have improved in his speaking, but he certainly gets along in his reading."

The collision with Colonel S., and other circumstances, made this address rather of the satirical order, than of the grave and sublime character of that at Prince Edward court. Severe repartees and remarks creating great mirth at the expense of others, overshadowed in a measure the able and eloquent view he took of the politics of that day.

On this, or on some other occasion about that time, having been often interrupted with much heat by the same Colonel S., who was not only of a highly respectable family, but was highly respectable himself, yet a little too warm in party politics, Mr. Randolph was admonished to keep cool and not to be provoked to rashness. "I am as cool," said he, "as the centre seed of a cucumber."

He had all the deliberation, self-possession and outward calmness that would belong to a man who was cool, and he was guarded; still I thought his mind and passions were roused to the highest pitch of excitement. The fiery vengeance that burns and flashes in the eyes of an enraged tiger cannot be mistaken for coolness, however deliberate he may be in preparing to make his spring.

When Jerman Baker was a rival candidate for Congress, Mr. Randolph treated him with great kindness and forbearance, considering his usual treatment towards his opponents.

On one occasion, when Mr. Baker was promising what he would do, if elected, Mr. Randolph, in reply, said: "The gentleman and I stand on very different ground. I stand on fourteen years' hard bought experience. He is in the land of promise which always flows with milk and honey;" and presently afterwards he said, "A new broom sweeps clean, but an old one knows where the dirt lies."

As Mr. Baker stood no chance of election, and was moderate in his abilities, there was no great interest in that canvass.

When Mr. Austin was a candidate, and Mr. Randolph declined a reëlection to Congress, expecting to go to Europe for his health, he took leave of his constituents by riding around to the elections, and addressing the people in the morning, before Mr. Austin began. These addresses were of a character wholly different from any made by him on any other occasion, that I ever knew of. They were filled with grave and solemn advices, and the most pathetic appeals to the sympathies of the district, without the least allusion to party or feud.

I remember *verbatim* a portion of the commencement of a speech he made at Charlotte court, which, from its peculiar style of parenthesis, will be recognized by all who were acquainted with his manner of expression. He was excusing himself, on the ground of ill health, for declining the service of the people, after their long continued 'confidence in him. He said:

"I am going across the sea to patch up and preserve a shattered frame —a frame worn out in your service, and to lengthen out, yet a little longer, (hitherto certainly,) not a very happy existence; for, excepting the one upbraided by a guilty conscience, no life can be more unhappy, than that, the days of which are spent in pain and sickness, and the nights in travail and sorrow."

During this address he remarked: "I was going to say in the sincerity of the poet, but the sincerity of the poet is somewhat doubted;—I can say with a truth, in the language of the poet,—

'Fare ye well; and if forever,
Still forever, fare ye well.'"

Just as he had concluded, and was putting on his hat (he always spoke with it off), as he was stepping down to the next step, weak and somewhat tottering, he said: "The flesh is indeed weak,'though the spirit is strong."

Mr. J. Robinson, a clergyman of distinguished ability, dined with me the day on which he made this speech. He was opposed to Mr. Randolph in politics, but was a great admirer of his genius. He remarked: " He had not supposed that Mr. Randolph had any pathos, as he had never before heard him in that strain, but that now he was forced to confess, after having heard all the distinguished orators of the then just past age, from Patrick Henry down, that Mr. Randolph was the most pathetic man he ever heard open his lips."

I certainly saw tears roll down the cheeks of men who hated him then, and would curse his memory now if he were named in their presence.

I think these addresses did more to make firm his popularity, which, during the war, had been a little shaken, than anything he ever did. They soothed, softened, and set aside much of the bitterness which had been engendered during those bitter party conflicts.

Though this was the first and only time I ever heard Mr. Randolph deliver a speech *wholly* in this strain of pathos, and sober wisdom and counsel, I had often witnessed touches of the same in other speeches, and his power of fascination in private, when he chose to exert it, with wonder and amazement."

We once asked one of Mr. Randolph's old constituents to tell us which of all his speeches he considered the best. He replied, the one he made at Charlotte Court-house, soon after the adjournment of the Virginia Convention of 1829. In this address he gave an account of his stewardship and the proceedings of said convention. On this occasion he is reported to have used the following language: "I appear here to take my leave of you for the last time. Now what shall I say? Twenty-eight years ago you took me by the hand, when a beardless boy, and handed me to Congress. I have served you in a public capacity ever since. That I have committed errors I readily believe, being a descendant of Adam, and full of bruises and putrifying sores, from the crown of my head to the sole of my feet. People of Charlotte! which of you is without sin?" (A voice in the crowd exclaimed, 'Gracious God! what preaching.')"

Speaking of the trust committed to him by his confiding

constituents, the duties of which he had so long discharged, he made use of the following expression: "Take it back, take it back," at the same time moving his hand forward towards the multitude. Mr John Henry, son of the immortal Patrick Henry, who was present, says he instinctively shrank back, feeling as if the speaker was about to roll a tremendous stone upon him. Just as the orator concluded, and while still under the intoxicating effects of his eloquence, Mr. Henry's brother turned to him, and exclaimed, "He is almost a God!"

For the following description of Mr. Randolph's style of speaking, we are indebted to Mr. William H. Elliott:

"It has been said by some, who have heard Mr. Randolph both in Congress and on the hustings, that on the latter theatre he made his most fascinating and brilliant displays. I never heard him in Congress, but I cannot conceive that anything he uttered there could possibly surpass what I have heard on the hustings.

Most generally, whenever it was expected he would speak, a large proportion of the crowd would anticipate his arrival by some hour or two, and gather around the stand to secure a close proximity to the speaker. But when he was seen to move forward to the rostrum, then the courthouse, every store, and tavern, and peddlar's stall, and auctioneer's stand, and private residence, was deserted, and the speaker saw beneath him a motionless mass of humanity, and a sea of upturned faces. When he rose, with a deliberate motion he took off his hat, and made a slight inclination of the body, a motion in which grace and humility seemed inexplicably blended. Now the grace was natural, but the humility was affected, but with such consummate address as to pass for genuine, except among those who know that *artis est celare artem*. His exordium was brief, but always peculiarly appropriate. His gestures were few and simple, yet exactly no more or fewer than what the occasion called for. With many public speakers there seems to be an unpruned luxuriance of gesticulation, laboring most painfully to bring forth a mouse of an idea. But, in the case of Mr. Randolph, the idea was sure to be bigger than the gesture that accompanied it. His voice was unique, but yet so perfect was his pronunciation, and so sharp the outlines of every sound, that, as far as his voice could be heard, his words could be distinguished. In short, his speaking was exquisite vocal music. An accurate ear could distinguish, as he went along, commas, semi-colons, colons, full stops, exclamation and interrogation points, all in their proper places. In adverting to what he conceived to be the overruling agency of Providence in the affairs of man, no minister of the gospel could raise his eyes to heaven with a look more impressively reverential. If the reader will look at Hamlet's advice to the players, and conceive it to be punctually followed to the letter, Shakspeare will give him a better idea of Randolph's oratory than he can derive from any other source.* He seemed to have discarded from his vocabulary most of those sonorous *sesquipedalia verba*, which enter so largely into the staple of modern oratory, and to have trimmed down his language to the nudest possible simplicity consistent with strength. When he had gotten fully warmed with the subject, all idea of anything nearer to perfection in eloquence was held in utter abeyance, and when he concluded all felt that they had never heard the like before, for the speeches of this remarkable man were characterized by all that is conclusive in argument, original in conception, felicitous in illustration, forcible in language, and faultless in delivery."

We purpose now to lay before the reader a highly interesting sketch of a speech made by Mr. Randolph at Halifax Court-house, in the year 1827. It is from the pen of the late Dr. C. H. Jordan, formerly a citizen of Halifax county, Virginia, but a resident of the State of North Carolina at the time of his death. Dr. Jordan was a gentleman of the purest type, and, as the reader will discover, a most forcible writer.

Accompanying his Randolphiana, he addressed to us a letter in which he says: "The lapse of time has greatly increased the difficulties of doing him and his subject the justice which I so much desire. Forty years ago, I could have repeated whole paragraphs from his various arguments; but now I cannot do it.

---

*Hamlet, act III, scene II.

In many instances, when I put his words in quotation marks, the language is precisely his. In others, I have used the quotations with a less vivid recollection of his precise words. But for fear some one might think that I was disposed to appropriate to myself what rightfully belonged to Mr. Randolph, I have also used them, especially where my recollection of the sentiment is distinct."

The article referred to is headed: "Mr. Randolph's Great Speech at Halifax Courthouse in the Spring of 1827."

Dr. Jordan says:

Mr. Randolph's was a peculiar physical organization, encasing one of the most astute, philosophic minds of his or any other day. No statesman ever looked into or predicted the future of any governmental policy with more accuracy than did Mr. Randolph.

But to give those who never saw him some idea of his personal appearance and presence, I may say that he was tall, slender, delicate and feeble, with a short body, long legs and arms, and the longest fingers I ever saw. His head was not very large, but was symmetrical in the highest degree. His eyes were brilliant beyond description, indicating to a thoughtful observer a brain of the highest order. No one could look into them without having this truth so indelibly impressed upon his own mind that time's busy fingers may strive in vain to efface the impression. His eye, his forefinger and his foot were the members used in gesticulation; and, in impressing a solemn truth, a warning, or a proposition to which he wished to call the attention of his audience particularly, he could use his foot with singular and thrilling effect. The ring of the slight patting of his foot was in perfect accord with the clear musical intonations of that voice which belonged only to Mr. Randolph. In his appeals to High Heaven, the God of the Universe, the Final Judge of all the Earth, with his eyes turned heavenward, and that "long bony finger" pointing to the skies, both gradually lowering as the appeal or invocation closed, the moral effect was so thrilling that every man left the scene with (for the time at least) a better heart than he carried there.

The "long bony finger" really appeared, when used in gesticulation, to have no bone in it; for when it had accomplished what it had been called into action for, it would fall over on the back of his hand, almost as limp as a string, as if, having done its work, it sought repose.

But I have digressed from what I set out to write, viz: Mr. Randolph's great speech at Halifax Court-house in the Spring of 1827. I would that the task had fallen to hands more skillful than mine; that the power of that mighty effort had been portrayed by an abler pen, before force of circumstances devolved the duty upon me. Of the vast multitude there assembled, only a few remained to witness the fulfillment of the ominous predictions of the illustrious speaker. These should aid in preserving from oblivion the almost prophetic warnings they then received.

He came to breast the flood then rolling on from the western portion of the State for a convention. In spite of all his efforts, however, the stream increased, until it found temporary rest in the convention of 1829. It had been known, for a long time, and for many miles around, that he would be there upon that occasion, and would address the people on that question. The time drew nigh; the people everywhere were talking about it; expectation ran high. The day arrived and the crowd was immense, the largest I ever saw at a country gathering, variously estimated at from six to ten thousand, representing all the bordering counties in Virginia and North Carolina.

As the hour approached every countenance beamed with anticipation, or was grave with anxiety, for the weather was a little inauspicious, and Mr. Randolph's health was bad. It was known that he had reached Judge Leigh's, but fears were entertained that he might be deterred by the weather. About 10 o'clock, however, the thin clouds vanished, and about 11 news passed like an electric current through the vast multitude that he was coming. In an instant the crowd began moving slowly and noiselessly towards the upper tavern. Scarcely had they reached the summit of the slope between the court-house and the tavern when they saw him coming on horseback, his carriage in the rear, driven by one of his servants. As he drew near, the crowd simultaneously divided to each side of the street, making a broad avenue along which he passed, hat in hand, bowing gracefully to the right and to the left, until he reached the lower tavern. The people, with uncovered heads, silently returned the graceful salutation. As he passed on to the lower tavern, the multitude followed in profound silence, not a shout nor a word being heard. Alighting and going in for a few moments he soon reappeared, crossed the street, ascended the steps leading over to the court-house, and began by asking:

"Fellow-citizens:—Why in my feeble condition am I here? Love of your liberty, as well as my own, compelled me to come!" A mighty effort he said was being made by politicians to call a convention to alter the constitution of the State. He warned them against the danger of tinkering with the constitution; said that few if any had ever been bettered by so doing; reminded them that change was not always improvement; that the change then sought began in the west for sectional power; that it was the work of 'mushroom politicians,' seeking place and power in the only way in which they could attain them.

He next adverted to the social, civil and religious liberty the people of Virginia enjoyed, and asked what more they wanted. "Ah! but," said he, "politicians want more! They want the right of suffrage extended! And for what? Only that upon it they may ride into office!" And here he denied the right upon sound governmental principles of any man to vote to tax, or impose any other State burden upon the people of Virginia to-day, and to morrow set out for Pennsylvania or New York, there to remain beyond the reach of accountability for injuries inflicted on Virginia. He admitted the difficulty of prescribing exact limits to the right of suffrage, but believed that Virginia had come nearer to it than other States, viz: in allowing it to none but those who had a "permanent interest in the soil." This restriction he said had been adopted as a part of her constitution after mature deliberation by some of the wisest and purest statesmen and sages the world had ever produced.

Here he dwelt at considerable length on State and national authorities, defining the boundaries of each, and cautioning the people against conflict with the powers delegated to the General Government, maintaining that delegated power was all that it could claim, and all not thus obtained belonged to the States severally, or to the people. He admonished them to make no encroachment on the rights of the Federal Government, and to suffer none to be made on their own; said that a reckless disregard of these powers, or a false interpretation of these them by unqualified men in power, had on several occasions come very nigh destroying our beautiful political fabric, then being watched with jealousy by every monarchist on earth. He adverted to Shay's and Shattock's war in Massachusetts, the whiskey insurrection in Pennsylvania, &c., as instances of the precipitate action of hasty, incompetent men; and in the same connection severely animadverted on the Missouri compromise as a political measure of like character, hasty, ill-advised, weak, and fraught only with present humiliation and future danger.

Here he drew a striking and vivid picture of "the Old Ship of State" sailing amongst these breakers, and, with extended arms and eyes raised to heaven, he threw his body forward (as if to catch her), crying as he did so in a half imploring, half confident tone, "God save the Old Ship!" It was the most solemn, the most impressive gesture I ever saw from any human being; and so powerful was the impression made, that the whole multitude, many with extended arms, seemed to move involuntarily forward, as if to help save the sinking ship."

After portraying many of the evils of an extended ballot, he raised his eyes to heaven, and in an humble, Christian-like manner, thanked God that in all our difficulties we yet had a pure *judiciary*. "Fellow-citizens," said he, "keep your judiciary pure, and your liberties are safe. Let it become contaminated by political strife, and all will be gone! The name of liberty alone will remain to you a phantom, a will-o'-the wisp, to lure you on to degradation, and the destruction of all that is dear to you now.' From the bench to the jury box these feelings would gradually find their way, until courts of justice would become mere instruments for rewarding friends and punishing opponents. Let the candid observer of passing events say how far these predictions have reached their fulfilment.

Mr. Randolph reminded his hearers that during a long life in Congress he had often been taunted with—"You never propose anything!" "You are always trying to tear down other men's work!" Pausing a moment, with that long finger pointing back from the top of his forehead, he said: "True, and I regard it as the brightest feather in my cap. My whole aim has been to prevent, not to promote, legislation. Our people need but few laws, couched in plain, simple language. Litigation would then be rarer, and our troubles would almost cease!" He said it was with pain and misgivings that he beheld the tendency throughout the country to excessive legislation, and called attention to the prediction he would then hazard, that if this country should ever be destroyed it would be by 'excessive legislation.'

He next gave an outline of his course in Congress, his opposition to the Tariff and to the United States Bank; said there was no warrant in the constitution for any such institution as the latter; that ours was intended for a "hard money" government; that he had it from many of the fathers of the constitution; that he had lived in their day, and was familiar with their sentiments on that subject. He said he would be the veriest dunce on earth if he were unacquainted with the fundamental principles of government, for he had grown up and become familiar with many of the leading men of Virginia who had assisted in the conception and erection of the mighty political fabric under which we lived, and enjoyed all the blessings of a free and happy people. Said he, " Mind, gentlemen, how you touch it; how you set about with innovation. Once gone, you may never restore it. Revolutions never go back, but on and on they roll; no returning tide brings repose; no bow of promise spans their dark horizon. On and on they go, until all is swallowed up in the abyss of anarchy and ruin!''

During the long and entertaining speech, every man, of both races, seemed bound to the earth on which he stood; not one moved.

The convention, however, was called; Mr. Randolph was elected to it; served with characteristic fidelity, and returned to Halifax in 1829, to give an account of his stewardship. By his arduous labors in that body his health had suffered greatly; he was too feeble to speak out doors, and the county court, then in session, tendered him the court-house, which he gratefully accepted. As he moved up to the bench, it was apparent to every one that he lacked the physical ability to entertain the people as he had done on the previous occasion. Taking his stand on the county court bench, and supporting himself with one hand on the railing, and the other on his cane, he began by returning his thanks in a polite and graceful manner to the worshipful court for their kindness in suspending their business to accommodate one who needed so much their consideration. He told them it must be plain to all that it was the last speech he should ever make in Halifax. He gave a succinct statement of all the various alterations (he would not call them amendments) proposed to the constitution, and advised the people to vote against them.

He then showed what he called a trick of the convention in submitting the ratification or rejection of the proposed alterations to the vote of the people.

"Who called the convention?" he asked. "The freeholders! Who had the right to say whether the work was done according to their wishes but those who ordered it? No one! The non-freeholders, according to all the rules of legitimate induction, had no more right to vote on that question than the people of Hayti."

Mr. Randolph was, in every respect, a great man. As a statesman he had no superior, and but few equals. As a philosopher and student of history he stood in the foremost ranks, while as an orator he would compare with any that the 19th century has produced.

His voice was uncommonly shrill, but was of that soft flute-like character that always elicited admiration, and feeble as he was for nearly his whole life, he could always so modulate it as to make every member of the largest assemblies distinctly hear every word that he uttered, and that without the least strain on his vocal or respiratory organs.

For the following curious incident we are indebted to Colonel Thomas S. Flournoy, who, though a lad at the time, has a vivid recollection of the scene he describes.

He says that, in the year 1829, he and his father were on their way to Halifax Court-house; about sunset they stopped at Roanoke; Johnny, Mr. Randolph's body servant, met them, and informed his master of their arrival. They were invited into Mr. Randolph's bed room, and what followed we will give as nearly as possible in the language of our witness. Colonel Flournoy is a man of national reputation, and we are glad to have such undoubted authority for the strange statement which he makes. He says: "My father inquired after Mr. Randolph's health. His reply was: 'John, I am dying; I shall not live through the night.'

"My father informed him that we were on our way to Halifax court. He requested us to say to the people on Monday, court day, that he was no longer a candidate for the convention; that he did not expect to live through the night, certainly not till the meeting of the convention.

"He soon began to discuss the questions of reform and the proposed changes in the constitution. Becoming excited, he seemed to forget that he was a 'dying' man. In a short time we were invited to tea, and when we returned to his room we found him again in a 'dying' condition; but, as before, he soon began to discuss the subject of the convention; and becoming more and more animated, he rose up in bed—my father and myself being the only auditors—and delivered one of the most interesting speeches, in conversational style, that it was ever my good fortune to hear, occupying the time, from half past eight, until midnight.

"The next morning, immediately after breakfast, Mr. Randolph sent for us again. We found him again in a 'dying' condition. He stated to us that he was satisfied that he would not live through the day, and repeated his request that my father would have it announced to the people of Halifax that he declined being a candidate for the convention. Once more he became animated while discussing the convention, and kept us till 10 o'clock at his house. When we were about to start he took solemn leave of us, saying: 'In all probability you will never see me again.'

"Before we reached Clarke's Ferry, five miles distant, I heard some one coming on horseback, pushing to overtake us, which proved to be Mr. Randolph, with Johnny in a sulky following.

"We traveled on together until we came to the road leading to Judge Leigh's. Mr. Randolph then left us, to spend the night with Judge Leigh. The next morning, Monday, he rode nine miles to court, where an immense crowd of people had assembled to hear him. He addressed them in the open air on the subject of the convention in a strain of argument and sarcastic eloquence rarely equalled by any one."

We will close this chapter with the following graphic description of Mr. Randolph's personal appearance and style of speaking, by Mr. James M. Whittle, a distinguished and gifted member of the bar of Pittsylvania county, Virginia. The article is headed: "Boyhood's Recollections of John Randolph of Roanoke."

At March term 1821 of Prince Edward county court, it was expected that Mr. John Randolph of Roanoke would be present, on his way home from Washington city, on the close of the then recent session of Congress. I was then a boy at school in the neighborhood—in my sixteenth year. The universal expectation of this event, as usual, induced a general desire among the people to look upon this strange man, as much so to those who had seen him from his youth up, to his constituents, whom he had represented in Congress for more than twenty years, as to those who had derived their impressions of him from the tongue of rumor alone. It was near the time of the congressional election, for which he stood a candidate; and in the session just ended had been settled, as was supposed, the "Missouri question," after convulsive struggles of two sessions. The crowd found at court was much larger than usual, and throbbing with anxiety to see—hopingly—to hear a man, so extraordinary in all respects, that a promiscuous mingling with my race, in many differing phases, in the long years which have since rolled away, has failed to furnish me with a suggestion—much less a likeness—of him.

In a short time after reaching the court-house, groups of people were seen hurrying to a spot down the road, some hundred yards off. Joining the throng, I followed on, and discovered a dense crowd surrounding a person in a sulky, drawn by a gray horse, and behind it a negro seated on another of the same color, apparently its match. The heads of these animals were lifted high above the spectators, and looked down upon them with disdainful pride. On approaching it was observed that the sulky and harness were deep black, with brilliant plated mountings, the shafts bent to a painful segment of a circle, the horses of the best keep, as doubtless they were of the highest blood. The servant, who was of the profoundest sable, carried a high black portmanteau behind him, and was attired in clothing of the same hue. Quite a strong contrast—possibly designed—was exhibited between the masses of intense darkness and the plating, the horses, the teeth and shirt collar of the servant. The order of the whole equipage was complete. The tenant of the sulky was as frail a man as I have ever seen. He was conversing pleasantly with the people.

I heard nothing he said. He soon bowed gracefully to the crowd, which gave way before him, and he passed on, it following him. The throng increased as he proceeded to an old-fashioned Virginia inn near the court-house, by which time it was swollen by the addition of most of the persons on the ground, and became a dense mass. A twitch was felt by some of the spectators, at observing so delicate a man at the mercy of apparently so terrific a horse, which seemed to have its driver completely in its power, but which he managed with entire composure. Mr. Randolph alighted with a feeble step, passed through the porch of the inn, into a passage, followed by a crowd, and disappeared within a room, the door of which was immediately closed. The people remained before the door of the inn, awaiting his reappearance, without noise or confusion. After lolling awhile, Mr. Randolph came out and proceeded toward the court-house. The crowd followed—keeping a respectful distance; by his side walked some of his elderly and prominent constituents, with whom he conversed familiarly on the way. It happened to me to have a position from which I could discern his form and action. He was the merest skeleton of a man; any boy of fifteen could, likely, have mastered him. His extreme emaciation may have magnified his apparent height, which was about six feet. There seemed to be a want of action about his knees, which were somewhat in-turned. He drew them up in walking, and did not throw his feet boldly forward. More than the usual amount of the bottom of the feet was seen as he moved, and he placed these directly forward as the Indians do. On reaching the court-house pale, he stopped and conversed with a good many people, when a lawyer came up and introduced one of his brethren to Mr. Randolph. The latter passed through the introduction with commanding dignity and grace. Having passed over the steps within the court-house yard, some of his constituents solicited him to speak to the people; this he seemed reluctant to do, but after some importunity he consented, and retired to a bench near by, put his elbows about his knees, inserted his head between his hands, and seemed to be in profound meditation for a few moments. In this position, the want of proportion between the length of his body and of his lower limbs was striking, so much so that his knees seemed to intrude themselves into his face. He then approached the steps with a languid and infirm tread, ascended them, took off his hat, and made his bow to his audience in the most impressive and majestic manner that can be conceived. It may be doubted whether there lives in America a man who can do this as he did it. His countenance and manner were solemn—funereal. Subsequent information enabled me to account for what would seem to have been without occasion. He had just emerged from a contest in Congress, running through two sessions, into which he had thrown his whole power, the result of which had filled him with apprehensions of the ruin of the Union, and from the rebound of the loosened tension he was left sick and solemn. The outer man was now fully presented to those before him. He was evidently a great sufferer from disease, and likely the sturdy working of his impatient intellect had strained too severely the feeble case which contained it. He appeared to be the Englishman and Indian mixed. The latter assuming the outer, the former the larger part of the inner man. His dress was all English—all over. His hat was black; his coat was blue, with brilliant metallic buttons and velvet collar; his breeches and vest drab, with fair-topped English boots and massive silver spurs—likely they were ancestral; his watch ribbon sustained a group of small seals—heirlooms, it may be, from times beyond Cromwell. His age must have been about forty-three; his hair was bright brown, straight, not perceptibly gray, thrown back from his forehead and tied into a queue, neither long nor thick. His complexion was swarthy; his face beardless, full, round and plump; his eye hazel, brilliant, inquisitive, proud; his mouth was of delicate cast, well suited to a small head and face, filled with exquisite teeth, well kept as they could be; his lips painted, as it were, with indigo, indicating days of suffering and nights of torturing pain. His hands were as fair and delicate as any girl's. Every part of his dress and person was evidently accustomed to the utmost care.

His face was the most beautiful and attractive to me I had almost ever seen. There was no acerbity about it that day, his manner was calm and bland, though sustained by a graceful and lofty dignity. It was apprehended that a body so frail encased a group of shattered and tremulous nerves, and that the prominence of his position, and what was expected of him, might put these in an ague of agitation. Though he was as much excited as a speaker could well be, yet he did not betray his emotion by any quivering of a lip, tremor of a nerve, or hurry of a word. He seemed in this, as in most other respects, to differ from all other men. He was calm, slow and solemn throughout his address. The text of it, as has been intimated, was the "Missouri compromise," and he expended not more than fifteen minutes in its delivery. His manner was deliberate, beyond any speaker I have ever heard. This so differed from my expectation of him, as to dispel the ideal of tempestuous rapidity, which his cynic and impassioned reputation had inspired. It was obvious, however, that the supreme mastery which he had over himself was essential to the deadly aim of his arrow, and the fatal mixing of the poison in which he dipped it. He stood firm in his position, his action and grace seemed to be from the knee up. His voice was that of a well-toned flageolet, the key conversational, though swelled to its utmost compass. The grandeur of his mien and his impressive salutation may have composed his audience into the deep silence which prevailed, but the uttering of a few words disclosed a power of engaging attention which I have met with in no other man—his articulation. Without this, it is hard to conceive how, in the open air, he could have been so distinctly heard by so large a mass. He was greatly aided too by his self-possession, as in his feeble state it must have been essential, to command every faculty and every art which could contribute to the result desired. Not only every word and syllable, but it seemed that every letter of every word in every syllable was distinctly sounded. There was a perceptible interval it appeared between each of his words as they dropped one by one from his lips, and that he had supplied himself with a given *quantum* of speech before he commenced, determined by its judicious use to accomplish a proposed effect.

These words, written and read, would hardly occasion any remark, except perhaps that if he had not a foresight, which was extraordinary, there was a rare coincidence between what he said would occur, and what, forty-four years afterwards, actually did occur at Appomattox Court-house—the overthrow of *that Union* under which we *then* lived, and that it resulted from the causes which he indicated.

But his words were only a part of the performance, the uttering of but a few of those showed that he was an actor. They were few, so were his gestures, but they were as expressive as his words. I had studied some of the orations of Cicero, and had read of Roscius; but I could not understand the power of the latter over his spectators until that day. Had Mr. Randolph lived when pantomine was in vogue, it is not unlikely that he could have communicated his thoughts and feelings effectually, though he spake never a word. As he proceeded, the impression was, there is Cicero and Roscius combined, two men in one, Cicero within, Roscius without. The auditors of course yielded themselves prompt and willing captives. This combination required deliberation for its display, otherwise it cannot be conceived how so much time was consumed in uttering so few words without any apparent impatience of his hearers, or that throbbing twitter which is felt when expectation is excited, and held too long in suspense.

I did not comprehend the subject he was discussing, nor know even its leading facts, but he dwelt chiefly on the dissolution of the Union as the effect of the compromise; and here Roscius did well act his part. As if startled by the bursting asunder of the materials of some massive building, in which he was, he drew up his shoulders, his head seemed to sink between them, his bust was bent forward, and his face filled with horror. His concluding words: "We fought manfully the good fight, and we are beaten," seem inadequate to any oratorical effect; but Roscius took them up, and equipped them for their work. The speaker must allude to the faithful valor of the combat—how "manfully" it was fought—here the fever-parched lips were compressed, the finger pointed to the skies, and bowing in sad but lofty recognition of his fate, and with a countenance hung with pictures of anxiety, came the words—"We are beaten," and he retired.

In the Congress just ended, the State of Maryland was represented in the Senate by William Pinckney, Esq., who is deemed to have delivered the ablest speech on the "Missouri question" which had ever been made in this country. Had Mr. Randolph been as ambitious of fame as Mr. Pinckney, and had devoted himself as he had done to the preparation of his speeches, and the manner of their delivery, it is not unlikely that Mr. Pinckney could with more propriety have made the motion in the Senate, which Mr. Randolph did in the lower House, when the former was about to speak: "I move that this House do now adjourn, to hear the first orator of this or any other age."

CHAPTER VI.

His Economy—Acts of Kindness—"Flowers Produce Fruit"—"Genius Not Desirable"—Reproof to a Schoolboy for Cutting a Cane in his Forest—Obituary of Joel W. Watkins—Treatment of Mrs. Royal—Preaching to his Slaves—Scene in the Library—"The Bible is True"—Incidents by Dr. Isaac Read.

IN digesting our notes of Mr. Randolph, we found that the dark side increased rapidly, while we had comparatively few *data* with which to build up the bright side.

One of his biographers dismisses the latter branch of his subject in very short order. After enumerating all of his bad qualities, he says: "We may be asked, were there no virtues, no redeeming traits in the character of Mr. Randolph; as a counterbalance to this long array of antagonistic ones?" He is forced to admit "some of a negative kind," which he enumerates in less than a dozen lines.

We have been particular to note down every incident furnished us by Mr. Randolph's old neighbors and acquaintances, illustrating his good qualities, or mitigating the bad. Our effort is to draw him as he was.

He is represented as being terribly repulsive to his foes; but to his friends he was often gentle, kind and fascinating. He did not always outrage the feelings of an opponent. We find from the manuscript of Mr. Bouldin, that when Jerman Baker was a rival candidate for Congress, he treated him with great kindness and forbearance.

He was exceedingly cleanly in his habits, and dressed with great neatness and care; and "the neatness of his household affairs," says Mr. Bouldin, "was truly remarkable." His table was furnished with food of the best quality, dressed in the most palatable manner, and his cellar was furnished with wine and other spirits of the finest description. His economy in housekeeping was praiseworthy and remarkable. And not only that, but his whole style of living was creditable to him. For a long time he lived in a log house, never in a fine one. He had no unnecessary furniture, but what he had was, for the most part, of the best materials.

Those who were unacquainted with his real condition, who saw only his visible effects—his large tracts of land and his hundreds of negro slaves, were not in every instance disposed to commend his economy. Doubtless there were those who thought he ought to have built a fine dwelling, and rivalled in hospitality and display his ancestors of Colonial times. This is the reason why Mr. James W. Bouldin remarked in his sketch of Mr. Randolph, that if his *indebtedness* was generally known it was not generally borne in mind by those who have spoken of him. Mr. W. B. Green, in his recollections, states that he happened to know that he was nearly always hard run for money, having himself been under the disagreeable necessity of calling his attention to the settlement of a small amount which had been due for several years. He states that he was also acquainted with other facts, in relation to his pecuniary affairs, which showed a want of promptitude in the settlement of accounts. It is true that he inherited a large and princely estate, by far the largest in the county, yet it was under a heavy British mortgage. Mr. Green states that this mortgage was not entirely extinguished until after his mission to Russia. "The receipt of salary and outfit," remarks Mr. Green, "enabled him to pay all his debts and purchase the 'Bushy Forest' estate."

To show how minutely attentive he was to his plantation

affairs, we will make an exact copy of a slip of paper in Mr. Randolph's own hand-writing, which was found between the leaves of one of his books, purchased at the auction sale of his effects after his death:

"*The Beds are to be shared as follows: eight yards of oznaburgs to a bed.*

Middle Quarter.	Lower Quarter.
Simon & Effy	' Abram & Sarey
Essex & Jenny	' Quashee & Molly
Mingo & Jenny	' Archer & Nancy
Amos & Agga	Jerry (Heffy's daughter.
Jim & Jenny	' Henry & Lavinia
Rogers & Hannah	' Moses & Phoebe
Othello & Nancy	' Phil & Amelia
Peter (Smith) & Jenny	Nancy (Anthony's wife)
Maria	Anna (Remus's wife)
nine	Old Jane
Ferry Quarter	Old Aggey
Molly, Robinson's wife	' Isham & Finey
Nancy, Isham's wife	
Betty, Johny's wife	Chloe
' Geoffrey & Phoebe	
' Jim & Garmonth	Savery
' York & Amy	Aggy & Effy
' Abram & Lavania	Little Quashee
Farrar (Pompey's wife	seventeen beds
' Nero	

Maria	9
' John & Lucy	14
Katy	17
Isbel	—
fourteen beds	40 a
	8 yards
	—
	320 yards
	219

Stockings to be given two pair apiece to each of the men above mamed * and also to the following. See over leaf. *except Little Quashee & Old Quashee who have had here. Also Waggoner Jimmy has had. Aaron & little Henry have also had stockings here.

Sent by Quashee.

Stockings shared to the twenty-two men and the women on the other page who are to have beds and the following in addition.

Middle Quarter	Lower Quarter	
Sam	Hampton	
Phil, Essex's son	Cæsar	
Phil Carpenter	Manuel	
Billy (Smith)	Guy	
Billy Carpenter.	Isaac	
Isham & Simon's son	5	
Paul	forty-three men ⎱	No. of pair
Isham & Nero's son	2 pair apiece ⎰	86
Ned Carpenter	Thiry-four women	
Ben	1 ditto ditto	34
Berkley	.	
Harry Carp'r		120
12	Sent by Quashee	
Terry	Ten dozen pair	120
Jim Boy		
Billy (Milly's son)		
Isaac		

Note—The men are forty three in number, viz, 22—12—5—4. They must have two pair apiece and the women one pair (except those who have a line drawn under their names. There are thirty seven women of whom Molly Jane & Chloe at the Lower Quarter and Nanny (Othello's wife) at the Middle Quarter are to have no stockings."

Even these little memoranda, written in Mr. Randolph's own hand-writing, point to several traits of character—his attention to the details of business, his power to contract his ample mind to the humblest duties of life. He also kept a diary during the greater portion of his life, commencing his first entries in youth. R. A. Brock, Esq., of Richmond, has a copy of it, the original being in the possession of the grand niece of Mr. Randolph, Mrs. Cynthia B. Coleman, of Williamsburg, Va.

Mr. Randolph was a good master to his servants, as a general rule. Though he occasionally flew out into violent fits of rage against them, he was for the most part very kind to them. He always provided well for their physicial, and was not inattentive to their spiritual wants. His negroes lived in fear of him, but they were bound to respect him. There was something so lofty in the bearing of their master, so brilliant and comprehensive in his genius, that, to their humble minds, he appeared almost a God. His servants were the best and politest in the county. One of his male servants could have been invariably recognized by his taking off his hat when he met a white man in the road; a female servant would always make a courtesy. Mr. Randolph himself never failed to speak to his field hands, and he knew the names of all of them. His manner was to take off his hat when he addressed his overseers. In his intercourse with his neighbors, to whom he took a fancy, he was punctual in performing all the offices of neighborly kindness.

The following circumstance will show that he knew how to confer a great favor, and in the most becoming manner; unlike some, who cancel in a measure the obligation by the unhappy style of conferring it.

One of Mr. Randolph's young friends once went from home leaving his crop in a very bad condition. It was in great danger of being eaten up by the grass. To his great surprise and relief, when he came home he found a large number of plows and horses sweeping over his corn fields at the grandest rate. He did not know what to make of it. Having asked nobody for help, he was totally at a loss to discover to whom he was indebted for such an unusual act of kindness.

They were the hands of Mr. Randolph. The overseer was told by him to watch the farming operations of his young friend, and whenever he found that he needed assistance, to render it without his asking.

Mr. Randolph's conversational powers impressed every one that came within the sound of his voice. We shall not soon forget the pleasant hour we spent with Mrs. Joseph M. Daniel, the venerable wife of the witness in the will case, whose testimony we shall place before the reader in another chapter.

She informed us that Mr. Randolph used to visit her house frequently, and that he made himself highly entertaining. In the Summer time she said he frequently came riding on horseback, dressed in white pantaloons, white flannel coat, white vest, and white paper wrapped round his beaver hat. He had the most ghostlike appearance of anything she ever beheld. But as unprepossessing as was his personal appearance, he could make himself perfectly fascinating in his conversations, even upon the commonest subjects. His transcendent genius, his wonderful powers of description, his splendid imagination, seemed to create a new interest in everything he touched. His pictures of the objects constantly before her possessed a magical charm. She saw beauties which she never saw before—new beauties of *form*, soft notes, which had escaped her ear; and the garments which failed to attract her attention, when drawn by him, appeared rich and gorgeous as those of the bride decked for the hymeneal alter.

Mrs. Daniel is a very old woman, and yet Mr. Randolph's description of the mocking bird is fresh and bright in her memory.

The following incident, related also by Mrs. Daniel, shows that the heart of the man who was "nearly devoid of pity," and who too frequently trampled without scruple or remorse upon the feelings of others, was softened by the artless attentions of little children.

On one occasion, says Mrs. Daniel, while he was on a visit to her house, one of her little girls went into the garden and selected a bouquet of beautiful flowers, and presented them to him. He seemed highly gratified: said "she had chosen the old man for her valentine."

The next time he came over he brought the sweet little girl some delicious fruit, saying—"Flowers produce fruit."

Sometime afterwards a member of the family visited the solitary home of the recluse, and found the same bunch of flowers, preserved in water, sitting upon his centre table.

We pass on now to the memoranda furnished us by another of Mr. Randolph's old acquaintances, who told us of the visit which a certain young gentleman frequently made to Roanoke, and how "modest, pining merit" was raised from despair, and a clouded eye given "a golden hour."

It appeared that the gentleman alluded to was a young man of good solid sense, but had no pretensions to genius. He had commenced the study of one of the learned professions, and with that modesty, which is of itself the sign of merit, mistrusted his own abilities.

Mr. Randolph poured the oil of consolation into his drooping breast, by assuring him that he had nothing to fear; that all he had to do was to persevere; that he had the right kind of talents to ensure success. He said that "genius was not desirable; that it rendered the possessor miserable," and pointed him to several men of his acquaintance, who, without splendid abilities, had solely by industry and perseverance succeeded well in their professions.

The young student invariably returned home from his visits to his distinguished counsellor greatly encouraged, and in due time the best hopes of himself and his friends were realized.

Mr. Randolph was very respectful to ladies while in their presence, though sometimes he would animadvert with sarcastic bitterness on their foibles in his public speeches.

A young gentleman of considerable parts once met with Mr. Randolph at the house of a friend. He was delighted at his good fortune in having an opportunity of conversing on political subjects with the famous Virginian orator and statesman. But whenever he introduced the subject of politics, Mr. Randolph, after politely answering any question propounded to him, changed the conversation to something else.

It was thought that he did it out of respect for the ladies who were present; that he considered it out of taste to discuss such matters in their presence.

Very handsomely done! A well merited rebuke!

That he did not respect as a lady every female dressed in petticoats will sufficiently appear from the following anecdote. The scene described was in the county of Charlotte, and therefore comes appropriately under the head of *home* reminiscences.

But we must first acquaint the reader with the fact, if he be not already cognizant of it, that at one time, in the city of Washington, resided a certain mischievous old woman by the name of Royal. She edited, to the infinite vexation of the officials in the city, a paper called "The Paul Pry," afterwards "The Huntress." The paper was sent without solicitation to every member of Congress, and perhaps to other high officials at the Capitol. But though he might not have requested her to send the aforesaid paper, woe to the member who went home without paying the subscription price. He was first threatened with secretary "Sal;" and if he still refused to pay, he was advertised in the paper, and the number containing the advertisement was sent home to the neighbors of the delinquent debtor.

One evening two members of Congress were walking arm in arm up the streets of Washington, when they were suddenly confronted by the redoubtable Mrs. Royal. She began immediately addressing herself to one of them: "Sir, I understand you have turned true blue Presbyterian and a clock pedlar."

She had no sooner said this than the other member beat a precipitate retreat, leaving his companion to extricate himself as best he could.

The reader has some idea now of what sort of woman Mrs. Royal was, and he has doubtless a curiosity to know how Mr. Randolph would treat such a person if he should meet her.

He was driving out one morning in his coach along the public road near his house when he met the stage in which Mr. John C. Calhoun happened to be traveling from the South on his way to Congress. He ordered the driver to stop that he might speak to the distinguished traveler.

The two great statesmen had no sooner recognized each other than Mrs. Royal put her head out of the window, saying, at the top of her voice, "Good morning, Mr. Randolph."

She had scarce uttered the salutation ere Mr. Randolph clapped his fingers to his nose, and making a sound, which indicated that he smelt an insufferable stench, told the driver to drive on, and thus left Mr. Calhoun to reflect upon the eccentric nature of the man of Roanoke.

The scene now changes, and our hero appears in a new role. Again we select from the MSS. of Mr. Elliott, who was living at the time that he generously donated them to us, but who has since gone to that wide eternity, where all at last must find a place. William H. Elliott was a genius, and was the author of several pieces of poetry of great merit—one, the "Cockiad," was not only published with flattering notices in the newspapers of this country, but was copied into the London periodicals.

But to return to our subject. In his "Schoolboy Reminiscences of John Randolph," Mr. Elliott records an incident which illustrates a peculiar phase in his character. He says:

I sometimes on Friday evening accompanied my school-fellow, Tudor Randolph, who was an amiable youth, to Roanoke, to hunt and fish and swim.

The house was so completely and closely environed by trees and underwood of original growth, that it seemed to have been taken by the top and let down into the bosom of a dense virgin forest. Mr. Randolph would never permit even a switch to be cut anywhere near the house. Without being aware of such an interdiction I one day committed a serious trespass. Tudor and I were one day roving in the woods near the house, when I observed a neat hickory plant, about an inch thick, which I felled. Tudor expressed his regret after seeing what I had done, saying he was afraid his uncle would be angry. I went immediately to Mr. Randolph and informed him of what I had ignorantly done, and expressed regret for it. He took the stick, looked pensively at it for some seconds, as if commiserating its fate. Then looking at me more in sorrow than in anger, he said: "Sir, I would not have had it done for fifty Spanish milled dollars!" I had seventy-five cents in my pocket, at that time called four-and-sixpence, and had some idea of offering it to the owner of the premises as an equivalent for the damage I had done, but when I heard about the fifty Spanish milled dollars, I was afraid of insulting him by offering the meagre atonement of seventy-five cents. I wished very much to get away from him, but thought it rude to withdraw abruptly without knowing whether he was done with me. "Did you want this for a cane?" No, sir. "No, you are not old enough to need a cane. Did you want it for any particular purpose?" "No, sir, I only saw it was a pretty stick, and thought I'd cut it." "We can be justified in taking animal life, only to furnish us food, or to remove some hurtful object out of the way. We cannot be justified in taking even vegetable life without having some useful object in view." He then quoted the following lines from Cowper:

> "I would not enter on my list of friends,
> Tho' graced with polished manners and fine sense,
> Yet wanting sensibility, the man,
> Who needlessly sets foot upon a worm."

"Now God Almighty planted this thing, and you have killed it without any adequate object. It would have grown to a large nut-tree, in whose boughs numerous squirrels would have gamboled and feasted on its fruit. Those squirrels in their turn might have furnished food for some human beings." Here he made a pause, but looked as if he had something more to say, yet only added, "I hope and believe, sir, you will never do the like again." "Never, sir, never!" He got up and put the stick in a corner, and I made my escape to Tudor in an adjacent room, where he had remained an invisible but sympathizing auditor of this protracted rebuke. It was some time before I could cut a switch or a fishing rod without feeling that I was doing some sort of violence to the economy of the vegetable kingdom. When reflecting on this passage of my boyish history, I have thought that Mr. Randolph's tenderness for vegetable life, as evinced on this occasion, was strangely contrasted with the terrific onslaughts he sometimes perpetrated on human feelings. But Mr. Randolph was not a subject for ordinary speculation. He would sometimes surprise his enemy by unexpected civility, and anon, mortify his friend by undeserved abruptness. He was an edition of Man, of which there was but one copy, and he was that copy. Sometimes he would take the whole world in the arms of his affection. When in a different mood, he seemed ready to hurl the offending planet into the furnace of the sun.

Mr. Randolph would sometimes unbend himself in small talk with little boys, but not often. On one occasion C. C., a distant relation of Mr. Randolph, accompanied Tudor and myself on a visit to Roanoke. At the close of a long Summer's day, after having hunted squirrels, climbed trees, swam in the river, and played marbles to satiety, we composed ourselves to rest, all in the same apartment—we three boys on a pallet of liberal dimensions, spread upon the floor, Mr. Randolph on a bed to himself, where stretched out at full length, and covered by a single sheet, he looked like a pair of oyster tongs. He had a book and a candle by him reading. At length he dropped the book, looked up at the ceiling, and commenced thus: "Boys! why may not the earth be an animal?" Our researches into natural history did not enable us to advance any striking hypothesis on such a subject. All continued perfectly silent. Mr. Randolph no doubt did not expect any ingenious suggestion in support of his theory, but asked the question merely for the purpose of introducing his own fanciful strain of remarks. He resumed: "Now the ocean may be regarded as the heart or great receptacle of the blood, the rivers are the veins and arteries—the rocks are the bones." Here C. C. being a sprightly youth, whispered in my ear, "there is not much marrow in them bones." This sally well nigh cost me an irreverent chuckle—" the trees are the hair of this animal, and men and other vermin inhabit these hairs. If we dig a hole in the earth, or wound it in any way, we find that it has a tendency to heal up." Tudor, who was a corpulent youth, and overcome by the exercises of the day, commenced snoring. Randolph's quick ear caught the sound—he turned his head in our direction—his eyes flashed indignation:—" Is that beef-headed fellow asleep already?" but as he received no further response than a confirmatory snort from the same quarter, he extinguished his candle with an impatient jesture—wheeled himself over towards the wall, and seemed to seek in sleep an oblivion of his disgust."

There was a soft place in Mr. Randolph's heart. There is in every one's.

He was telling Mr. Bouldin, one day, that he and his brother went hunting, when they were boys, and found where two little hares had been hanged by the neck. Mr. Bouldin said he saw the tears suspended in the eye of Mr. Randolph as he related to him this act of wanton cruelty.

The tenure of his friendship has been pronounced "too frail to render it secure or ardent." He was certainly very changeable, except in very rare instances. This is the case, however, with nearly all dyspeptics. His friendship could stand less opposition than any man's we ever heard of. Where there was difference of opinion, his absolute spirit almost invariably severed the tie. He assumed the dictator, and all who opposed him were regarded as rebels to his authority. He had but few friends who were not subservient to him. One had to advance his interest and harmonize with his opinions, or else be deprived of his favors.

Mr. Randolph's friendship, while it lasted, was indeed valuable. The late Judge Thomas T. Bouldin, when he was a young man, was called on one occasion to the discharge of his professional duties in a strange place, where he was but little known. Being required to give security on some kind of bond, perhaps as trustee, he found some difficulty in giving the required security. It reached the ears of his distinguished friend, who raised his shrill voice above the noise of the crowd, saying he would endorse for him. Judge Bouldin said it at once lifted him out of his dilemma, and placed him on a high elevation.

It is true that in after life his friendship was estranged; but at the death of Mr. Randolph all was forgotten, except the acts of kindness. Gratitude in the noble breast of the recipient of such timely and efficient aid, caused him at that sad hour "to cast every bitter remembrance away," and to guard and protect with scrupulous care the remains of his former friend.

While on a visit to Dr. Joel W. Watkins, of Charlotte, we noticed a neat little frame suspended from his parlor wall. It contained a paper in the hand-writing of John Randolph, found among other papers after his death. It was an obituary of the grandfather of the gentleman above named, and as every stroke of the pen of Mr. Randolph is eyed by the world with curiosity, we requested a copy of it, which was kindly given. Nowhere had we ever seen what sort of obituary he could write. The reader's curiosity shall be gratified.

"On Sunday, the 2d of January, 1820, departed this life at

an advanced age, beloved, honored and lamented by all who knew him, Colonel JOEL WATKINS, of the county of Charlotte, and State of Virginia.

"Without shining abilities, or the advantages of education, by plain and straight forward industry, under the guidance of old-fashioned honesty and practical good sense, he accumulated an ample fortune, in which it is firmly believed, by all who knew him, there was not *one dirty shilling*.

"The fruits of his own labors he distributed with a promptitude and liberality seldom equalled, never surpassed, in suitable provision to his children at their entrance into life, and on every deserving object of private benevolence or public spirit, reserving to himself the means of a generous but unostentatious hospitality.

"Nor was he liberal of his money only. His time, his trouble, were never withheld on the bench, or in his neighborhood, where they could be usefully employed.

"If, as we are assured, the peace-makers are blessed, who shall feel stronger assurances of bliss than must have smoothed this old man's passage to the unknown world?"

Gracefully, beautifully and truthfully done.

Dr. Johnson once said of Mr. Campbell that he "was a good man, a pious man." He "was afraid he had not been in the inside of a church for many years; but never passed by a church without pulling off his hat; this showed he had good principles."

If he made this remark of Mr. Campbell, who merely pulled off his hat as he passed a church, what would the Doctor have said of Mr. Randolph who stood up in the aisle at Bethesda—once—the whole time that the Rev. Clement Read was preaching, with his hat off, and who, when he landed in London, went straightway to St. Paul's, and was so earnest in his devotions as to attract universal attention.

He once rode up to a church where the congregation had gathered, and services were about to begin. He dismounted, tied his horse, went in, and selected a seat near the pulpit, and was so exceedingly devout and solemn in his appearance, that the minister invited him to take a seat with him in the pulpit, which he politely declined to do, but knelt down, however, during prayers, and preserved his gravity during the whole time. When the services were concluded, he mounted his horse and rode off. The eyes of the whole congregation were upon him from first to last.

Mr. Randolph and the Rev. Dr. Rice had been speaking at Charlotte Court-house nearly all day. A clergyman of the Baptist denomination had attentively listened to them during the whole time. That night he went home with a brother minister: "Brother," said he, "did you hear the speakers?" "Yes." "Well, brother, we ought to study our sermons more."

It is not improbable that they preached better ever afterwards.

If Randolph and Henry had been born in the county of Charlotte, our native county, we should have been proud of the honor. As it is, we have in keeping their sacred remains. But it was in the possession of these great men, while living in their glorious prime, which was truly valuable. In the case of Mr. Randolph, this priceless intellectual jewel was possessed by the people of Charlotte for upwards of twenty years. They could not claim Henry so long, but still he remained in their midst a sufficient time to sow the most precious seed.

Who knows how much the immortal Henry is indebted for his eloquence to the inspirations of some divine who stirred from its deep foundations his mighty genius? Who knows but that the first and most powerful stimulus given to the genius of Randolph was received when—a youth—he stood behind the judges' seat and drank with rapturous delight the words of Henry? And who can tell in the breasts of how many youths the generous spirit of emulation was roused and kept alive by the noble example of Randolph constantly before their eyes.

The advantage to be derived to any community from having among them for so long a time a man of such great abilities and high sense of honor cannot be well calculated. The words of this brilliant orator formed an important part of the education of the people of Charlotte. Hundreds of persons might say, in the language of the gifted William H. Elliott, whose pleasing reminiscences we have already quoted, that "they could not recollect the time when the idea of John Randolph did not occupy a large space in their minds; that his high position, his transcendent genius, his fascinating manners and imposing presence all conspired to render him in their views as prominent and necessary an object in our human world as the sun in the solar system." And more than one can say, that for all he possesses, which is most valuable of the art of public speaking, he is indebted to the orator of Roanoke.

Such was the curiosity which was attached to the memory of Mr. Randolph, that every slip of paper in any way relating to him was preserved by his old constituents as a precious memorial.

The following letter from the Rev. Abner W. Clopton was handed to us by the Rev. E. W. Roach, who found it among some old books which he purchased at Mr. Randolph's sale.

"CHARLOTTE COURT-HOUSE, August 23, 1832.

"DEAR SIR:—If it should meet your view I will preach the funeral of your servant Billy at 4 o'clock in the afternoon of the second Sabbath in

September. Such of your black people as may attend the meeting at Mossingford on that day may reach your house by that time, and the meeting will be closed in time for them to reach their homes by night.

"As I was satisfied it would not meet your convenience to have the funeral preached on any day but the Sabbath, and as my services are already pledged for every Sabbath forenoon, I perceived, after I saw you last, that from previous engagements I could not obey your call at an earlier day.

"This consideration, together with my necessary absence from home, almost every day since I saw you, may serve I trust as an apology for my silence until the present time.

"Be good enough to inform me by Mr. C. whether the proposed arrangement will meet your wishes.

"I am glad to hear that your health is improving. That renewed mercies may excite in your heart a more lively gratitude, and in your life a more devoted service to the Father of all mercies, is the desire and prayer of your friend.

ABNER W. CLOPTON."

This Mr. Clopton was a minister of the Baptist church, a man of fine abilities, great integrity and piety, and a friend of Mr. Randolph. We were glad to be put in possession of this memento. It brought to mind several incidents with regard to our subject which might otherwise have been forgotten. Among other things, it reminded us of how Mr. Randelph used to deal with his negroes in a religious point of view.

Mr. Randolph frequently employed ministers of the gospel to preach to his negroes, and sometimes when the sermon was over, he would make remarks himself.

He once invited the Rev. Mr. Clopton to pray for him. Mr. Clopton began, but was soon arrested in his petitions. "Stop, sir," said he, "if that is the way you are going to pray, you must go into the garden or garret."

On another occasion he said, "Stop, sir, if you pray after that manner God Almighty will damn us both."

For the following contribution, bearing upon the same subject, we are indebted to the Rev. E. W. Roach, of Charlotte county, Virginia, who received his information from the Rev. A. W. Clopton. From the high standing of the witnesses, the facts stated cannot be doubted.

Mr. Randolph, from the dignity of the Rev. A. W. Clopton's character, became peculiarly attached to him. He frequently invited him to his house to preach to his negroes, and on these occasions he would have them collected from his different plantations, to the number of several hundreds, to hear him.

On one occasion, after Mr. Clopton had closed his discourse, Mr. Randolph undertook to deliver an appendix.

He dwelt on the gratitude that was due to God for his kindness, and illustrated by his own kindness to his servants. He spoke of the ingratitude shown to the Creator, and illustrated by their ingratitude to him. "My ancestors," said he, "have raised all of you, save one, whom I bought from a hard master for sympathy's sake. I have cherished and nourished you like children; I have fed and clothed you better than my neighbors have fed and clothed their servants. I have allowed you more privileges than others have been allowed. Consequently any good heart would have shown gratitude even to me.

But, oh! the ingratitude of the depraved heart! After all my superior kindness, when I was in my feeble health, sent a minister to Russia, you all thought I would not live to return, and you and the overseers (damn you—God forgive me) wasted and stole all you could, and came well nigh ruining me. But come back, and I will forgive; come back to God, and He will forgive. My negroes, hear what the clergyman says: He stopped, and said, "Don't think I mean any disrespect by calling you negroes, for I must inform you that negro is only a Spanish word for black."

When the services closed, he took the clergyman into his library, a room full of shelves and books arranged in good order. Passing on to a corner, he called for two chairs, and sat down to relate his Christian experience.

In that corner was stored a fine family Bible, with a number of works for and against its authenticity. "Mr. Clopton," said he, "I was raised by a pious mother (God bless her memory), who taught me the Christian religion in all its requirements. But, alas! I grew up an infidel; if not an infidel complete, yet a decided deist. But when I became a man, in this as well as in political and all other matters, I resolved to examine for myself, and never to pin my faith to any other man's sleeve. So I bought that Bible; I pored over it; I examined it carefully. I sought and procured those books for and against; and when my labors were ended, I came to this irresistible conclusion: The Bible is true. It would have been as easy for a mole to have written Sir Isaac Newton's Treatise on Optics, as for uninspired men to have written the Bible."

What a strange compound is man! and the strangest of men was John Randolph of Roanoke.

That is striking testimony which he gives in favor of the Bible, but who can account for his sudden burst of passion in the midst of a religious exhortation?

When he said, "I resolved to examine for myself, and never to pin my faith to any other man's sleeve," he spoke the truth. There never lived a man who was freer from flunkyism, or of more personal independence.

If a jury of twelve of Mr. Randolph's old constituents and neighbors were summoned to sit upon his conduct, with a prosecutor sworn to do the accused justice, as well as the commonwealth, it would be no bad method of getting at his true character.

In drawing the outlines of a picture of our subject, we were obliged to rely solely upon the observations of others. Much to our sorrow, Mr. Randolph went out of the world a little while after we came into it. Much to our sorrow we say, because we would rather have laid our eyes upon him than any man living or dead.

This being the case, we never failed, when the opportunity presented, to ask one of his old countrymen what sort of man he was. And though his character was said to be so difficult, we always received a prompt and decided response.

In spite of all that has been stated of the delicacy of the task, we found ourselves thinking that they really understood Mr. Randolph better than they understood anybody else.

Not that there were no secret springs which they could not see into; but his main points were so prominent. His eye, his voice, his demeanor were more vividly impressed upon them than any man's they had ever seen; and the distinctive traits of his moral and intellectual character were equally striking and prominent.

These pages contain opinions, formed not only from reading his written life, but also from the conversations of those who were well acquainted with him. Nor are they our opinions alone, but also the opinions, for the most part, of the witnesses, whose testimony we have weighed and placed before our readers.

But we do not expect the jury to take our word for them, for we have endeavored so to arrange it that our subject may exhibit himself, that he may be seen himself.

Mr. Randolph was very much diseased in body. Many allowances ought to be, and have been, made for him on that account; for this reason we were anxious to have a physician empannelled. We knew an old gentleman who, in his day, was a distinguished physician, who was also a neighbor of Mr. Randolph's.

This gentleman informed us that he used to say, "Mr. Randolph was like the toad, who had a pearl in his head, but poison in its bowels." But he afterwards had cause to somewhat modify his opinion.

He said he could give a little incident, but he doubted whether it would harmonize with what we had written. He was aware of the harsh opinion of Mr. Randolph, which had gone to the world; asked us if we had not made him all gall and bitterness.

We told him we had drawn him quite bitter, but not more so we thought than he deserved. Still we were anxious to insert anything tending to mitigate that opinion. He said, for the sake of truth, it would be gratifying to him to have an interview, which he had with our distinguished subject, published to the world. He thought it might give a better opinion of his power of forgiveness. The facts might be stated, and the unprejudiced reader would be enabled to draw his own conclusion. They might sustain him or not in his view.

Mr. Robert Carrington, a neighbor and personal enemy of Mr. Randolph, applied to the county court of Charlotte for the opening of a road through the plantation of the latter. Viewers were appointed to decide upon the expediency of establishing the road; a writ of *ad quod damnum* awarded, and a jury of twelve freeholders of the vicinage impanneled.

When the said jury had met on the land of the proprietor named in the writ, at the place and day specified, he, the proprietor, made a long speech. While Mr. Randolph was speaking, a quantity of provisions was brought by his servants to the ground. The speaker informed the jury that he had it prepared for them, thinking they would be fatigued and hungry before they got through.

During his remarks, he took occasion to abuse the C. family very much. Mr. C. would have attempted a reply, but for the advice of a friend, who persuaded him he could not contend with his antagonist on that arena. By the way, Mr. C. was one of the few persons who was not afraid of Mr. Randolph.

This is the occasion on which our old friend, the Doctor, was present, and which gave rise to the interview to which we just now alluded.

The Doctor was invited by Mr. C. to dinner, but declined.

He told him, however, that if his house was much further than it really was, he would go cheerfully with him, provided he could get him and Mr. Randolph to be good friends.

Mr. C. replied, if the difficulty could be honorably adjusted, he would have no objection.

The conversation occurred in the presence of several of Mr. Randolph's personal friends.

Some time after that, Mr. Randolph took rooms at Mr. Wyatt Cardwell's hotel, at Charlotte Court-house. His stomach was in such a delicate state, at that period of his life, that he could not digest the fare he met with abroad, and he brought snacks with him from home generally, when he put up at the hotel aforesaid.

One day he sent his servant down to the Doctor's for some of his sweet potatoes; said he preferred the small ones, that they were sweeter.

The Doctor had his basket filled with such as he liked, but on the top placed a very large one. Mr. Randolph was highly delighted with the big potato; called it a real "negro potato."

The next time the invalid saw the Doctor, which was at Charlotte Court-house, he invited him to his room, doubtless, to thank him for his nice present.

During this visit, the Doctor took occasion to say to his distinguished host that, in his recent speech, he had given utterance to a sentiment which he admired exceedingly.

"And what is that, sir?"

"You observed that the forgiveness of an enemy was the highest attainment of moral virtue."

"But you recollect I said I had not attained it."

"Mr. Randolph from that went on to remark how magnanimous it was to forgive an enemy; giving a most beautiful lecture, equal to old Dr. Hoge in his best days."

And this accords with the testimony of a truly devout old lady, who lived within a few miles of that singular man. She avers she never heard such a beautiful and pathetic discourse on the subject of religion in all her life as he delivered on one occasion at her house. The impression was made upon her mind that he must be a *Christian.*

But to return to our narrative:

The Doctor told him he should like to have a practical illustration of what he had said.

Was he willing to make up the difficulty between himself and Mr. C?

"With all my soul, sir," replied he, without a moment's reflection.

His expression of countenance, and the promptness with which he met the proposal, induced his companion to believe he was entirely sincere.

High hopes were entertained of establishing friendly relations between them.

A flag of truce, as it were, had been agreed upon by both belligerents.

When the peacemaker informed a friend on the street of what he had done, that friend was greatly astonished, and would not believe it. Was Mr. Randolph ever known to settle a difficulty in that way? he inquired; and, like the doubting Thomas, he must see before he believed.

But the difficulty was settled, and the matter taken out of court.

We have thus laid before the inquisitive reader the anecdote of our old particular friend, which he said he wanted to go in in mitigation of the character of his great fellow-man. He admitted that he was "full of subtlety" (that was his expression). Nor did he maintain that he was of a forgiving temper, but merely thought that too much bitterness had been given to it.

The foregoing incidents were related to us by Dr. Isaac Read, of Charlotte county, Virginia, who lived to be 92 years of age; but his testimony was taken twelve years before his death.

We purpose to give another proof that Mr. Randolph was not all gall; but this time we shall have to draw upon what has already been published.

The following is an extract from a letter of his to his nephew, Dr. Theodorick Dudley, published in 1834, selected from a mass of others of the same tone. The Mr. Curd spoken of was his overseer.

"ROANOKE, Sept. 22, 1811.

"Indeed, my attention had been, in some measure, distracted by the scene of distress which my house has exhibited for some 'time past. Mr. Curd breathed his last on Thursday morning, half past three o'clock, after a most severe illness, which lasted sixteen days. I insisted on his coming up here, where he had every possible aid, that the best medical aid, and most assiduous nursing could afford him. During the last week of his sickness I was never absent from the house but twice, about an hour each time, for air and exercise; I sat up with him, and gave him almost all of his medicines, with my own hand, and *saw* that every possible attention was paid to him. This is to me an unspeakable comfort, and it pleased God to support me under this trying scene, by granting me better health than I had experienced for seven years. On Thursday evening I followed him to the grave; and soon after, the effects of the fatigue and distress of mind that I had suffered, prostrated my strength and spirits, and I became ill. Three successive nights of watching were too much for my system to endure; I was with him, when he died without a groan or a change of feature."

CHAPTER VII.

Critical—Sarcastic—Revelations of his Overseer—His Manner of Dealing with Overseers—Midnight Ride—Whips his Cook—Testimony of Joseph M. Daniel in the Will Case—" Hot Toddy"—" Boiled Pants"—The Effect of Liquor on Him—Recollections by W. B. Green, Dr. I. B. Rice and others.

ABOUT two days after a severe spell of sickness, Mr. Randolph was seen driving up to Watkins's store. Everybody was daily expecting to hear of his death. Those who saw him could hardly believe that it was he; but it was indeed the "dying man."

Mr. Randolph drove up before the door, and observing the gentleman who had waited upon him during his illness said: "You hardly expected to see me out so soon." His friend was indeed astonished at the rapidity with which he could recover from a spell of sickness.

Mr. Randolph called for some red flannel. The young gentleman who acted as salesman brought out the article called for. Mr. Randolph inquired how much there was in the piece? The merchant replied: "I cannot tell precisely without measuring it, but I *reckon* there are ten yards."

"*Reckon!*" reiterated the critic. "A young *man* reckoning! I thought it was *women* who kept a reckoning, and that only at particular times!"

Mr. Randolph once put up at one of those "miserable inns between here and Washington," as he styled them. As soon as he seated himself at the table, he turned up his nose at the plate before him, saying it was "nasty." The lady of the house blushed up, and replied that he was mistaken; the plates were clean. She took it off the table, however, and washed it with her own hands. Still he insisted that it was "nasty." The hostess tried to turn it off in a joke, by remarking: She "had heard it said that we all had to eat our peck of dirt during our lives."

"Yes," rejoined Mr. Randolph, "but I don't want to take all of mine at once."

Mr. Randolph bought a plantation of Mr. H. Read, and was somewhat behind in paying for it. He had been dunned for it repeatedly, but he had never found it convenient to pay. On one occasion, when Mr. Read went to Roanoke to collect the debt if possible, he was met by the distinguished debtor, who accosted him thus:

"Sir, had it not been for your exceedingly genteel appearance, my dogs would have torn you to pieces."

Mr. Randolph bought the "Bushy Forest" tract of land on Roanoke creek of Mr. Howel Read. Mr. Read was very reluctant to sell it, but after repeated solicitations he consented. When the papers were all signed, Mr. Randolph turned around and chided him for selling the graves of his forefathers. Mr. Bedford, who was present at the time, regarded it as a most unjustifiable piece of ill-nature. The tall poplar tree was pointed out to us, under the shade of which the memorable transaction took place.

Upon being asked the direct question what sort of man was John Randolph, nine out of ten of his neighbors would reply at once, without a moment's reflection, that he was the most sarcastic man they ever knew. We do not remember to have conversed with a single individual, learned or unlearned, friend or foe, who did not remark upon this trait of his character.

Speaking of his powers of ridicule and sarcasm, a gentleman informed us that Mr. Randolph was once inflicting upon a certain individual one of his severest and most unmerited chastisements, when a man in the crowd, no longer able to endure the scene of mental agony, exclaimed, "Stop, stop, Mr. Randolph, I would not treat a dog so."

What must have been the ill-nature which dictated remarks calling forth such an exclamation under such circumstances? It would not have been more cruel to have thrust a knife into the flesh of his victim.

Mr. Thomas Cardwell, a great admirer of talent, once asked the Hon. James W. Bouldin to tell him who, in his opinion, was the greatest man that the county of Charlotte had raised.

Mr. Bouldin replied: "Mr. Randolph could force more down the throats of the people than any man he ever knew, and that, with the exception of Mr. Randolph, the Rev. Moses Hoge was the most eloquent."

Mr. Randolph would drive a man as far as he could be driven; had no mercy on him. In fact, he took a pleasure in seeing how many humiliating things he could force a fellow creature to do. He would make sport of him in his own house, and laugh him to scorn at his own table. He was familiar with the faults of everybody in reach of him, and when he wanted a man to move, he knew exactly where to apply the goad. But when he could not drive, he would not insist on it. His knowledge of human nature enabled him to determine who was a proper subject to be operated on. When he found that he had mounted the wrong horse, he frequently got right off and complimented him for his independent spirit.

He once sent for all his overseers. We have this from Mr. William P. Harvey, now living in the county of Pittsylvania,

Virginia, one of the few overseers who was not afraid of him. It so happened that Messrs. H., C. and G. rode up at the same time. John, Mr. Randolph's body-servant, met them at the door, and requested them to pull off their shoes, saying his master was quite sick, and could not bear a noise. John's request was complied with, and they all went in in their stocking feet. Mr. H. states that he found Mr. Randolph sitting up in bed, far from being in the condition represented.

In a few days he sent for all his overseers again, with the injunction that they should come as soon as possible. John was at the door as before, holding in his hands several pairs of stockings for the overseers to slip on before they entered his master's chamber. Mr. G. pulled off his shoes as before; but Mr. H. says the game could not be played on him again. He had no objection to taking off his shoes if he had supposed there was a necessity for it, but he had no idea of doing it when he believed that it was all "pretense with Mr. Randolph about being so sick."

John informed him that his orders were positive not to let any one in with his shoes on. Mr. H. told him "if he did not stand aside he would knock him down."

As they entered, Mr. Randolph said: "Good morning, G.; I can afford to call you G.; but"—addressing himself to Mr. H., "I shall have to call you *Mr.* H.

Mr. H. replied: "It mattered not with him what he called him."

"Shut your mouth, sir," said Mr. Randolph.

Mr. H. being very much incensed opened wide his mouth right in Mr. Randolph's face. They then had some bickering words. At last Mr. Randolph remarked: "See, now, you have gotten mad with a gouty old man." He then invited them to take a drink. Mr. W. C., who was sitting on the bed with the sick man, conducted them into the next room. After they had gotten there, Mr. C. remarked: "We have to swallow some hard things here." Mr. H. replied: "Yes; I have been swallowing chestnut burs, but I do not intend to do it any longer."

Mr. Harvey says he witnessed the following:

Mr. ———, one of his overseers, was leaning his chair back against the wall when the following dialogue ensued:

"Were you ever in a gentleman's house?"

"Yes, sir."

"Leaning your d—n greasy head against the wall?"

"Yes, sir."

"As d—ned a fool as you are, the wonder is how you ever" * * * * * * * * *

"Yes, sir."

And that was all he could get out of him.

A highly respectable old lady in Charlotte told us the following:

Shortly after Mr. Randolph had in a spree, as she supposed, killed several of her husband's finest hogs, he was visited by the injured party for the purpose of finding out the cause. He nerved himself up to the point of intimating that if his neighbor's dogs did not stop killing his hogs he might possibly shoot them.

Mr. Randolph informed him that if he killed his dogs he would shoot the best cow he had on his plantation. Afterwards he threatened to shoot his best horse, and finally said: "If you kill my dogs I will kill you."

The husband being a quiet, easy sort of man, did not resent it, but his wife was

"Gathering her brows like gathering storm,
Nursing her wrath to keep it warm."

She determined to take revenge in the best way she could. At any rate, the next time she met him she would give him to understand that if he was Mr. Randolph she was Mrs. ———.

As good luck would have it, she one day overtook him in the road. He was riding in his coach; she in a buggy with a fleet horse. As he was going along at a slow gait she passed him. But when they came to a wide space in the road he increased his speed and passed her.

Again she reined up her spirited steed, and putting the lash to him with all her might, distanced him a second time. As she drove by, Mr. Randolph gave her an awful look, and she returned the glance. He looked at her, and she at him. He passed her, and she passed him:

> "Then the fight became a chase;
> She won the day; who won the race?"

When they came to the fork leading to her house she was ahead, and turning exultingly round in her buggy she bid him "Good bye."

In a few days afterwards Mr. Randolph sent for her husband, and asked him the value of his hogs. Upon being informed, he gave him an order on Mr. C. for the amount specified.

Mr. Robert Carrington and Mr. Randolph were at variance. In fact they were mortal enemies. It appears that the latter had to pass through the plantation of the former to get to his lower quarter. Mr. Carrington determined he would put a stop to all passing on the part of all persons from the premises of his hostile neighbor, so he posted a servant at his gate, with a loaded gun in hand, with the necessary orders. Pretty soon Mr. P., an overseer of Mr. Randolph's, came by. The sentinel halted him, telling him the nature of the instructions he had received, at the same time requesting that he would see his master before 'he passed through. Mr. P. went to Mr. Carrington, who informed him that *he* might go anywhere he pleased on his plantation. Some time afterwards Mr. Randolph drew an instrument of writing condemning the conduct of Mr. Carrington, and requested his overseer to endorse it. His overseer promptly refused, saying Mr. Carrington had always treated him in a very gentlemanly manner, and that he had nothing to say against him. Mr. Randolph thereupon informed him that he had no further use for him. "And I have none for you," replied his overseer, and left him.

' Mr. Randolph insisting that he had the right to go from one of his plantations to another through Mr. Robert Carrington's, the latter addressed him a short note, prohibiting him, and informing him plainly that if he attempted it he would shoot him. Knowing of what stuff Mr. Carrington was made, Mr. Randolph did not venture. Mr. Carrington told Judge F. N. Watkins, of Prince Edward, that in reply to his curt note, Mr. Randolph wrote him four pages of foolscap, which Mr. Carrington said was as brilliant as anything Mr. Randolph ever wrote, and in which, in his way, he said a great many things of severity.

When Mr. Carrington afterwards became a candidate for the house of delegates, although all personal intercourse between the parties had ceased, Mr. Randolph was one of the first to record his vote (then *viva voce*) for Mr. Carrington, with some very complimentary remark.

Mr. W. P. Harvey states that he was present on one occasion when Mr. P., one of his overseers, came after being sent for several times to get his wages for the previous year. Mr. Randolph was then living up stairs. Mr. Hundley was also present.

"Harvey," said Mr. Randolph, "go and invite him up."

Mr. Harvey went, and reported that P. had to go out.

"Has he the b—y ache?"

This created quite a laugh. Mr. Harvey invited him as many as three times before he could be induced to go up stairs. Mr. Randolph received him in a very friendly manner.

"Mr. P.," he inquired, "why have you not been after your money?"

"I could not come sooner," replied Mr. P.

"Well, sir, I shan't pay interest on it, as I was not able to go to you, and you would not come to me. There is the money. Count it out to him, Harvey."

Mr. Harvey counted it.

"Is it right?"

"Yes, sir."

"Count it over again."

"Right, sir."

"Mr. Hundley will you count it?"

Mr. H. (not Harvey, but the other gentleman present) counted the money, and detected a five-franc piece among the silver.

"That's right now, sir," said Mr. Randolph, "sign this receipt without interest, else it will be said of me that I am not an honest man in not paying interest, when it was your fault."

Mr. P. stated that he preferred not to sign it. Mr. Randolph then requested Mr. Harvey to talk to him; but Mr. P. still declined to sign the receipt. Mr. R. requested the other gentleman present to talk to him. Mr. P. holding to his resolve, Mr. Randolph said to him: "You are the d——st fool I ever saw. You are as d——ed a fool as my Bull," a negro whose name he had changed to Bull.

Mr. Harvey says he never saw a man sign his name as quickly before. Mr. Randolph was in bed propped up. He sent both hands under the sheets, and P. thought he was after his "bull dogs," as he called them—meaning his pistols.*

Mr. Harvey states that while Mr. Randolph was kind to his servants, he was the strictest master he ever knew. He said disobedience to orders was the greatest crime a negro could commit. Mr. Harvey states that he has heard Mr. Randolph say to his negroes if their overseer told them to set fire to the granary, corn house, stables or barns, if they did not do it he would kill them.

Mr. Harvey says: He was at his house when one of his slaves ran from his overseer at Lower Quarter, and came to Mr. Randolph, complaining that his overseer was going to kill him, and he wanted to see master before he did.

As soon as he said that, Mr. Randolph told Mr. Harvey to take him out and kill him. "D—n him, kill him. I have plenty negroes to kill one every other day."

Mr. Harvey took the "run-a-way" and gave him a thrashing. When he brought him back, Mr. Randolph remarked: "I told you to kill him,"

"Stand there, sir," said Mr. Randolph to the negro, while he wrote a note to the overseer.

"Take that, sir; give it to your overseer.

Mr. Harvey states that he never had one to come to him after that. He remarks that "this harsh chat and strict orders were to save him from annoyance. Had it not been for that, his negroes would have been running from overseers to 'master' all the time."

---

*Mr. Randolph's conduct on this occasion was adduced, on the trial of his will case, as evidence of his derangement; but, to our mind, it seems in perfect keeping with his character.

Mr. Harvey states that when he was overseer for him, Mr. Randolph had four hundred and nine slaves.

He says he has frequently heard Mr. Randolph speak of an overseer he once had by the name of Cumbey. He said: "Cumbey could do anything." They were riding in the plantation one day together when they came to a framed house, Mr. R. remarked: "He wished he had it for a storehouse." He said in two days afterwards it walked up into his yard—everything complete, except the chimneys.

Mr. Harvey mentions another of Cumbey's performances.

Mr. Randolph, he says, showed him a barn forty by twenty feet; stated that that was the "turn-round barn." Cumbey had it built in his absence. He told him it was in the right place, but that it was set wrong; it ought to have been north and south. The next day he said he rode by and it was all right. He therefore named it the "turn-round barn."

Mr. Harvey says Mr. Randolph once had horses saddled at dead of night, to ride to a certain point in the plantation. As they (Mr. Harvey and Mr. Randolph) rode along, Mr. Randolph's horse became dreadfully frightened at a bush. Mr. Randolph stuck the spurs deep in his side, and the horse plunged and reared at such a rate that Mr. Harvey became alarmed for the safety of the rider, and so expressed himself. Mr. Randolph remarked: "It was as easy to throw a new girth from a saddle as to throw him." He did not desist until he made his horse go up to the bush. When they had arrived at a certain place, Mr. Randolph observed:— "There is the place I want you to begin the ditch."

Mr. Harvey says Mr. Randolph drank very hard, and took great pains to conceal it. Johnny would sooner put his head in the fire than invite a gentleman into his master's room while he was drinking. He always carried liquor in his carriage pockets; kept a great variety in his cellar; and, what is curious, he always stopped the key-hole.

On one occasion, Mr. Randolph asked Mr. Harvey what he would have to drink; said, "he had everything."

Mr. Harvey says he thought he would call for something out of season, that he might baulk him; so he asked for cider. To his suprise, Johnny was ordered to go into the cellar and bring up cider, which was very fine.

When intoxicated, Mr. Harvey says, he was profane and obscene. He kept at least six candles burning all night long. The excuse he made was, that if he dreamed anything he could take his lap desk and write it down, and then he would never forget it.

He once directed Mr. Harvey to give Queen Betty, his cook, a whipping, complaining that, instead of making him a plum pudding she made him a pudding with a plum in it. After she had been chastised, he said, "she always made them right, and greatly improved in her soup."

When entirely sober he always called old Essex "father." One day, the old servant came into his master's room, where there were several gentlemen present, in his every-day clothes. Mr. Randolph remarked: "Essex, if your friends came to see you, I would put myself in a condition to see them." Pretty soon afterwards Essex came back, the finest dressed man almost that Mr. Harvey had ever seen.

Mr. Randolph's orders to his negroes were to take off their hats whenever they spoke to a white man. He himself spoke to each of his negroes as he came to them in the field. He always spoke to his overseers with his hat off.

Mr. Randolph once got one of his overseers to do some writing for him. When the letter came to be backed, the overseer wrote "*Va.*" Mr. Randolph repeated, "'*Va.*,' d—n your '*Va.*,'" and tore the letter to pieces and threw them against the wall. He wanted it written "*Virginia*," in full.

The above closes our memoranda from Mr. Harvey. We are glad that we had an opportunity of interviewing him, which was done about ten years ago, and the result carefully written out and filed away among the other interesting papers which we were keeping until the time should arrive when we had leisure to arrange our Randolphiana for a book. We say we are glad we took notes from him, because we feel that we must draw Mr. Randolph as he really was.

We now turn to the reminiscences of Dr. R. B., whose high standing entitles him to the highest credit.

He states that in the latter part of Mr. Randolph's life he sent for him in great haste. It was known all over the neighborhood that he was sick abed. Dr. B. went promptly to see what Mr. Randolph wanted with him. Upon entering the room, he found him lying on a bed which was literally covered with books and papers. The moment he made his appearance, Mr. Randolph pointed to a box, and requested him to hand him a certain paper, describing it. After an hour's search, the paper was found and handed to him. Mr. Randolph took it and bid him good morning; and that, before his guest showed any indications of his intention to leave. Dr. B. had scarcely gotten off his horse at home, before the same messenger who went for him the first time rode up and said that his master desired him to return immediately. On his entering the room, Mr. Randolph requested him to look in a certain box for another paper, which, he stated, it contained. The paper was found and placed in his hand. He looked at it for a few moments, and handed it back to his friend, with the request that he would put it back in the box and "seal it with the sign of the cross." This latter injunction was somewhat embarrassing to the doctor; but he placed the paper away and made the sign of the cross with his finger, which seemed to satisfy the mysterious patient. So soon as this was was done, Mr. Randolph again bid adieu to his visitor in the same unceremonious style.

The Hon. James W. Bouldin prefaces his Randolphiana, the manuscript of which is now before us, with the following remark:

"In order to make many of the following facts intelligible, consistent, or even credible, it will be necessary to mention two facts in relation to Mr. Randolph, which, if they were generally known, have not been generally borne in mind by those who have spoken of him, his character and peculiarities."

We will not in this chapter quote the first of the facts mentioned by Mr. Bouldin, but the second. He says:

From the first time I ever saw Mr. Randolph, to the last—say from about 1808 or '9 till his death, he drank very hard—great quantities of all kinds of intoxicating drink. He generally drank the best, whether wine or distilled spirits; but he would drink bad if he could not get good.

This had various and very singular effects on him. Sometimes he became drunk in the ordinary way—lost the use of his limbs, including his tongue, and his mental faculties became almost entirely obscured. This, however, I presume was seldom, as I do not recollect of having seen it happen more than two or three times in all my acquaintance with him. Generally the more he drank the stronger and the more brilliant he became, until after weeks sometimes he would become suddenly prostrate and sink, and so after a time he would recover.

Although he drank much in public, he drank still more in private, and although this fact was known to so many, yet it is a matter of great surprise to nine-tenths of persons to be told that he drank to excess. He scarcely ever drank with the illiterate or vulgar at all, even during the highest electioneering times. I scarcely ever saw him drinking with gentlemen, but he drank more than any of them. Still he had the power of fascination and charm to such an extent on most men, that though he drank much, they thought it had no effect upon him. One of the most talented men I ever knew, General J., told me he knew that when he boarded with Mr. Randolph, at Crawford's, he drank more brandy (fifth proof French brandy) than any man he ever saw.

If any one doubts that the brilliant intellect of the great statesman and orator was sometimes maddened by strong potations, let him read the testimony of Mr. Joseph M. Daniel, one of the witnesses (and a more truthful witness never testified in any cause) at the trial of his celebrated will case at Petersburg. A manuscript report of Mr. Daniel's testimony was kindly donated to us by his venerable wife, who still survives him. From this manuscript we extract as follows:

I saw Mr. Randolph at Charlotte Court-house, November court 1831, but observing that he received many of his old friends with more indifference than usual, I did not approach him.

A few days afterwards some fox-hunters ran their dogs through his yard, and when they reached my plantation I joined the chase. During the chase Mr. Randolph sent for me, and when I reached his house, the first thing he said to me was: "I am sorry you have turned fox-hunter." He inquired after the health of my family, but was less particular in his inquiries than usual about them, and less cordial in his reception of me. He inquired if I would accept the office of postmaster at Tucker's, a new office he wished to establish near him. I told him it would be inconvenient to me, and was going on to assign my reason for not accepting, but he stopped me, and in a rather crabbed manner said, "that is sufficient." He then turned off and addressed himself to Mr. L., who was also then talking to him about his horses.

During the same month I received a note from him, one night about dark, urging me to come to his house on some matters of business. I accordingly went. He met me at the door, and received me more cordially, and apologized for sending for me in the night. The business related to an overseer of his, named ———, whom he had that day discharged from his employment.

He said that the overseer had destroyed more than he had made. He suspected, he said, and verily believed, that the overseer had, at that time, in his wagon, a quantity of wool, leather, and some other articles I do not remember, and demanded of me a search warrant to enable him to search the wagon. He took the necessary oath and I issued the warrant.

In a few days after, he returned from Prince Edward court, the same month. He again sent for me. ——— appeared in the afternoon, according to his promise to the constable, to answer the charge of stealing the wool and leather. After sitting with Mr. Randolph a short time, he proposed that we should go and try ———. As soon as he came in sight of ——— he appeared to get very mad; made a great many charges against him, and said he would swear to them. By way of getting rid of him, I told him he had already been sworn. I then asked him if he had no other evidence of his guilt. He said, "yes." Mr. P. (his overseer) and Mr. T. (the constable) would be ample witnesses of guilt; for they had found some of the leather in his chest.

From the evidence of P. and T. (I did not examine Mr. Randolph) I thought the case ought to be enquired into, and committed him to jail, he being unable to find security for his appearance.

The evening Mr. Randolph obtained the search warrant he complained of his negroes also. He said he had no doubt there was a combination between ——— and several of his negroes that he named, in relation to taking and carrying off the wool. "He had," he said, "the tanner's receipt for twenty-eight hides," I think, and the overseer had only accounted for a small proportion of them—I think about half.

The next time I saw him was a month or two afterwards. He complained that a great many lies had been told about his conduct in Saint Petersburg and of his appearance before the Emperor of Russia; showed all his clothes, and, using a quotation from Shakspeare, said, "they were rich but not gaudy." He then took up a volume of Shakspeare, and said he would read me the whole story. He commenced reading; but before he finished, Mr. W. M. W. came in. I went off shortly afterwards.

I saw him again about the last of February, or the first of March, 1832. I found him in the garret room, in bed. He complained that I had not visited him; said that that was black Monday with him; that, during his absence in Europe, his negroes had all turned rogues—those on the hill worse than any. When he left he thought they were as honest and correct negroes as any he knew. Indeed, he said there were but few men he would sooner rely on or believe than Daddy Essex and some others whose names I do not remember. But, he said, old Essex had taken to hard drink, and had been drinking some time before he found it out; that the habit was so confirmed and the propensity was so strong it had caused the old man to resort to dishonest means to procure it.

He had made a will, he said, before he went to Russia, leaving his negroes, particularly those on the hill, as free as the laws of his country would permit; that he had left his brother Harry their nominal master, and had made ample provision for their suppport. But, he said, since his return, and since he found how badly they behaved in his absence, he had changed his mind, and none of them should be sold within five hundred miles of that place.

While I was there, he had Queen in the room, searching for money which, he said, had been stolen from him some few weeks before. She searched all over the room, and said she could not find it. He was in a great passion with her; abused her very much, and asked her if she had examined under the head of the bed. She then examined under the head of the bed, and pulled out a pair of blue broadcloth pantaloons, very much rumpled, and on examining them found the money in the watch pocket, as she said, and as I believe.

Mr. Randolph's rage seemed to be more violent, if possible, than before. He said he would convince me or any other person that she had put the money in the pocket herself; and, raising himself up in the bed, with the pantaloons in his hand, he handed them to me, and said: He would swear they had been boiled and well washed, and if the money had been there it would have been defaced or destroyed. At the same time he handed me the money to show it was uninjured. The money was not injured, nor did I think that the pantaloons had been washed.

I saw him again about the middle of March of the same year, 1832. I found him as before in the garret in bed. He asked me if I did not think he was dying. I told him I thought not. He then asked me if I thought him capable of making a will, or if he was in his right mind. I answered I hope you are. He handed me a paper, which he said was his will. He said he was blind, and could see but little, but felt on the paper for a wax or wafer seal. He said: "I acknowledge this to be my hand and seal, act and deed."

His name was signed to the paper, which he said he had written in a great hurry, expecting to die every minute. I witnessed it, and he then, requested me to send for some other witness. I accordingly sent for Mr. H. and Mr. C., who came and also witnessed the paper.

He advised me if I had any money owing to me to collect it, or owing from me to pay it. Spoke of South Carolina nullification; said that dreadful times were coming. The United States Bank would be broke; troops would he marching through the country; breadstuffs would be very high. He advised us to make grain and no tobacco; said he would not take Mr. Gerard's or Mr. Bruce's bond for eighteen cents. He had, he said, a large sum of money in bank, and wanted me to write a check in favor of Henry Saint George Tucker, president of the Court of Appeals, to enable him to draw it all in gold and silver, not in notes, which he considered no better than trash.

When he first called on me to witness the paper he told me to take it, and to take care of it, and made me promise to deliver it to the clerk immediately after his death; then warned me against letting it be known, and said if his negroes found it out they would burn my house over me. After I had witnessed it, however, he changed his mind, and concluded to send it to his brother by an express, which I understood he did. He frequently repeated the words: "Take notice, I am in my right mind."

I saw him again in April, the morning of the day he went to the courthouse. He seemed to be in a stupor; received me politely, and taking one of my hands between both of his, pressed it, and closing his eyes said, in a voice hardly audible, "I am dying." Asked me if I noticed that Nero, his dog, did not bark at me when I came in; said that he had been a good guard, but now the devil had gotten into him, and he would bark at nobody.

We then went into the house. His servant, John, came in after us. He told John to hand him old Colonel Morton's cane. He then gave it to me to keep; said he expected to die, and wished good care taken of it. In this time John went out, and locked the door after him. He asked me if I did not see devils, or blue devils, I forget which, standing around the room. I said I did not; at which he seemed greatly surprised.

He said he had a portrait of my mother—a better one than I had. He pointed to a watch hanging up, which he said I might have. John, he said, was above wearing it. The watch needed some repair. Send it to Lynchburg, said he, and I will pay for it.

He had just found out, said he, how it was that the portrait of my mother, which he said he had, was better than mine. Asked me if I had not observed that there was a harshness in the features in the portrait which I had, and accounted for it by saying that at the time it was taken my mother was looking at these blue devils. He then said I must go home, as he knew I was fond of home; took hold of my hand and pressed it to his bosom, and said he loved me, and that I must not forsake him.

The next time I saw him was in the month of September, or last of August. I thought him free from all excitement.

The result of the prosecution of ——— was, that he was examined by the court and acquitted.

I believe Mr. Randolph had not a portrait of my mother in his possession. When ———'s case was before me, Mr. Randolph asked me to swear him as a witness. I told him that he had been sworn to get rid of him. I did not think he was in a situation to give evidence. He was violently excited, and in a great rage.

When asked the question: "Did you think him insane when he made the will in March?" Mr. D. answered: "I was not certain. I thought he had been drinking, as I smelt spirits very strong, and he sent me out of the room several times. On another occasion he sent me out of the room in the same manner, two or three times. Once he sent me out with a watch into another house to ascertain the time of day. When I came back I thought he smelt stronger of spirits than before, and did not seem to care about knowing what o'clock it was. He sent me again to find his English papers, saying that the servants could not find them. I brought them to him, and he pressed them in his hands, with the remark, that they were his only source of amusement."

"Did you perceive that he was more abusive to his servants, and punished them more frequently after his return from Russia than before?"

"Answer. He was more abusive, but I do not know that he punished them more frequently."

His servants were excellent. As far as I know, there was no foundation for the charge made against them by Mr. Randolph. I had a suspicion that they did trade improperly, and that some of them were guilty of theft while he was in Russia. But old Essex I had seen sometimes at the tavern in the neighborhood.

Mr. Randolph sent for me in February, 1832, the evening before he went to Watkins's, and asked me to ride that night with him to some magistrate to have the acknowledgment of some deeds taken. He said he had to send them off by next morning's mail. He detained me at his house reading a letter to me, and I thought it was too late to go. It was also very cold, and I objected to going with him. He said I must not lie, but must go with him. He wished me to ride in the carriage, but I declined. He then said, I had better push on as if I was mounted on a plow horse.

He told me to go to Watkins's store and wait for him. I rode there and waited about an hour and a half. As he did not come, I started to go home; but met him on the road, and hailed him. He said he should be sorry to make orphan children that night, and insisted that I should get into the carriage, as it was so cold I should otherwise freeze. I declined; but he still urged me, when I told him it would make me sick to ride in the carriage. He said that I must have one of his bottles of hot water. He handed one to me, and I took it in my hands, and put it back. He then said I must have some hot toddy, which he made and handed me. I drank part of it and gave him back the rest, which I presume he drank, as he did not throw it out.

We went on a little farther, when he stopped and asked me to take another drink, which I declined, saying one was enough. He stopped some time. What he was doing, I do not know. He again stopped a third time, but did not again ask me to drink. We then went on to Watkins's store. When he got out of the carriage, he put his cloak over one of the horses. When we went in, he returned to see about some sugar which he said had been spilt in the carriage. I remained in the house, and when he came back he was rubbing his hands saying: "I am frost-bitten. I am frost-bitten." He then sat down and wrote letters, and I wrote the acknowledgments, which, I believe, he dispatched to the post-office that night.

I went home and left him there. I did not hear any of the letters read.

He was excited I thought by drinking, but I considered him capable of transacting business. He said he must send them off that night, as his honor was pledged to do so. I do not know when the deeds were made. I understand that they conveyed lots in Farmville. I am under the impression that the deeds were inclosed and sent off that night by a boy.

I am a very near neighbor of Mr. Randolph's. Before he went to Russia he was in the habit of visiting me frequently, but he did not visit me after his return from Russia.

A few pages of the manuscript of Mr. W. B. Green will come in very appropriately here. He says:

Mr. Randolph always professed to be an orthodox Christian, and consequently recognized the personality of the devil on all proper occasions.

It was, I think, in the winter preceding his death, or perhaps the winter before, that he set out from home in a deep snow, late in the afternoon, to visit me, for the purpose of having some deeds certified for lots in Farmville, which he had sold. On his way to my house he learned (or imagined that he had) that the devil had gotten after me, and that I had left home and gone up to the Rev. Clement Read's (my father-in-law) to get him to pray for me. Hearing this on the road, he turned back at Overby's store and went to Captain Watkins's, where he remained all night. It was from him that I learned these particulars. The Captain also informed me that Mr. Randolph kept him up nearly all night burning and drinking burnt rum. He had doubtless made a free use of rum on the road. I was at the time at home, and quite happy.

I have always considered it fortunate for myself that he did not come to my house that night, for if he had I should have been summoned to Petersburg instead of Captain Watkins, as witness in the will case. Captain Watkins, and several other gentlemen from Charlotte, were witnesses, and the former, when giving testimony before the court, mentioned what has been above stated.

This was, however, by no means the first time that Mr. Randolph's imagination had been disturbed by the devil. Many years before he had been in a high state of excitement, which continued for a considerable length of time. The devil took advantage of this, and through key-holes and crevices insinuated himself into the bed rooms and all parts of the house, until the annoyance could no longer be borne. Mr. Randolph posted off a messenger to the Rev. Mr. Clopton, requesting him to come to his aid and abate the nuisance. I do not know whether Mr. Clopton went or not; I presume he did not go.

We will now lay before the reader the Randolphiana, furnished us by Dr. I. B. Rice, who resided on the Staunton, about eight miles above Mr. Randolph's, a man of sterling integrity, upon whose statements the reader may implicitly rely. He pleads Mr. Randolph's ill health in mitigation of much of the irregularity of his conduct.

After stating that "Mr. Randolph appeared among men as a towering oak amongst the undergrowth of the forest," he proceeded to furnish us with the Randolphiana, which occurred to him at the time we made our request. We copy literally from his manuscript.

On one occasion, I met with him at Mrs. D.'s, in the county of Charlotte, on a morning visit to her. He was very agreeable; asked me "How is Dr. ——— this morning?" I remarked he was still very ill; that he would not take the advice of physicians, but practiced on himself. "That," said Mr. Randolph, "reminds me of an old Spanish adage, that 'a man who practiced on himself had a fool for a physician.'"

He found Mrs. D. busily engaged in making clothes for the Greeks. (At that time there was considerable sympathy expressed in this country for the Greeks in their effort to throw off the Turkish yoke. Mr. Randolph opposed the resolutions introduced in Congress, and on that occasion made one of the great speeches of his life.) As he left, after the door was closed, he saw two ragged negroes passing by. He told them to stop. He again knocked, and Mrs. D. returned. He pointed at the negroes, and said to her: "Madam, *the Greeks are at your door,*" and passed rapidly away.

He once set his hands to pulling fodder on the Sabbath. A lady remarked to him that it was sinful. "No," said he, "it is the pulling my ass and ox out of the mire."

In the Virginia Convention Mr. Benjamin Watkins Leigh was at a loss for an epithet with which to designate the Western people of Virginia. "Call them horned cattle," said Mr. Randolph.

On another occasion in the Convention, when Alexander Campbell was replying to some personal allusions to himself, among other things he said: "The gentleman's remarks had no more effect than the falling of the last leaf in Autumn." Mr. Randolph replied: "I perceive my shot has stuck."

He had made a long absence from home. On his return he learned that his negroes had been sick, and that one had died. Mr. Randolph asked if a physician had been sent for, and was replied to in the negative. "Then," he said, "the poor fellow had a fair chance, and died a natural death."

His passion for fine horses was great, and he had many of his own to admire. Two of his favorite horses were once presented to public view; one (Gascoigne) under size, and in other particulars defective, which he earnestly eulogized; the other (Janus) a horse of great beauty and merit. He was asked by a gentleman what he had to say for *him?* " Nothing," he replied; " *he* stands for himself."

I heard a gentleman ask after his health on one occasion. His reply was: " Dying, sir; this continent was not made for the white man, but the red man." On another occasion his reply was: " This church-yard cough will surely kill me."

My opinion for a long time has been that Mr. Randolph's mind was as sound as any man's, and that much of the irregularity of his conduct proceeded from disease of body and inebriety. I believe that he never had an hour of good health, nor was he ever free from physical suffering. A great deal of his suffering was of that class of diseases which are mitigated by *stimuli*, which he used freely, until they brought his system into a terrible state of mental excitement and physical debility, and until the use of them was a fixed fact with him, necessary to sustain his bodily energies and even his life.

Besides two valuable letters furnished us by Judge F. N. Watkins, we are indebted to him for some interesting notes concerning Mr. Randolph. We give them in his own language. He says:

When I went to the bar, the Honorable James W. Bouldin was still in practice. In calling the docket in the county court, Mr. Randolph had been a party to some motion or suit. He having died, it was necessary to revive it, or let it go off in some way. Many of the old justices were afraid of Mr. Randolph (in his latter days especially). When the clerk called the case there was quite a pause and silence. Neither court (justices) or counsel seemed disposed to say a word. Mr. Bouldin in his very peculiar and amusing way said, so that all the court could hear: "Mr. Randolph is dead now; you need not be afraid of him now."

Mr. Randolph drove up to the old hotel in Farmville, during the last year or two of his life, in his carriage and four. Juba went promptly to the heads of the leaders, and Johnny to the carriage door. Messrs. M. and J. were sitting in the porch. Seeing Mr. Randolph's feeble condition, they hastened to the carriage to help him out and up the steps of the hotel. Petulantly he called Juba, and reproving him for not helping him out the carriage, struck him with a little cane several times. Juba reminded him that his own orders required him to promptly stand at the horses' heads, while Johnny's duty was to help him out. Messrs. J. and M. assisted him to his room on the first floor, and Randolph threw himself on the bed. They asked whether "they could serve him, and what were his wishes," &c. "I gave orders," said Randolph, "to have a *private* room prepared for me, and here I am, where I can't be alone." Of course the gentlemen at once retired.

CHAPTER VIII.

The Secret of his Success—How he carried Elections—Highly Dramatic Scenes—An Overseer scared out of his Wits—a Religious Lecture suddenly cut short—A Georgian run clean out of the Country—Anecdotes by Henry Carrington, Esq.

IN one respect, Mr. Randolph's life may be regarded a perfect success. From the time that he made his first appearance upon the political arena, to the last year of his life, he held high and responsible positions in the affairs of the nation.

"For more than thirty years," says Mr. Benton, "he was the political meteor of Congress, blazing with undiminished splendor during the whole time. His parliamentary life was resplendent in talent, elevated in moral tone, always moving on the lofty line of honor and patriotism, and scorning everything mean and selfish. He was the indignant enemy of personal and plunder legislation, and the very scourge of intrigue and corruption." "During the first six years of Mr. Jefferson's administration," adds the same high authority, "he was the Murat of his party, brilliant in the charge, and always ready for it, and valued in the council as well as in the field. In England we are informed that "his company was sought after by the nobility and gentry, and on one occasion royalty itself condescended to admit him within the same tent." Lord L. was forced to acknowledge that his conversations were most dazzling even in London.

His example of lofty purpose, untarnished honor and

manly bearing, was worth a great deal to the nation. It is true that there are few great measures of civil polity which his admirers can lay their hands upon, and say: "This is Randolph's work!" Mr. Baldwin says: "None." Mr. Sawyer admits that "there were some important measures for which the nation is indebted to his oratorical powers, as the originator and successful defender;" and he mentions the substitution under the appropriate heads, of specific, instead of general and indefinite appropriations, which he brought about after a warm and extremely powerful discussion with Mr. Lowndes, of South Carolina, who advocated the old system. The standing appropriation of $200,000, for arming the whole body of the militia, is also placed to his credit.

The reader doubtless remembers that in his speech at Halifax Court-house, in 1827, he plead guilty to the charge of "trying to pull down other men's work," and boasted that "it was the brightest feather in his cap." "My whole aim," he said, "has been to prevent not to promote legislation."

But it is to Mr. Randolph *at home* that we wish to devote ourself mainly. He exerted an influence which no other man in his district or any other district ever did. His power was almost supreme. We stated that he never was defeated but once before the people, and that was by Mr. Eppes, who he charged was imported like a stallion, for the purpose of being run against him.

Mr. Baldwin, in his Party Leaders, says "he was defeated, and without a murmur bowed his head to the stroke."

We say emphatically that is not Mr. Randolph. He may have gone about in a more pleasing shape than that of a roaring lion, but he certainly sought whom he might devour. His resentment was high and lasting. He never did forgive those who voted against him. Mr. Baldwin invests him with a degree of Christian patience, which he was far from possessing. Of all the men upon the face of the earth, we should say he was the least disposed to bow to a stroke of that sort. One of his old constituents once told us that he frequently alluded to the canvass with Eppes, in which he was defeated, and in no pleasant manner. We were forcibly reminded of this remark when we read the manuscript report of the last speech he made to the people of Charlotte nearly twenty years after the canvass with Eppes. This speech, as reported by one who heard it, and took it down at the time, is now before us, and in it we find him cutting at those who assisted in returning him, "to be discharged from the confidence of his old constituents." We once heard one of the keenest observers of human nature say, that notwithstanding Mr. Randolph visited on terms of friendship at her brother's, she fancied she could see in his eye, beneath all that was superficial, that he remembered her father's political opposition long years before.

The question is sure to rise in the minds of intelligent readers, how did Mr. Randolph gain such continued support of the people? What made them vote for him?

We have the greatest respect for Mr. Benton's "Thirty Years" view of Mr. Randolph *in Congress;* but not much value could be placed upon a picture of Mr. Randolph *at home*, taken from his observatory at Washington. In our estimation, the likeness drawn by Hon. James W. Bouldin, who saw him in his house, on his plantation, and on the court green, is much more valuable.

When Mr. Benton informed us that he never saw Mr. Randolph affected by wine, we were somewhat surprised; but we were still more so when he intimates that his popularity was founded upon the love and affection of his people. A member of Congress for sixteen years with him, and who afterwards published a biography of him, after speaking of his strong and lasting friendship for Mr. Tazewell, says: "So with many others, and preëminently so of his constituents—the people of his congressional district—affectionate and faithful to him, electing him, as they did, from boyhood to the grave."

Again, Mr. Benton says, his friendship with Mr. Macon was historical. It is true that his friendship for a few, very few, of his neighbors, and constituents in the different counties composing his district, was proverbial; but it is equally true that his capacity for friendship was very small.

In conversing with the old men of Charlotte, they will talk a long time about how Mr. Randolph flattered this one to carry his point; how he barbecued another for merely differing with him in opinion; how he drove men clean out of the country who offended him; how ridiculous he sometimes made his acquaintances appear; we say they will entertain you a long time in this way, before they will mention one word about his friendship for anybody, or anybody's for him.

The means which a master spirit employs in gaining his influence and establishing himself firmly upon his throne, must ever be a subject for curious speculation. This is particularly the case in regard to Mr. Randolph. But, really, we should never get at the secret of his success if we relied on the books that have been written; they being inconsistent with themselves and with one another upon this point.

His first biographer attributes his popularity to his "acts of neighborly kindness," and his "free and easy manners." Another says, "his want of charity was his greatest defect;" and laments that, "to the constancy and intrepidity of Mr. Randolph were not allied the suavity and gentleness of manner, which had made those stern attributes to be beloved as well as admired."

Mr. Baldwin states that Mr. Randolph was "eminently unsocial, proud, reserved, uncommunicative," and that "he never made a speech that he did not make more enemies than converts. How then did he manage always but once to be elected? And what becomes of Mr. Benton's theory of the affection of his constituents, electing him, as they did, from boyhood to the grave? And there is something almost laughable in the idea that Mr. Randolph owed his success to "his acts of neighborly kindness." He did not owe it to his "free and easy manners," nor to his "imposing presence," nor to the affection of his constituents gained by any means; but he owed it to his commanding genius, to the force of his will and the great strength of his moral and physical courage. And it was chiefly by flattery, by domineering, by bullying, that he obtained his unparalleled sway. But his was not the fulsome adulation applied without discrimination; nor was he an ordinary street bully. In all his acts he was infinitely above ordinary men. His knowledge of human nature was miraculous, and he had the greatest facility for applying his knowledge. He had unwavering supporters; but for the most part they were men who had no affection for him, who had never received any favors at his hands. Some voted for him because he was an able and fearless exponent of their principles; but it was, as we stated, chiefly by arts of flattery and bullying that he obtained his almost supreme power in his district. There is much truth in what Miss Mary Bouldin replied, when we asked her how Mr. Randolph gained his position in society: "By kicking every body else out of their places and getting in himself," she said. She went on to state, that if there was a man who stood high in the community before Mr. Randolph came to the county himself, a man of great talents and virtue, he soon gave him to understand that he, Randolph, must be foremost, and that he did not intend to join in the worship of him. If a citizen of his county held a prominent position and opposed him, he immediately set to work to pull him down—and that must have been a solid foundation which his destructive hand could not demolish.

No one *flattered* more his friends than he did; none were capable of doing it in finer style. Few could resist his arts. A young man of talent and promise, upon whom he chose for some cause or other to lavish his favors, might be conscious of his insincerity, might have received the solemn warnings of his friends, still he would remain under the spell of his influence. Nor could he be led away from the snare by his father even, until the tempter changed his better nature, and "by some devilish cantrap slight," suddenly forced him from his presence. Then followed tears of repentance, for having neglected the advice of his parent who, from long observation, had discovered how easily Mr. Randolph's friendship was estranged, and how deadly his resentment against those he once pretended to love.

When he chose to make himself agreeable, there was a charm about him which was irresistible. The pious old lady, who religiously observed the second commandment, never having seen Mr. Randolph, might grieve to find her husband worshiping an idol below, but when she too came to know him well, found herself kneeling at the same idolatrous shrine. We should like to know how many of those he determined to win ever failed to be won. The only way of escape, we imagine, was to flee. To remain within the sound of that voice, when in tune, to gaze upon that eye when "the fire was quenched," was certain and hopeless captivity. It is curious how that eye and that voice could be made at one time the instrument of such pleasure, and at another of such pain; how his presence should be so fascinating to his friends, and so terrible to his foes. But it is no wonder that with these extraordinary physical advantages and his genius he "raised emotions never felt before," and produced effects which the world despaired of ever witnessing again.

But, like Swift, Mr. Randolph coveted the fear of his fellow man more than his love or admiration. His genius was idolized, but the man was not beloved. He possessed the art of making people in love with themselves, but not with him. He mixed very little with society at home, and had none of those qualities which drew his supporters near. He looked upon mankind in the light in which they are represented in the Scriptures, but without charity. Hence he preferred to govern by fear rather than by love; to drive, instead of leading them gently by the hand.

We are not mistaken in saying that he possessed an influence in his district which no other man ever did. During a long career of public service, as stated before, he was never defeated before the people but once. His conduct, in consequence of that defeat, his never forgetting it, his high resentment against those who voted against him, and the means he adopted of repairing his loss and ensuring his next election, lets us into the secret of his great success, and utterly dispels the illusion about his "bowing his head to the stroke without a murmur."

In some places we are informed the people voted for his opponent *en masse*. He found out the leading men in all the neighborhoods which went against him. It is astonishing what a knowledge he had, not only of the public affairs of others, but of their private concerns. It seemed he knew everything that was going on, heard everything to be heard, and saw everything in sight, and what he could neither see nor hear, he had some one to tell him, even if it was a negro.

So it was one court day he sought out a certain Mr. S., who he knew had carried a certain precinct almost unanimously for Mr. Eppes. He met him with malice prepense, but with all the forms of the greatest politeness and friendship.

Now let the reader bear in mind that whenever Mr. Randolph stopped for a moment on the street, the people began to collect around him, and if he remained long at a place talking politics to any one, the whole court green was gazing at him, and eagerly catching in every word he said.

Mr. S. being artfully drawn into a political discussion, Mr. Randolph propounded to him some of the most difficult questions that ever were conceived of, questions which perhaps Webster himself could not have answered.

His opponent being a plain farmer, who made no pretensions to deep learning, failed of course to solve the abstruse problems. Mr. Randolph would then express the greatest astonishment that a man of his sense and weight in the community had not turned his attention to those matters.

Mr. Randolph raising his voice to a pitch resembling a speech, by this time had gathered a tremendous crowd around him, who witnessed the agonizing scene. Mr. S. would have given his right arm for a chance to escape; but the inexorable schoolmaster held him on to his lessons. To break off and run before everybody, and with a fire in rear, was what he could not stand.

Mr. Randolph kept putting knotty questions to him, which he failed to answer, whereupon he would repeat his expressions of astonishment. Still, all was done in such elegant style, that no offence could be taken. But no school-boy on examination ever suffered more at being found deficient than did Mr. S. on this memorable occasion.

The sympathies of the spectators were all against the ignorant man who undertook to control the votes of others. For, we may rest assured, that Mr. Randolph, before he was done with him, made them believe that his antagonist had committed an unpardonable sin. We would not be surprised if they were enraged both against themselves and him—themselves for following the blind and him for presuming to lead.

This thorough examination and exposure, before a large collection of people, we are informed, completely destroyed the confidence of the neighbors in the political sagacity of the said Mr. S. At the next election Mr. Randolph carried the precinct by an overwhelming majority.

This unmerciful chastisement was to be, moreover, a warning to all who should dare to take an active part against him for all time to come.

Few men who, if they had the ability, have the heart to expose a man after this manner. But, we must recollect, Mr. Randolph could stand no opposition, and individual feeling was never in his way. Nor did he regulate the punishment according to the offence. If he were thwarted in the least, he would crush the very soul of his opponent.

Attacks upon the feelings and opinions of others was one of the means he adopted of maintaining his supremacy. But he also made people afraid of the dirk which he wore in his pocket. Generally, he could pierce a man through with that long bony finger; but those who were insensible to that, he wished to keep in dread of the solid metal.

His plan was to make people afraid of him physically, as well as mentally. He frequently talked about shooting people. He threatened to shoot Mr. S., and actually called for him at a sale for the purpose; but Mr. S. stood firm and Mr. Randolph abandoned what he pretended was his purpose.

He also threatened the son of Mr. S., and scared him terribly, for talking about whipping his servant, Juba.

As to his servants, he kept them in terror of him.

After his return from Russia, and after the Southampton insurrection, he gave orders that all his negroes should change quarters. Those at the lower should be moved to the upper plantation, and *vice versa*. At the same time he instituted a general search for stolen goods.

In one of the cabins he found some wood, which he said he was convinced was stolen. He shut himself up in the same room with the suspected negro, told him he could not live in the same world with such a rascal, and gave him one gun, and he took another. The poor slave, alarmed nearly to death, ran up stairs and jumped out of the window.

All this was for effect. He knew his servant was afraid to defend himself; nor had he the slightest idea of shooting him; his sole object was to place the negro in terror.

His method of dealing with his overseers is well known in the county. We have seen how he dismissed one for not joining in his abuse of a neighbor, and how he made another pull off his shoes before he went in to see him; we will now state how he served another for a slight variation of orders.

In a spirit of spiteful annoyance to a gentleman who resided on the opposite side of Staunton river, and who kept a ferry, he established another, offering its use gratuitously. One day Mr. Randolph rode down and found York, the ferryman, absent from his post. The overseer was immediately summoned to explain why it was so.

Mr. Randolph asked him if he did not tell him that York was to be on the bank?

The overseer replied that he had merely sent him a little

way off to worm some tobacco, which he thought he could do, and attend to the ferry besides.

"The next time you disobey my orders," said Mr. Randolph, "I wish you to understand that you are to be cashiered."

Mr. Randolph has the reputation of being one of the strangest men that ever lived; and we have no doubt the reader, when he opened this volume, expected to find a record of some of his extraordinary deeds. If not already satisfied that there never lived a human being like him, we are confident he will be when he peruses the following incidents, written at our solicitation by the late Henry Carrington, of Charlotte county, Virginia, a gentleman of the highest standing, who was an eye witness to the scenes described, and whose statements are entitled to the utmost credit. We are glad to be able to lay them before the reader in his own words and graceful style. Mr. Carrington says:

In 1818 I lived in Mr. Randolph's neighborhood—received much hospitable attention from him, and heard many things from him highly interesting to me at the time. He was, at that time, unconnected with the politics of the country, having declined a reëlection to Congress. The year was also memorable in the history of Mr. Randolph, as being the time at which he made a profession of religion, had family prayers, and preached to his servants on Sunday.

Many incidents that were interesting at the time have passed away. I recollect, however, one or two, which perhaps it may be well to preserve.

In the above mentioned year, Mr. Randolph failed in his supply of tobacco plants at his lower quarter, where a man by the name of P. was overseer. About the first of July he ascertained that he could get plants from Colonel C., in Halifax. He wrote to P. to take a boat belonging to the estate, cross the river to Colonel C.'s, get the plants and plant his crop.

Some two days afterwards, he learned that the overseer had not obeyed the order. He was aroused. He wrote to me to meet him on the estate at nine o'clock next day. On going to the place, according to his appointment, I found him on the ground, and also Colonel C., Captain W., Captain J. S. and Mr. A. G. He proposed to us to ride with him over the estate and view the condition of the crops. We found everything in bad order, the tobacco ground particularly out of order for planting.

After consuming some hours in the survey, he conducted us to the granary. There were gathered together the plantation implements of every description, and, in the midst, were standing two negro girls, each with a mulatto child in her arms. The assemblage was remarkable, and I anxiously expected a scene. He enquired of the girls where was P. They said that, after collecting the various articles then in our view, he disappeared.

Mr. Randolph said he had ordered him also to be present; but he disobeyed because he could not stand the ordeal to which he was to be subjected. Then, turning to Mr. G., a plain but respectable citizen, who had, some years before, acted as steward for Mr. Randolph, he said: "I have invited you here to-day, Mr. G., to make to you publicly, in the presence of these gentlemen, all the reparation in my power for the great injury I have done you."

Mr. G. seemed greatly startled. He assured Mr. Randolph that there was no occasion for explanation; that he had always treated him very well.

"Sir," replied Mr. Randolph, "you are greatly mistaken. For more than a year past, I have endeavored to show by my bearing towards you, my disgust with you and my contempt for your character. But I am undeceived. This fellow, P., had induced me to believe that you were the father of the children now before us. But, I now know that he, P., has carried on the intercourse which he charges upon you, and that these are his children."

Never was man more astonished than was Mr. G. He reiterated,— "never, Mr. Randolph, was there a greater lie." * * * Mr. Randolph all the time assuring him that he knew that he had wronged him, and therefore he was anxious to make the most ample apology and reparation.

He then turned to the gentlemen present and said: "Look at these girls; they are my crop hands. See how their heads are combed; how oily their hair. Do they look like they had stood the blasts of Winter or Summer's sun. No, sirs; they have been in his harem."

The scene was highly dramatic; the acting, if it could be so regarded, unsurpassed.

After this scene at the granary, Mr. Randolph proposed to us to go to the house and get some fresh water. Mrs. P. brought us the water. Mr. Randolph, in our presence, said to her, he was aware of the infidelity of her husband, and felt for her the deepest compassion.

Mr. P. had, in the mean time, taken himself to some house in the neighborhood, where, from great perturbation of spirit, he fell ill. Mr. Randolph sent for a lawyer and instituted several suits against him. But, hearing that he was seriously ill, his feelings relented. He told me it did not become him, a professing Christian, to persecute the man to death. "I must go and see him," said he; and he did so, with the hope of curing and relieving him.

He told P. that he must not let this difficulty depress him; that the suits he had ordered against him must be prosecuted to judgment, as an example to his successors, but that no execution should be issued.

Mr. Randolph asked him what he intended to do. Mr. P. told him he wished to move west. Mr. Randolph asked him if he had money for the purpose. Mr. P. replied, he had not; but that he proposed selling the negro boy who waited on him. Mr. Randolph asked the price. Five hundred dollars, was the reply. Thereupon Mr. Randolph agreed to purchase the boy, and paid the price.

Mr. Carrington continues:

In August of the year 1818, there came to Mr. Randolph's a man by the name of M., who represented himself to be a citizen of Georgia, but staying at present with G. B., whose lands adjoined Mr. Randolph's, that he was negotiating with said B. for his land, and that he had called on Mr. Randolph to get some information in regard to the dividing lines between him and B.

Mr. Randolph said to him, that he must decline going into the matter of the land; but there was one subject which his conscience required him to bring to his mind. "Sir," said Mr. Randolph, "there is a subject of vastly more importance than *land*—the salvation of your soul. It is strongly impressed upon me that you are a great sinner. It is too probable that you have already committed the unpardonable sin; but possibly this may not be the case." And he urged upon him the importance of attending to this great matter.

M. was amused at the freedom of Mr. Randolph's remark, and concluded to indulge in some freedom in return in regard to Mr. Randolph.

He said: "Mr. Randolph, you can't tell me what I am thinking about." Mr. Randolph replied: "I should be very poorly employed in guessing your thoughts."

M. at length said: "Mr. Randolph, I must tell you what I am thinking about—I am thinking you are an eunuch."

Mr. Randolph immediately assumed the loftiest attitude. "Sir," said he, "if you had used this language to me at any other period of my life, you would have been instantly a dead man. Nothing restrains me from taking your unprofitable life but the fear of God and the grace that is here," (laying his hand upon his heart). "Go, sir; leave me, lest I be tempted to sin."

M. left in 'great consternation.

Mr. Randolph came into the room where were assembled Mr. ——, Dr. —— and Dr. ——. He was greatly excited; talked till late bed-time on the subject. Next morning, about day-break, he came into the room where the three gentlemen slept; awoke them, and said that he had made this M.'s conduct the subject of much reflection and of prayer; and he had come to the conclusion that, by no law, human or divine, ought such a wretch to live; that he had loaded the guns and ordered an early breakfast and horses, and they must all go and put him to death.

All was hurry and preparation, and soon they were on their way to shoot M. Mr. Randolph declared that it was said to him in answer to prayer that the wretch must die.

Arrived at the place, M. was called out, and told to take his stand, that they came to take his life.

M. was greatly alarmed and agitated. He fell on his knees and begged for life.

Mr. Randolph made every demonstration of his deadly purpose, but suddenly seemed to relent, and said that as he so eagerly desired to live, and certainly was in no condition to die, he would grant his life, but on the condition that he should immediately leave the county and state, and never be heard of here again. Moreover, he should advertise him as a swindler and imposter.

M. was too glad to accept the terms, mounted his horse, and rode off at a rapid pace.

Mr. Randolph advertised in the *Enquirer* newspaper, in a few days thereafter, the said M. as a swindler and imposter, and a purchaser of pretended titles to land.

It is said, we know not how truthfully, that the last time M. was seen in these parts was at Halifax Court-house, riding at full speed and looking behind him. The image of Mr. Randolph was doubtless more indelibly impressed upon his mind than that of any other object on earth, and remained the dark cloud of his existence.

This is the way Mr. Randolph resented insults from nerveless men. His conduct on this occasion was not that of an *ordinary* man with strong feelings, but of an *extraordinary* man, arbitrary, vindictive, with almost absolute power over others, yet under the dominion of his own violent passions. It is the conduct of one whose *heart* but not *head* is deranged.

Are we wrong in saying that Mr. Randolph was the most vindictive man that ever lived? For a remark, which was not intended as an insult, he humbled his victim to the very dust, and pronounced a judgment upon him more terrible and speedy in its effects than any which could proceed from a court of justice. We have no doubt that the reader is satisfied with the proof which we have adduced, and that he has rendered a verdict of guilty.

Well may it be said of him, that he did things which nobody else could do, and made others do things which they never did before, and of which they repented all the days of their lives, and that, on some occasions, he was totally regardless of private rights, and not held amenable to the laws of the land.

CHAPTER IX.

An Amusing Incident—Reception at a Private House—Could not have Written Don Juan.

THE following little incident was told to us by Honorable James W. Bouldin. It amused us, and may the reader. He says:

Mr. Randolph once rode up to his house, saying he had lost his way. (They lived about fifteen miles apart.) He dismounted, and made himself highly entertaining. Mr. Bouldin says he knew it was all put on about his missing his way, and he determined to retaliate. So he went to Mr. Randolph's soon afterward and inquired for the overseer. After sitting an hour or two in high chat, he reminded his host of the object of his visit. Mr. Randolph caught his meaning in an instant. Said he, pulling out his watch: "If you really want to see my overseer, he may be found at this hour in a certain part of my plantation," naming it.

"I was once deputed," said Mr. Bouldin, "to ask him whether we ought to send from our county delegates to the Charlottesville Convention on the subject of internal improvement."

Said he: "Sir, I am against cabals of all sorts. As to internal improvement it begins here—striking his breast."

Said I: "How do you account for wise men meeting to deliberate what to do with the fund for internal improvement when that fund has no money?"

"Very easily."

"How, sir?"

"They are not wise men."

"The Chief Justice was there, I think, with many other able men—men that he always admitted to be able."

The foregoing little incidents were thrown in without any relation to the remarks which follow.

The reader can but remember the impression made upon him from reading Mr. "Garland's Life of John Randolph"— how the latter complained of the want of society—how dreary and lonely he was at Roanoke.

From the developments already made, it cannot be a matter of surprise that he had very few visitors. We have heard, and we believe truly, that when some of his friends from a distance designed to pay him a visit, they would stop at a neighbor's house to find beforehand what sort of humor Mr. Randolph was in. If he was in an agreeable mood they paid the visit; if not, they returned to await a more favorable frame of mind.

He visited very little himself. When he did visit his neighbors, who were plain, unpretending people, but highly cultivated, and some of them wealthy, he created quite a sensation. He was helped out of his carriage, escorted into the house, and the whole plantation placed at his command, from the services of the landlord to those of the humblest slave; from the bed-chamber of the landlady to a room in the garret. He has been known to accept the bed-chamber of his hostess repeatedly. Yet he never regarded the inconvenience he was putting people to; seemed to think it all right that he should be waited upon as no other man was, forsooth, because there was no other man equal to him.

And this reminds us of a very interesting scene which the late Dr. William A. Fuqua, of Charlotte county, described to us.

He says on one occasion Mr. Randolph drove up in his coach-and-four to the house of his friend Mr. A., on his way to Buckingham. He was attended by two servants. The most unusual attentions were paid to the distinguished guest. Such a brushing of rooms; such cooking in the kitchen, and stir generally among all on the plantation, white and black, never was seen. Nothing could be clean enough for him; nothing too good for him. His friends, whom he visited, were afraid not to know what food suited his fastidious taste. Hence, at the table they always handed him something he was fond of. If it happened to be fish, the modest hostess was overwhelmed with compliments, and he would talk about fish for perhaps a half an hour.

His arrival at Mr. A.'s excited the curiosity of some nice young ladies, residing near by, to see the strange and unaccountable man. They sent over to know if Mr. Randolph could be seen; the host sent to know of his guest.

After spending some time at his toilet, and when everything was ready for the curtain to rise, the young ladies were ushered in. Mr. Randolph was reclining upon a sofa, with his head leaning upon one of his hands, and looking as if he was ready to expire. He showed off handsomely before the spectators. His polished manners and fine address charmed them.

But before the performance concluded, he said something to make the company feel that they were "handled." He rang the changes on the name of one of the young ladies to her great embarrassment, and wound up by telling her to tell her mother to change her name, for she had named her after "a very great rascal." But, nevertheless, the young ladies went home highly gratified at having seen John Randolph.

Dr. Joel W. Watkins was once fox hunting: his dogs ran

on Mr. Randolph's plantation; his overseer informed him he was sorry he should have to report him, his orders were imperative from Mr. Randolph, whose land was posted. That night Mr. Randolph sent a servant with a note, saying he did not post his land against gentlemen who rode Roanoke horses, but against those who rode grass-g—ted horses. His (Dr. W.'s) horse could jump over any fence his (Randolph's) d—n lazy overseer would make.

An old lady who resided for years near Mr. Randolph's solitary abode, on the banks of the Staunton, informed us that she was one day sitting alone in her chamber, when suddenly appeared before her a woman dressed in white in the dead of winter. She was described as a beautiful creature, but she had lost the bloom of youth, and was as pale as death itself. She talked about her lover. She said, "he would never prove false to his plighted faith; Mr. Randolph would marry her yet."

When told that she had better cease to think of him, for that he would never marry her, "Yes, he will," she replied.

She talked incessantly of him, nor could she be induced to believe that he did not love her. Presently there came riding by a young gentleman leading a horse with a side saddle on. She darted out of the house and asked permission to ride a few miles. The young man politely gave his consent; but what was his astonishment when she mounted astride like a man and rode off. Though greatly embarrassed, he had nothing to do but to escort his strange companion to the end of her journey.

We are informed by the same truthful lady that this same strange woman occasionally visited Mr. Randolph from time to time for several years. There was no doubt upon the mind of our informant that Mr. Randolph was greatly annoyed by his fair visitor. He sometimes rid himself of her by putting her on a horse with a servant to escort her, and sending her away in that manner.

Had the poor creature lost her mind? We had not supposed that any woman ever loved Mr. Randolph to that extent. An old lady once remarked to us that she never heard any of her female acquaintances acknowledge that she aspired to the hand of Mr. Randolph, or speak of him in the light of a beau. The thought of "catching" him never seemed to occur to them. Nor had we ever associated Mr. Randolph in our mind with love scrapes and adventures such as are indulged in by most other men. When therefore we were informed that a young lady had fallen desperately in love with him, so as either to have dethroned her reason, or made her take extraordinary means of counterfeiting derangement, in order to procure an interview with him, we were surprised. And yet there was nothing unnatural about the story.

Mr. Baldwin expresses the opinion that Mr. Randolph might have been the author of Childe Harold. We agree with him. But brilliant as was his imagination he never could have written Don Juan. There are thoughts and scenes described in that poem which he could not have painted, because he had no conception of them. The pleasures of *illicit* love were the bane of Byron—Randolph never knew them. The love of the one, was ardent, passionate; that of the other, pure, Platonic. How could he have been the author of the scene commencing—

"Twas on the sixth of June, about the hour
Of half-past six—perhaps still nearer seven—
When Julia sate within as pretty a bower," &c.

He might have sung:—

> "'Tis sweet to hear
> At midnight on the blue and moonlit deep
> The song and oar of Adria's gondolier
> By distance mellowed, o'er the waters sweep:
> 'Tis sweet to see the evening star appear;
> 'Tis sweet to listen as the night winds creep
> From leaf to leaf: 'tis sweet to view on high
> The rainbow, based on ocean, span the sky."

All this he had doubtless felt, and might have sung as well as Byron himself. But how could he have concluded this long catalogue with the following outburst of feeling:

> "But sweeter still than this, than these, than all,
> Is first and *passionate* love."

The fair and fading woman, who left her distant home, and wandered in the dead of winter in search of her lover, returned from the shades of Roanoke as pure and undefiled as she came.

CHAPTER X.

General Wilkinson's Challenge to Mr. Randolph to Fight a Duel—Mr. Randolph's Reply—Duel with Clay.

MR. WILLIAM TOWNES, now eighty-six years of age, has in his possession a scrap-book of Thomas Jefferson's, purchased at his sale by the late James C. Bruce, of Halifax county, Virginia, and presented to him by Mr. Bruce, in which there is a letter from John Randolph to General James Wilkinson of the United States army, in reply to a challenge of General Wilkinson to fight a duel. As we have never seen the correspondence in print, we take pleasure in placing it before the public.

In a letter offering us a copy of it, dated March 26, 1877, Mr. Townes writes:

"The quarrel between General Wilkinson and Mr. Randolph had its origin in the grand jury room at Richmond at the trial of Aaron Burr. Mr. Randolph was foreman of the grand jury which indicted him. Colonel Henry E. Coleman, of Halifax, was also a member of the grand jury, and from him I was informed of the particulars shortly after the quarrel took place."

Mr. Randolph believed that General Wilkinson was implicated in the treason of Burr. When he, Wilkinson, entered the grand jury room as a witness, he was in *full uniform* as an United States General, with his side arms. Mr. Randolph instantly ordered the marshal to "disarm James Wilkinson," not even giving him a title, which the marshal did; and it seemed to give great offence to General Wilkinson.

The following correspondence took place afterwards in the city of Washington:

WASHINGTON, Dec. 24th, 1807.

SIR:—I understand several expressions have escaped you, in their nature personal and highly injurious to my reputation. The exceptionable language imputed to you may be briefly and substantially comprised in the following statements: That you have avowed the opinion that I was a rogue—that you have ascribed to me the *infernal* disposition to commit murder to prevent the exposition of my sinister designs, and through me have stigmatized those citizen soldiers who compose the military corps of our country. No person can be more sensible of the pernicious tendency of such cruel and undeserved reflections in their application to public men, or private individuals than yourself; nor is any man more competent to determine the just reparation to which they establish a fair claim. Under these impressions I have no hesitation to appeal to your justice, your magnanimity and your gallantry, to prescribe the manner of redress, being persuaded your decision will comport with the feelings of a man of honor—that you will be found equally prompt to assert a right or repair a wrong. I transmit this letter through the post-office, and shall expect your answer by such a channel as you may deem proper.

I have the honor to be, sir,
Your obedient servant,

JAMES WILKINSON.

The Hon. JOHN RANDOLPH.

To this letter Mr. Randolph replied as follows:

DECEMBER 25TH, 1807.

SIR:—Several months ago I was informed of your having said that you were acquainted with what had passed in the grand jury room at Richmond last spring, and that you declared a determination to challenge me. I am to consider your letter of the last night by mail as the execution of that avowed purpose, and through the same channel I return you my answer. Whatever may have been the expressions used by me in regard to your character, they were the result of deliberate opinion, founded on the most authoritative evidence, the greater part of which my country imposed upon me, to weigh and decide upon; they were such as to my knowledge and to yours have been delivered by the first men in the Union, and probably by a full moiety of the American people.

In you, sir, I recognize no right to hold me accountable for my public or private opinion of your character that would not subject me to an equal claim from Colonel Burr or Sergeant Dubbough. I cannot descend to your level. This is my final answer.

JOHN RANDOLPH.

Brigadier GENERAL WILKINSON.

Mr. Randolph did not decline General Wilkinson's challenge through fear. Mr. Randolph was a brave man, and had already shown it upon the field of honor by his exchange of shots with Mr. Taylor; and he was yet to prove it upon a most signal occasion in his duel with Henry Clay. That duel was fought during the administration of Adams, and while he was United States senator. Mr. Randolph believed every word of the story of Cremer, and it was the following allusion to the charge of bargain and corruption which caused the challenge of Mr. Clay: "This until now unheard of combination of the black-leg with the Puritan; this union of Black George with Blifil" (an allusion from Fielding's novel of "Tom Jones").

Referring to this, Mr. Parks remarks: "Language could not have been made more offensive. But the fruitful imagination of Mr. Randolph was not exhausted, and he proceeded with denunciation, which spared not the venerable mother of Mr. Clay, then living—denouncing her for bringing into the world 'this being so brilliant, yet so corrupt, which, like a rotten mackerel by moonlight, shined and stunk.'"

This drew from Mr. Clay a challenge, and a meeting was

the consequence. We purpose to give Mr. Benton's account of it, which Mr. Clay said was strictly correct.

Mr. Benton says:

It was Saturday, the first of April, towards noon, the Senate not being that day in session, that Mr. Randolph came to my room at Brown's hotel, and (without explaining the reason of the question) asked me if I was a blood-relation of Mr. Clay? I answered that I was; and he immediately replied that that put an end to a request which he had wished to make of me; and then went on to tell me that he had just received a challenge from Mr. Clay, had accepted it, was ready to go out, and would apply to Colonel Tatnall to be his second. Before leaving, he told me he would make my bosom the depository of a secret which he should commit to no other person: it was that he did not intend to fire at Mr. Clay. He told it to me because he wanted a witness of his intention, and did not mean to tell it to his second or anybody else; and enjoined inviolable secrecy until the duel was over. This was the first notice I had of the affair. The circumstances of the delivery of the challenge, I had from General Jesup, Mr. Clay's second, and they were so perfectly characteristic of Mr. Randolph that I give them in detail, and in the General's own words:

"I was unable to see Mr. Randolph until the morning of the first of April, when I called on him for the purpose of delivering the note. Previous to presenting it, however, I thought it proper to ascertain from Mr. Randolph himself, whether the information which Mr. Clay had received— that he considered himself personally responsible for the attack on him— was correct. I accordingly informed Mr. Randolph that I was the bearer of a message from Mr. Clay in consequence of an attack which he had made upon his private as well as public character in the Senate; that I was aware no one had the right to question him out of the Senate for anything said in debate, unless he chose voluntarily to waive his privileges as a member of that body. Mr. Randolph replied, that the constitution did protect him, but he would never shield himself under such a subterfuge as the pleading of the privilege as a Senator from Virginia; that he did hold himself accountable to Mr. Clay; but he said that gentleman had first two pledges to redeem: one that he had bound himself to fight any member of the House of Representatives who should acknowledge himself the author of a certain publication in a Philadelphia paper; and the other, that he stood pledged to establish certain facts in regard to a great man, whom he would not name; but he added he could receive no verbal message from Mr. Clay—that any message from him must be in writing. I replied that I was not authorized by Mr. Clay to enter into or receive any verbal explanations—that the inquiries I had made were for my own satisfaction and upon my own responsibility—that the only message of which I was the bearer was in writing. I then presented the note and remarked that I knew nothing of Mr. Clay's pledges: but that if they existed as he (Mr. Randolph) understood them, and he was aware of them when he made the attack complained of, he could not avail himself of them—that by making the attack I thought he had waived them himself. He said he had not the remotest intention of taking advantage of the pledges referred to; that he had mentioned them merely to remind me that he was waiving his privilege, not only as a Senator from Virginia, but as a private gentleman; that he was ready to respond to Mr. Clay, and would be obliged to me if I would bear his note in reply; and that he would in the course of the day look out for a friend. I declined being the bearer of the note, but informed him my only reason for declining was that I thought he owed it to himself to consult his friends before taking so important a step. He seized my hand, saying, 'You are right, sir. I thank you for the suggestion; but as you do not take my note, you must not be impatient if you should not hear from me to-day. I now think of only two friends, and there are circumstances connected with one of them which may deprive me of his services, and the other is in bad health—he was sick yesterday, and may not be out to-day.' I assured him that any reasonable time which he might find necessary to take would be satisfactory. I took leave of him; and it is due to his memory to say that his bearing was, throughout the interview, that of a high-toned, chivalrous gentleman of the old school."

These were the circumstances of the delivery of the challenge, and the only thing necessary to give them their character, is to recollect that with this prompt acceptance and positive refusal to explain, and this extra cut about the two pledges, there was a perfect determination not to fire at Mr. Clay. That determination rested on two grounds: first, an entire unwillingness to hurt Mr. Clay; and next, a conviction that to return the fire would be to answer, and would be an implied acknowledgment of Mr. Clay's right to make him answer. This he would not do, neither by implication nor in words. He denied the right of any person to question him out of the Senate for words spoken within it. He took a distinction between man and senator. As a senator he had a constitutional immunity, given for a wise purpose, and which he would neither surrender nor compromise; as individual, he was ready to give satisfaction for what was deemed an injury. He would receive, but not return a fire. It was as much as to say, Mr. Clay may fire at me for what has offended him; I will not by returning the fire admit his right to do so. This was a subtle distinction, and that in case of life and death, and not very clear to the common intellect; but to Mr. Randolph both clear and convincing. His allusion to the "two pledges unredeemed," which he might have plead in bar to Mr. Clay's challenge, and would not, was another sarcastic cut at Mr. Adams and Mr. Clay, while rendering satisfaction for cuts already given. The "member of the House" was Mr. George Cremer, of Pennsylvania, who, at the time of the Presidential election in the House of Representatives, had avowed himself to be the author of an anonymous publication, the writer of which Mr. Clay had threatened to call to account if he would avow himself, and did not. The "great man" was President Adams, with whom Mr. Clay had had a newspaper controversy, involving a question of fact, which had been postponed. The cause of this sarcastic cut, and of all the keen personality in the Panama speech, was the belief that the president and secretary, the latter especially, encouraged the newspapers in their interest to attack him, which they did incessantly, and he chose to overlook the editors and retaliate upon the instigators, as he believed them to be. This he did to his heart's content in that speech, and to their great annoyance, as the coming of the challenge proved. The "two friends" alluded to were Colonel Tatnall and myself, and the circumstances which might disqualify one of the two were those of my relationship to Mrs. Clay, of which he did not know the degree, and whether of affinity or consanguinity—considering the first no obstacle, the other a complete bar to my appearing as his second—holding as he did, with the tenacity of an Indian, to the obligations of blood, and laying but little stress on marriage connections. His affable reception and courteous demeanor to General Jesup were, according to his own high breeding, and the decorum which belonged to such occasions. A duel in the circle to which he belonged was "an affair of honor," and high honor, according to its code, must pervade every part of it. General Jesup had come upon an unplesant business. Mr. Randolph determined to put him at his ease, and did it so effectually as to charm him into admiration. The whole plan of his conduct, down to contingent details, was cast in his mind instantly, as if by intuition, and never departed from. The acceptance, the refusal to explain, the determination not to fire, the first and second choice of a friend, and the circumstances which might disqualify one and delay the other, the additional cut, and the resolve to fall, if he fell, on the soil of Virginia, was all to his mind a single emanation, the flash of an instant. He needed no consultations, no deliberation to arrive at all these important conclusions. I dwell upon these small circumstances, because they are characteristic, and show the man, a man who belongs to history, and had his own history, and should·be known as he was. That character can only be shown in his own conduct, his own words and acts; and the duel with Mr. Clay illustrates it at many points. It is in that point of view that I dwell upon circumstances which might seem trivial, but which are not so, being illustrative of character and significant to their smallest particulars.

The acceptance of the challenge was in keeping with the whole proceeding—prompt in the agreement to meet, exact in protesting against the *right* to call him out, clear in the waiver of his constitutional privilege, brief and cogent in presenting the case as one of some reprehension—the case of a member of an administration challenging a senator for words spoken in debate of that administration, and all in brief, terse, and superlatively decorous language. It runs thus:

" Mr. Randolph accepts the challenge of Mr. Clay. At the same time he protests against the *right* of any minister of the Executive Government of the United States to hold him responsible for words spoken in debate as a senator from Virginia in crimination of such minister, or the administration under which he shall have taken office. Colonel Tatnall, of Georgia, the bearer of this letter, is authorized to arrange with General Jesup (the bearer of Mr. Clay's challenge) the terms of the meeting to which Mr. Randolph is invited by that note."

The protest which Mr. Randolph entered against the right of Mr. Clay to challenge him, led to an explanation between their mutual friends on that delicate point—a point which concerned the independence of debate, the privileges of the Senate, the immunity of a member, and the sanctity of the constitution. It was a point which Mr. Clay felt; and the explanation which was had between the mutual friends presented an excuse, if not a justification, for his proceeding. He had been informed that Mr.

Randolph, in his speech, had avowed his responsibility to Mr. Clay, and waived his privilege—a thing which, if it had been done, would have been a defiance, and stood for an invitation to Mr. Clay to send a challenge. Mr. Randolph, through Colonel Tatnall, disavowed that imputed avowal, and confined his waiver of privilege to the time of the delivery of the challenge, and in answer to an inquiry before it was delivered.

The following are the communications between the respective seconds on this point:

"In regard to the *protest* with which Mr. Randolph's note concludes, it is due to Mr. Clay to say that he had been informed Mr. Randolph did, and would, hold himself responsible to him for any observations he might make in relation to him; and that I (General Jesup) distinctly understood from Mr. Randolph, before I delivered the note of Mr. Clay, that he waived his privilege as a Senator."

To this Colonel Tatnall replied:

"As this expression (did and would hold himself responsible, &c.) may be construed to mean that Mr. Randolph had given this information not only before called upon, but in such a manner as to throw out to Mr. Clay something like an invitation to make such a call, I have, on the part of Mr. Randolph, to disavow any disposition, when expressing his readiness to waive his privilege as a Senator from Virginia, to invite, in any case, a call upon him for personal satisfaction. The concluding paragraph of your note, I presume, is intended to show merely that you did not present a note, such as that of Mr. Clay to Mr. Randolph, until you had ascertained his willingness to waive his privilege as a senator. This, I infer, as it was in your recollection that the expression of such a readiness on the part of Mr. Randolph was in reply to an inquiry on that point made by yourself."

Thus an irritating circumstance in the affair was virtually negatived, and its offensive import wholly disavowed. For my part, I do not believe that Mr. Randolph used such language in his speech. I have no recollection of having heard it. The published report of the speech as taken down by the reporters and not revised by the speaker, contains nothing of it. Such gasconade was foreign to Mr. Randolph's character. The occasion was not one in which these sort of defiances are thrown out, which are either to purchase a cheap reputation when it is known they will be despised, or to get an advantage in extracting a challenge when there is a design to kill. Mr. Randolph had none of these views with respect to Mr. Clay. He had no desire to fight him, or to hurt him, or to gain cheap character by appearing to bully him. He was above all that, and had settled accounts with him in his speech, and wanted no more. I do not believe it was said; but there was a part of the speech which might have received a wrong application, and led to the erroneous report; a part which applied to a quoted speech in Mr. Adams's Panama message, which he condemned and denounced, and dared the President and his friends to defend. His words were, as reported unrevised: "Here I plant my foot; here I fling defiance right into his (the President's) teeth; here I throw the gauntlet to him and the bravest of his compeers to come forward and defend these lines," &c. A very palpable defiance this, but very different from a summons to personal combat, and from what was related to Mr. Clay. It was an unfortunate report, doubtless the effect of indistinct apprehension, and the more to be regretted as, after having been a main cause inducing the challenge, the disavowal could not stop it.

Thus the argument for the meeting was absolute, and, according to the expectation of the principals, the meeting itself would be immediately, but their seconds, from the most laudable feelings, determined to delay it, with the hope to prevent it, and did keep it off a week, admitting me to a participation in the good work, as being already privy to the affair, and friendly to both parties. The challenge stated no specific ground of offence, specified no exceptionable words. It was peremptory and general for an "unprovoked attack on his (Mr. Clay's) character;" and it dispensed with explanations, by alleging that the notoriety and indisputable existence of the injury superseded the necessity for them. Of course this demand was bottomed on a report of the words spoken—a verbal report, the full daily publication of the debates having not then begun—and that verbal report was of a character greatly to exasperate Mr. Clay. It stated that in the course of the debate Mr. Randolph said:

"That a letter from General Salazar, the Mexican minister at Washington, submitted by the executive to the Senate, bore the ear-mark of having been manufactured or forged by the secretary of state, and denounced the administration as a corrupt coalition between the Puritan and black-leg; and added at the same time that he (Mr. Randolph) held himself personally responsible for all that he had said."

This was the report to Mr. Clay, and upon which he gave the absolute challenge, and received the absolute acceptance, which shut out all inquiry between the principals into the causes of the quarrel. The seconds determined to open it, and to attempt an accommodation, or a peaceable determination of the difficulty. In consequence, General Jesup stated the complaint in a note to Colonel Tatnall thus:

"The injury of which Mr. Clay complains consists in this, that Mr. Randolph has charged him with having forged or manufactured a paper connected with the Panama mission; also, that he has applied to him in debate the epithet of black-leg. The explanation which I consider necessary is, that Mr. Randolph declared that he had no intention of charging Mr. Clay, either in his public or private capacity, with forging or falsifying any paper, or misrepresenting any fact; and also that the term blackleg was not intended to apply to him."

To this exposition of the grounds of the complaint Colonel Tatnall answered:

"Mr. Randolph informs me that the words used by him in debate were as follows: 'That I thought it would be in my power to show evidence, sufficiently presumptive, to satisfy a Charlotte (county) jury that this invitation was manufactured here—that Salazar's letter struck me as bearing a strong likeness in point of style to the other papers. I did not undertake to prove this, but expressed my suspicion that the fact was so. I applied to the administration the epithet, Puritanic, diplomatic, black-legged administration.'"

In this answer Mr. Randolph remained upon his original ground of refusing to answer out of the Senate for words spoken within it. In other respects the statement of the words actually spoken greatly ameliorated the offensive report, the coarse and insulting words, "forging and falsifying," being disavowed, as in fact they were not used, and were not to be found in the published report. The speech was a bitter philippic, and intended to be so, taking for its point the alleged coalition between Mr. Clay and Mr. Adams with respect to the election, and their efforts to get up a question contrary to our policy of non-entanglement with foreign nations in sending ministers to the Congress of the American States of Spanish origin at the Isthmus of Panama. I heard it all, and, though sharp and cutting, I think it might have been heard, had he been present, without any manifestation of resentment by Mr. Clay. The part which he took so seriously to heart, that of having the Panama invitations manufactured in his office was, to my mind, nothing more than attributing to him a diplomatic superiority, which enabled him to obtain from the South American ministers the invitations that he wanted, and not at all that they were spurious fabrications. As to the expression, "*black-leg and Puritan*," it was merely a sarcasm to strike by antithesis, and which, being without foundation, might have been disregarded. I presented these views to the parties, and if they had come from Mr. Randolph they might have been sufficient, but he was inexorable, and would not authorize a word to be said beyond what he had written.

All hope of accommodation having vanished, the seconds proceeded to arrange for the duel. The afternoon of Saturday, the 8th of April, was fixed upon for the time; the right bank of the Potomac, within the State of Virginia, above the Little Falls bridge, was the place; pistols, the weapons; distance, ten paces; each party to be attended by two seconds and a surgeon, and myself at liberty to attend as a mutual friend. There was to be no practicing with pistols, and there was none; and the words, "one," "two," "three," "stop," after the word "fire," were, by agreement between the seconds, and for the humane purpose of reducing the result as near as possible to chance, to be given out in quick succession. The Virginia side of the Potomac was taken at the instance of Mr. Randolph. He went out as a Virginia senator, refusing to compromise that character, and, if he fell in defence of its rights, Virginia soil was to him the chosen ground to receive his blood. There was a statute of the State against duelling within her limits; but, as he merely went to receive a fire, without returning it, he deemed that no fighting, and consequently no breach of the statute. This reason for choosing Virginia could only be explained to me, as I alone was the depository of his secret.

The week's delay which the seconds had contrived was about expiring. It was Friday evening, or rather night, when I went to see Mr. Clay for the last time before the duel. There had been some alienation between us since the time of the Presidential election in the House of Representatives, and I wished to give evidence that there was nothing personal in it. The family were in the parlor—company present—and some of it staid late. The youngest child, I believe, James, went to sleep on the sofa—a circumstance which availed me for a purpose the next day. Mrs. Clay was, as always since the death of her daughter, a picture of desolation, but calm and conversable, and without the slightest apparent consciousness of the impending event. When all were gone, and she had also left the parlor, I did what I came for, and said to Mr. Clay, that, notwithstanding our late political differences, my personal feelings towards him were the same as formerly, and that, in whatever concerned his life and honor, my best wishes were with him. He expressed his gratificaion at the visit and the declaration, and said it was what he would have expected of me. We parted at midnight.

Saturday, the 8th of April, the day for the duel, had come, and almost the hour. It was noon, and the meeting was to take place at 4½ o'clock. I had gone to see Mr. Randolph before the hour, and for a purpose; and besides, it was so far on the way, as he lived half-way to Georgetown, and we had to pass through that place to cross the Potomac into Virginia at the Little Falls bridge. I had heard nothing from him on the point of not returning the fire since the first communication to that effect, eight days before. I had no reason to doubt the steadiness of his determination, but felt a desire to have fresh assurance of it after so many days' delay, and so near approach of the trying moment. I knew it would not do to ask him the question—any question which would imply a doubt of his word. His sensitive feelings would be hurt and annoyed at it. So I fell upon a scheme to get at the inquiry without seeming to make it. I told him of my visit to Mr. Clay the night before—of the late sitting—the child asleep—the unconscious tranquility of Mrs. Clay; and added, I could not help reflecting how different all that might be the next night. He understood me perfectly, and immediately said, with a quietude of look and expression which seemed to rebuke an unworthy doubt, "*I shall do nothing to disturb the sleep of the child or the repose of the mother;*" and went on with his employment (his seconds being engaged in their preparations in a different room), which was making codicils to his will, all in the way of remembrance to his friends; the bequests slight in value, but invaluable in tenderness of feeling, and beauty of expression, and always appropriate to the receiver. To Mr. Macon he gave some English shillings, to keep the game when he played whist. His namesake, John Randolph Bryan, then at school in Baltimore, and since married to his niece, had been sent for to see him, but sent off before the hour of going out, to save the boy from a possible shock at seeing him brought back. He wanted some gold—that coin not being then in circulation, and only to be obtained by favor or purchase—and sent his faithful man, Johnny, to the United States Branch Bank to get a few pieces, American being the kind asked for. Johnny returned without the gold, and delivered the excuse that the bank had none. Instantly Mr. Randolph's clear silver-toned voice was heard above its natural pitch, exclaiming, "Their name is legion; and they are liars from the beginning. Johnny, bring me my horse." His own saddle horse was brought him—for he never rode Johnny's, nor Johnny his, though both, and all his hundred horses, were of the finest English blood—and rode off to the bank down Pennsylvania avenue, now Corcoran & Riggs's—Johnny following, as always, forty paces behind. Arrived at the bank, this scene, according to my informant, took place:

Mr. Randolph asked for the state of his account, was shown it, and found to be some four thousand dollars in his favor. He asked for it. The teller took up packages of bills, and civilly asked in what sized notes he would have it. I want money, said Mr. Randolph, putting emphasis on the word, and at that time it required a bold man to intimate that United States bank notes were not money. The teller beginning to understand him, and willing to make sure, said inquiringly, you want silver? I want my money was the reply. Then the teller, lifting boxes to the counter, said politely, " Have you a cart, Mr. Randolph, to put it in?" "That is my business, sir," said he. By that time the attention of the cashier (Mr. Richard Smith) was attracted to what was going on, who came up, and understanding the question and its cause, told Mr. Randolph "there was a mistake in the answer given to his servant; that they had gold, and that he should have what he wanted."

In fact he had only applied for a few pieces, which he wanted for a special purpose. This brought about a compromise. The pieces of gold were received, the cart and the silver dispensed with; but the account in bank was closed, and a check taken for the amount on New York. He returned and delivered me a sealed paper, which I was to open if he was killed—give back to him if he was not; also an open slip, which I was to read before I got to the ground. This slip was a request to feel in his left breeches pocket, if he was killed, and find so many pieces of gold—I believe nine—take three for myself, and give the same number to Tatnall and Hamilton each, to make seals to wear in remembrance of him. We were all three at Mr. Randolph's lodgings then, and soon set out, Mr. Randolph and his seconds in a carriage, I following him on horseback.

I have already said that the count was to be quick after giving the word fire, and for a reason which could not be told to the principals. To Mr. Randolph, who did not mean to fire, and who, though agreeing to be shot at, had no desire to be hit, this rapidity of counting out the time, and quick arrival at the command "stop," presented no objection. With Mr. Clay it was different; with him it was all a real transaction, and gave rise to some proposal for more deliberateness in counting off the time, which being communicated to Colonel Tatnall, and by him to Mr. Randolph, had an ill effect upon his feelings, and aided by an untoward accident on the ground, unsettled for a moment the noble determination which he had formed not to fire at Mr. Clay. I now give the words of General Jesup:

"When I repeated to Mr. Clay the 'word' in the manner in which it would be given, he expressed some apprehension that as he was not accustomed to the use of the pistol, he might not be able to fire within the time, and for that reason alone desired that it might be prolonged. I mentioned to Colonel Tatnall the desire of Mr. Clay. He replied: 'If you insist upon it the time must be prolonged, but I should very much regret it.' I informed him that I did not insist upon prolonging the time, and I was sure Mr. Clay would acquiesce. The original agreement was carried out."

I knew nothing of this until it was too late to speak with the seconds or principals. I had crossed the little Falls bridge just after them, and come to the place where the servants and carriages had stopped. I saw none of the gentlemen, and supposed they had all gone to the spot where the ground was being marked off, but on speaking to Johnny, Mr. Randolph, who was still in his carriage, and heard my voice, looked out from the window, and said to me: "Colonel, since I saw you, and since I have been in this carriage, I have heard something which *may* make me change my determination. Colonel Hamilton will give you a note which will explain it." Colonel Hamilton was then in the carriage, and gave me the note, in the course of the evening, of which Mr. Randolph spoke. I readily comprehended that this possible change of determination related to his firing; but the emphasis with which he pronounced the word "*may*," clearly showed that his mind was undecided, and left it doubtful whether he would fire or not. No further conversation took place between us; the preparation for the duel was finished; the parties went to their places; and I went forward to a piece of rising ground, from which I could see what passed and hear what was said. The faithful Johnny followed me close, speaking not a word, but evincing the deepest anxiety for his beloved master. The place was a thick forest, and the immediate spot a little depression or basin, in which the parties stood. The principals saluted each other courteously as they took their stands. Colonel Tatnall had won the choice of position, which gave to General Jesup the delivery of the word. They stood on a line east and west, a small stump just behind Mr. Clay; a low gravelly bank rose just behind Mr. Randolph. This latter asked General Jesup to repeat the word as he would give it; while in the act of doing so, and Mr. Randolph adjusting the butt of his pistol to his hand, the muzzle pointing downwards, and almost to the ground, it fired. Instantly Mr. Randolph turned to Colonel Tatnall and said: "I protested against that hair trigger." Colonel Tatnall took blame to himself for having sprung the hair. Mr. Clay had not then received his pistol. Senator Johnson, of Louisiana (Josiah), one of his seconds, was carrying it to him, and still several steps from him. This untimely fire, though clearly an accident, necessarily gave rise to some remarks and a species of inquiry, which was conducted with the utmost delicacy, but which in itself was of a nature to be inexpressibly painful to a gentleman's feelings. Mr. Clay stopped it, with the generous remark that the fire was clearly an accident, and it was so unanimously declared. Another pistol was immediately furnished, and an exchange of shots took place, and happily without effect upon the persons. Mr. Randolph's bullet struck the stump behind Mr. Clay, and Mr. Clay's knocked up the earth and gravel behind Mr. Randolph, and in a line with the level of his hips, both bullets having gone so true and close, that it was a marvel how they missed. The moment had come for me to interpose. I went in among the parties and offered my mediation, but nothing could be done. Mr. Clay said, with the wave of the hand, with which he was accustomed to put away a trifle, "This is child's play," and required another fire. Mr. Randolph also demanded another fire. The seconds were directed to reload. While this was going on I prevailed on Mr. Randolph to walk away from his post, and renewed to him, more pressingly than ever, my importunities to yield to some accommodation, but I found him more determined than I had ever seen him, and for the first time impatient, and seemingly annoyed and dissatisfied at what I was doing. He was indeed annoyed and dissatisfied. The accidental fire of his pistol preyed upon his feelings. He was doubly chagrined at it, both as a circumstance susceptible in itself of an unfair interpretation, and as having been the immediate and controlling cause of his firing at Mr. Clay. He regretted this fire the instant it was over. He felt that it had subjected him to imputations, from which he knew himself to be free—a desire to kill Mr. Clay, and a contempt for the laws of his beloved state, and the annoyances which he felt at these vexatious circumstances, revived his original determination, and decided him irrevocably to carry it out.

It was in this interval that he told me what he had heard since we parted, and to which he alluded when he spoke to me from the window of the carriage. It was to this effect: That he had been informed by Colonel Tatnall that it was proposed to give out the words with more deliberateness, so as to prolong the time for taking aim. This information grated harshly upon his feelings. It unsettled his purpose, and brought his mind to the inquiry (as he now told me, and I found it expressed in the note which he had immediately written in pencil to apprise me of his possible change,) whether, under these circumstances, he might not "*disable* his adversary." This note is so characteristic, and such an essential part of this affair, that I here give its very words, so far as relates to this point. It ran thus:

"Information received from Colonel Tatnall since I got into the carriage *may* induce me to change my mind, of not returning Mr. Clay's fire. I seek not his death. I would not have his blood upon my hands—it will not be upon my soul if I shed it in self-defence—for the world. He has determined, by the use of a long, preparatory caution by words, to get time to kill me. May I not, then, disable him? Yes, if I please."

It has been seen, by the statement of General Jesup, already given, that this information was a misapprehension; that Mr. Clay had not applied for a prolongation of time for the purpose of getting sure aim, but only to enable his unused hand, long unfamiliar with the pistol, to fire within the limited time; that there was no prolongation, in fact, either granted or insisted upon; but he was in doubt, and General Jesup having won the word, he was having him repeat it in the way he was to give it out, when his finger touched the hair-trigger. How unfortunate that I did not know of this in time to speak to General Jesup, when one word from him would have set all right, and saved the imminent risks incurred. This inquiry, "May I not disable him?" was still on Mr. Randolph's mind, and dependent for its solution on the rising incidents of the moment, when the accidental fire of his pistol gave the turn to his feelings which solved the doubt. But he declared to me that he had not aimed at the life of Mr. Clay; that he did not level as high as his knees—not higher than the knee-band; "for it was no mercy to shoot a man in the knee," that his only object was to disable him and spoil his aim. And then added, with a beauty of expression and a depth of feeling which no studied oratory can ever attain, and which I shall never forget, these impressive words: "*I would not have seen him fall mortally, or even doubtfully, wounded, for all the land that is watered by the King of Floods and all his tributary streams.*" He left me to resume his post, utterly refusing to explain out of the Senate anything that he had said in it, and with the positive declaration that he would not return the next fire. I withdrew a little way into the woods, and kept my eyes fixed on Mr. Randolph, whom I knew to be the only one in danger. I saw him receive the fire of Mr. Clay, saw the gravel knocked up in the same place, saw Mr. Randolph raise his pistol—discharge it in the air; heard him say, "I do not fire at you, Mr. Clay;" and immediately advancing and offering his hand. He was met in the same spirit. They met half-way, shook hands, Mr. Randolph saying, jocosely, "*You owe me a coat, Mr. Clay*" (the bullet had passed through the skirt of the coat, very near the hip)—to which Mr. Clay promptly and happily replied, "*I am glad the debt is no greater.*".

I had come up, and was prompt to proclaim what I had been obliged to keep secret for eight days. The joy of all was extreme at this happy termination of a most critical affair, and we immediately left with lighter hearts than we brought. I stopped to sup with Mr. Randolph and his friends—none of us wanted dinner that day—and had a characteristic time of it. A runner came in from the bank to say that they had overpaid him by mistake one hundred and thirty dollars that day. He answered: "*I believe it is your rule not to correct mistakes except at the time, and at your counter.*" And with that answer the runner had to return. When gone, Mr. Randolph said: "*I will pay it on Monday: people must be honest if banks are not.*" He asked for the sealed paper he had given me, opened it, took out a check for one thousand dollars, drawn in my favor, and with which I was requested to have him carried if killed to Virginia, and buried under his patrimonial oaks—not let him be buried at Washington, with an hundred hacks after him. He took the gold from his left breeches pocket, and said to us (Hamilton, Tatnall and me): "Gentlemen, Clay's bad shooting shan't rob you of your seals. I am going to London, and will have them made for you," which he did, and most characteristically, so far as mine was concerned. He went to the herald's office in London and inquired for the Benton family, of which I had often told him there was none, as we only dated on that side from my grandfather in North Carolina. But the name was found, and with it a coat of arms—among the quarterings a lion rampant. That is the family, said he; and had the arms engraved on the seal, the same which I have since habitually worn; and added the motto: *Factis non verbis*, of which he was afterwards accustomed to say the *non* should be changed into *et*. But enough. I run into these details, not merely to relate an event, but to show character, and if I have not done it, it is not for want of material, but of ability to use it.

On Monday the parties exchanged cards, and social relations were formally and courteously restored. It was about the last high-toned duel that I have witnessed, and among the highest toned that I have ever witnessed, and so happily conducted to a fortunate issue—a result due to the noble character of the seconds as well as to the generous and heroic spirit of the principals. Certainly duelling is bad, and has been put down, but not quite so bad as its substitute—revolvers, bowie-knives, blackguarding, and street-assassinations under the pretext of self-defence.

CHAPTER XI.

MISSION TO RUSSIA.

A MONG the papers of the late William M. Watkins, of Charlotte county, Virginia, was found the following correspondence:

JUNE 2nd, 1830.

MY DEAR MR. RANDOLPH:

Infirm as your health is, your country has made another call upon you for your services. I have no right to ask, nor do I enquire whether you will accept of this highly honorable appointment. As a friend I have a right to say your country has no further claims upon you, and that you ought to consult your own comfort and happiness.

Should you accept the appointment, a long (tho' I trust not a final) separation must take place between us. My heart is too full to allow me to express my feelings, when I think of it, as I do now think of it.

Remember that in whatever situation you may be placed, I am your friend.

W. M. WATKINS.

The following is Mr. Randolph's reply:

ROANOKE, June 2nd, 1830.

I cannot express to you how deeply I am penetrated by your note which Peyton has this moment handed to me.

I have accepted the appointment in consequence of the manner in which it has been offered to me. Come and see me and I shall take pleasure in showing you the correspondence—that is, the letter of the P. and my reply.

Though "seas between us broad may roll," I too shall not be unmindful of "auld lang syne," and under every change of time and circumstance shall remain as I am, most truly your friend.

J. R., of Roanoke.

To W. M. W., Esq.

The allusion is to Mr. Randolph's acceptance of the mission to the Court of St. Petersburg. The following is the letter of the President offering him the post:

WASHINGTON, Sept. 16, 1829.

DEAR Sir:—The office of Envoy Extraordinary and Minister Plenipotentiary to Russia will soon become vacant, and I am anxious that the place should be filled by one of the most capable and distinguished of our fellow-citizens.

The great and rapidly increasing influence of Russia in the affairs of the world, renders it very important that our representative at that court should be one of the highest respectability; and the expediency of such a course at the present moment is greatly increased by circumstances of a special character. Among the number of our statesmen from whom the selection might with propriety be made, I do not know one better fitted for the station, on the score of talents and experience in public affairs, or possessing stronger claims upon the favorable consideration of his country than yourself. Thus impressed, and entertaining a deep and grateful sense of your long and unceasing devotion to sound principles, and the interest of the people, I feel it a duty to offer the appointment to you.

In discharging this office I have the double satisfaction of seeking to promote the public interest, whilst peforming an act most gratifying to myself, on account of the personal respect and esteem which I have always felt and cherished towards you.

It is not foreseen that any indulgence as to the period of your departure, which will be required by a due regard to your private affairs, will conflict with the interests of the mission: and I sincerely hope that no adverse circumstances may exist, sufficient to deprive the country of your services.

I have the honor to be, with great respect,
Your most ob't serv't,
ANDREW JACKSON.

The Hon. JOHN RANDOLPH, of Roanoke.

The following is Mr. Randolph's reply:

ROANOKE, Sept. 24, 1829.

SIR:—By the last mail I received, under Mr. Van Buren's cover, your letter, submitting to my acceptance the mission to Russia.

This honor, as unexpected as it was unsought for, is very much enhanced in my estimation by the very timid and flattering terms in which you have been pleased to couch the offer of the appointment. May I be pardoned for saying, that the manner in which it has been conveyed, could alone have overcome the reluctance that I feel at the thoughts of leaving private life and again embarking on the stormy sea of Federal politics. This I hope I may do without any impeachment of my patriotism, since it shall in no wise diminish my exertions to serve our country in the station to which I have been called by her chief magistrate, and under these "circumstances of a special character," indicated by your letter. The personal good opinion and regard, which you kindly express towards me, merit and receive my warmest acknowledgments.

I have the honor to be, with the highest respect, sir, your most obedient and faithful servant,

JOHN RANDOLPH, of Roanoke.

To ANDREW JACKSON, Esq , President of the U. S.

He had not been in St. Petersburg a week before he left for London. In the last speech which he made to the people of Charlotte, and which the reader will find reported in another chapter, he states his reasons for taking that step, which appear to us to be most excellent; the only wonder is, that he accepted the mission when he must have known that neither the duties of the office nor the climate of Russia would suit him.

Mr. Garland excuses him. "In accepting this appointment," he remarks, "he only carried out his original design of going abroad in search of health, while at the same time he served his country in a station pressed upon him as an evidence to foreigners of her distinguished regard." But Mr. Baldwin is very severe upon him. He says, he was physically unfit for the duties of the post; and besides, "he had won his influence as the great champion of the states by never taking pay or holding office from the Federal government."

In his speech on retrenchment and reform, delivered in the House of Representatives in 1828, he said: "I shall retire upon my resources; I will go back to the bosom of my constituents—to such constituents as man never had before, and never will have again; and I shall receive from them the only reward I ever looked for, but the highest that man can receive—the universal expression of their approbation, of their thanks. I shall read it in their beaming faces, I shall feel it in their gratulating hands. The very children will climb around my knees to welcome me. And shall I give up them and this? And for what? For the heartless amusements and vapid pleasures and tarnished honors of this abode of splendid misery, of shabby splendor, for a clerkship in the war office, or a foreign mission, to dance attendance abroad instead of at home, or even for a department itself?"

Who would believe that in one year seven months and twenty-three days from the time that he said this, Mr. Randolph would have accepted a foreign mission to any country, least of all to Russia?

It was well known to his constituents that until he received this appointment he was exceedingly hard pressed for the means to meet his engagements. It was also known that in the latter part of his life he became exceedingly fond of money. The presumption, therefore, is strong, that he accepted the appointment for the pay. We have it from an official source that he received pay as minister to Russia from June 9th, 1830, to July 17th, 1831, at the rate of nine thousand dollars per annum (nine thousand, nine hundred and fifty-seven dollars and seventy-one cents), and in addition thereto was granted the usual allowance of nine thousand dollars for an outfit and two thousand two hundred and fifty dollars for expenses in returning to his home.

It mars the symmetry of a beautiful political character; but we feel bound to state the facts as they were given to us by those who knew him, and to draw such conclusions as may seem to us reasonable and just.

But, notwithstanding the great blemish of his acceptance of the mission to Russia, Mr. Randolph may be regarded as the most consistent statesman which this country has ever produced.

CHAPTER XII.

Reminiscence by W. M. Moseley, Esq.—Mr. Randolph's Treatment of a Certain Young Politician of Buckingham.—Happy Retorts.

FOR the following sketch we are indebted to Mr. William M. Mosely, now of Danville, but who was an eye witness of the scene described, and at the time an influential citizen of Buckingham. Mr. Moseley gives us an illustration of the merciless manner in which Mr. Randolph dealt with his opponents and the supreme contempt which he was capable of expressing.

He says:

The last public speech of Mr. Randolph was delivered at Buckingham Court-house in the year 1833, he then being on his way to Philadelphia where he died shortly after. He was travelling by private conveyance, accompanied by his two favorite servants, Juba and John. His expected arrival had been previously announced, and it being the regular monthly term of the county court, as might have been expected, the attendance was unusually large, most of the old citizens of the county being prompted by a desire to see their former representative in Congress once more, and to hear him speak, perhaps, for the last time. Those who had never seen him, but who had heard of his reputation as a speaker, determined to avail themselves of this opportunity of seeing and hearing one of whom so much had been said.

He reached the village at about eleven o'clock A. M., by which time a large concourse of people had assembled upon the court yard, and along the principal street, all anxiously looking for the arrival of this distinguished personage; and when his carriage stopped in front of the hotel, it was immediately surrounded by a dense crowd—a proceeding by which

Mr. Randolph, in his weak and nervous condition, seemed to be greatly annoyed. This was clearly evinced by his abrupt command to his servant who was in the act of opening the door of the carriage, to let it remain closed until the crowd should retire; adding that he was no *wild beast* intended for public exhibition. The crowd, after some hesitation, retired to a respectful distance, whereupon, the door of the carriage was opened, and he descended with much difficulty by the assistance of his servants. He was immediately conducted to the court-house and occupied the judge's seat, from which, in a sitting posture, after the large court-room had become filled to its utmost capacity, he proceeded to deliver a speech, in the making of which he seemed to have had no special object other than that of giving his opinion as to matters and things in general. Public men and public measures of the past as well as of the present seemed to be passing in review before him, and for each of whom he seemed to have some unkind remembrance. His whole speech, if such it might be called, evinced an unhappy state of mind, if not a disordered intellect. No class and no profession escaped his bitter invective and withering sarcasm. Nothing either in church or state seemed to be progressing according to his liking.

At the close of his disconnected harangue but few even of his old constituents ventured to approach him with anything like familiarity, not knowing how such advances might be received. Among the vast assemblage there was but one individual who seemed willing to court his especial attention. This was a young lawyer of much self-importance who had shortly before been elected to a seat in the state legislature, where he had gained some notoriety by a speech he made in advocacy of the abolition of slavery, in the course of which he took occasion to make some very severe strictures upon Mr. Randolph as a cruel slaveholder. This course on the part of this young delegate had not met with the approval of his constituents, as had been evinced by their refusal to reëlect him. He took this occasion to set himself right before the people, by publicly acknowledging his political errors, and apologizing to Mr. Randolph for the supposed injuries he had done him. For this purpose, as soon as Mr. Randolph had concluded his speech, our young hero arose from his seat in the bar, and commenced by expressing his deep sympathy for the honorable gentleman in his seemingly great bodily afflictions, with the hope that his contemplated visit to Europe would result in the restoration of his health. He said he had always been a devoted admirer of Mr. Randolph, and felt it due to that distinguished gentleman, as well as to his fellow-citizens of Buckingham, that he should embrace that opportunity of making a public acknowledgment of his late political errors, as evinced by a speech which he had made when honored with a seat in the State legislature, and in the delivery of which he had taken occasion to speak disparagingly of Mr. Randolph as a tyrannical master to his slaves. His course, he said, he had reason to know, had not been in accordance with the sentiments of his constituents, and his personal attack upon his distinguished friend had been made without a personal knowledge of his mode of treatment to his slaves. He hoped his constituents would forgive his past errors, and he trusted to the well known magnanimity of Mr. Randolph for his forgiveness of the personal injury done him in a moment of heated debate upon an exciting subject, the wrong side of which he had unfortunately taken.

During the delivery of this ill-timed speech, Mr. Randolph sat with his head resting upon his hand, seemingly absorbed in deep thought; and at its conclusion he straightened himself up, and fixing upon his victim a penetrating gaze, he proceeded as follows: "I don't know you, sir; what might be your name?" The name was given, when Mr. Randolph continued his interrogatories: "Whose son are you? where did you make the speech you have been talking about? and what did you say you were trying to speak about?"

These questions were all answered in a hurried and confused manner, evidently showing that the young orator's situation was becoming unpleasant. Mr. Randolph, after asking a few more simple questions, the purport of which is not now remembered, concluded as follows: "I don't think I ever heard of you or your speech before; and, of course, I have no particular comment to make upon either. I knew your father, and have always thought he was a right good sort of a man; and I suppose you are a degenerate son of a noble sire—a thing that is becoming quite common in this country. I hope my old constituents, God bless them, will never again be *mis*represented in the legislature, or anywhere else, by such a creature as you have shown yourself to be."

It is needless to say, the applause throughout the court-room was tremendous; and it is not believed our young hero ever entertained as good an opinion of himself from that day until the day of his death, which occurred only a few months since.

We have recorded many of Mr. Randolph's short cutting thrusts, gathered from the recollections of his old constituents. We now purpose to give the reader a specimen of his wit, which Mr. Garland considers "the finest retort of the kind to be found in the English language." It was in reply to Mr. McLean, who on one occasion, during a speech delivered in Congress, stated "that the gentleman from Virginia (Mr. Randolph) had displayed a good head, but he would not accept that gentleman's head, to be obliged to have his heart along with it."

Mr. Randolph replied:

"It costs me nothing, sir, to say that I very much regret that the zeal which I have not only felt but cherished on the subject of laying taxes in a manner which, in my judgment, is consistent not merely with the spirit but the very letter of the constitution, should have given to my remarks on this subject a pungency, which has rendered them disagreeable, and even offensive, to the gentleman from Delaware. For that gentleman I have never expressed any other sentiment but respect—I have never uttered or entertained an unkind feeling towards that gentleman, either in the House or elsewhere, nor do I now feel any such sentiment towards him. I never pressed my regard upon him—I press it upon no man. He appears to have considered my remarks as having a personal application to himself. I certainly did not intend to give them that direction, and I think that my prompt disclaimer of any such intention ought to have disarmed his resentment, however justly it may have been excited. He has been pleased, sir, to say something, which, no doubt, he thinks very severe, about my head and my heart.

"How easy, sir, would it be for me to reverse the gentleman's proposition, and to retort upon him that I would not in return take that gentleman's heart, however good it may be, if obliged to take such a head into the bargain.

"But, sir, I do not think this, I never thought it, and therefore I cannot be so ungenerous as to say it; for, Mr. Speaker, who made me a searcher of hearts, of the heart of a fellow sinner? Sir, this is an awful subject, better suited to Friday or Sunday next (Good Friday and Easter Sunday), two of the most solemn days in the Christian calendar, when I hope we shall all consider it, and lay it to heart as we ought to do.

"But, sir, I must maintain that the argument of the gentleman is suicidal—he has fairly worked the equation, and one-half of his argument is a complete and conclusive answer to the other. And, sir, if I should ever be so unfortunate as, through inadvertence or the heat of debate, to fall into such an error, I should so far from being offended feel myself under obligation to any gentleman who would expose its fallacy, even by ridicule—as fair a weapon as any in the whole parliamentary armory. I shall not go so far as to maintain with my Lord Shaftsbury, that it is the unerring test of truth, whatever it may be of temper; but if it be prescribed as a weapon, as unfair as it is confessedly powerful, what shall we say (I put it, sir, to you and to the House) to the poisoned arrow, to the tomahawk and the scalping knife? Would the most unsparing use of ridicule justify a resort to these weapons? Was this a reason that the gentleman should sit in judgment on my heart? Yes, sir, my heart, which the gentleman (whatever he may say) in his heart believes to be a frank heart, as I trust it is a brave heart. Sir, I dismiss the gentleman to his self complacency—let him go—yes, sir, let him go, and thank his God that he is not as this publican."

Many of Mr. Randolph's sarcastic retorts have been published; we will repeat one more, taken from "The Memories of Fifty Years," by W. H. Sparks:

> I remember, upon one occasion, pending the debate upon the Missouri question, and when Mr. Randolph was in the habit of almost daily addressing the house, that a Mr. Beecher, of Ohio, who was very impatient of Randolph's tirades, would, in the lengthy pauses made by him, rise from his place and move the previous question. The speaker would reply: "The member from Virginia has the floor." The first and second interruptions were not noticed by Randolph, but upon the repetition a third time, he slowly lifted his head from contemplating his notes, and said: "Mr. Speaker, in the Netherlands, a man of small capacity, with bits of wood and leather, will, in a few moments, construct a toy that, with the pressure of the finger and thumb, will cry 'Cuckoo! Cuckoo!' With less of ingenuity, and with inferior materials, the people of Ohio have made a toy that will, without much pressure, cry 'Previous question, Mr. Speaker! Previous question, Mr. Speaker!'"—at the same time designating Beecher by pointing at him with his long, skeleton-looking finger. In a moment the house was convulsed with laughter, and I doubt if Beecher ever survived the sarcasm.

CHAPTER XIII.

Recollections by Dr. W. S. Plumer, D. D.—Extract from the *National Intelligencer.*

WE will now lay before our readers the recollections of Dr. W. S. Plumer, and we deem ourself fortunate in securing a contribution from a man of such national reputation, and one of the ablest and purest men living:

John Randolph, of Roanoke, was one of the most remarkable men of our country. He has now been dead over forty years, yet all over the land, in Virginia particularly, you hear his sayings reported as if they had been uttered but yesterday.

In early life he was frequently thrown into company with men more or less poisoned with French infidelity. Then appeared the power of maternal love and piety. He once said: "I should have been a French atheist if it had not been for one thing, and that was the memory of the times when my departed mother used to take my little hands in hers, and caused me on my knees to say; ' Our Father, who art in Heaven.' "

Many instances of Mr. Randolph's great eccentricity of character are still retained throughout the country. But in them the public is but little interested.

In pure Anglo-Saxon and in Latin Mr. Randolph was a good scholar. He was very familiar with Virgil. His ear was easily offended by the use of a wrong word, or the mispronunciation of the right word. Even in his last sickness, some one said: "Mr. Randolph, do you lay easy?" He replied: "I *lie* as *easily* as perhaps a dying man can."

Mr. Randolph often crossed the sea. He highly valued British honesty, British manufactures and British laws. He admitted very readily our indebtedness to the British constitution for many of our liberties, civil and religious. He carefully studied the writings of Edmund Burke. I long owned a copy of that statesman's writings, which once belonged to Randolph. It was often underlined, and in many places the margin was covered with pencil notes. Mr. Randolph's great speeches gave unmistakable evidence of his intimate acquaintance with Burke.

From early boyhood I had read and heard much of Mr. Randolph. His early speeches were commended by Patrick Henry and other great men. He was wholly opposed to the war of 1812. This made him many enemies. For a time it cost him his seat in Congress. He never spoke in high terms of Mr. Madison's administration. This was one of the points on which he and Mr. Clay widely differed. But Randolph greatly admired Mr. Monroe and his public measures.

In gaining a prodigious influence over his constituents, Mr. Randolph very successfully used two arts. One was to make young men afraid of his tongue. The other was to win over all the old men by special attention. He greatly praised, he even flattered old men. But his tongue was a terror to the young. Often at the hustings, and sometimes in Congress, he said: "No man ever had such constituents."

At one time Mr. Randolph seemed intent on vieing with others in raising fine horses. At a heavy cost he made one or two importations. The result was not satisfactory. He had a few fine animals for the saddle and sulky; but his own statement was that his horses were "too light for the draft and too slow for the turf."

I was once in a company of gentlemen from Virginia and North Carolina, when some one said Mr. Randolph seemed to have very little self-knowledge. One present replied, "However that may be, gentlemen, I think you will admit he knows a deal about other people."

Through life Mr. Randolph seems to have been a stranger to fear; no man ever saw his face blanched with terror. When a young man he was in Petersburg, Virginia. Being on the street some one told him of a desperado near the market, who had committed some outrage and refused to surrender to the officer of the law. "Where is he," said Mr. Randolph, and immediately started down Sycamore street. A number followed. Coming near the violent man, he fixed his eye on him, marched fearlessly up to him, laid his hand on him, and said, "Constable, do your duty."

Early in life Mr. Randolph took a lively interest and participation in the disputes and troubles arising out of the alien and sedition laws. This was in the days when the elder Adams was president. The election of Mr. Jefferson brought with it the early repeal of those odious measures, and was therefore hailed with joy by Mr. Randolph. To this time Mr.

Randolph referred, during the administration of the younger Adams, when he said: "I bore some humble part in putting down the dynasty of John the First, and, by the grace of God, I hope to aid in putting down the dynasty of John the Second."

It has sometimes been said that Mr. Randolph never originated or carried out any great measure. And this is true. But he thought*the world was too much governed. He believed that beyond the protection of the people in their rights, most of the measures proposed under the promise of immense benefit to the people, were delusive and injurious. Mr. Clay's "American System," the "Panama Congress," and all such schemes were objects of his strong aversion.

In 1829-'30, "the Mother of States and of Statesmen" was honored with a convention to make for her a new constitution. That was by far the ablest and most venerable body of men I have ever seen assembled on affairs of State. In it were two ex-Presidents—Madison and Monroe, the Chief Justice of the United States—John Marshall, Littleton Waller Tazewell, John Randolph of Roanoke, Richard Venable, Philip Dodridge, Briscoe G. Baldwin, Chapman Johnson, Richard Morris, Samuel Taylor, Benjamin Watkins Leigh, Judge Coalter, Henry St. George Tucker, and a large number of men of high consideration.

In this convention the policy of the East was to have as little change as possible. On the other side the desire was for great changes. Early in the session one gentleman used the phrase, "I protest." Mr. Randolph seeing that the member was likely to aid the party desiring change, undertook to destroy his influence by pouring ridicule on him for using language technically proper only in the British House of Lords.

Another member, before his election, had opposed any convention, or any change in the constitution. Subsequently he was a candidate for the convention, and agreed to favor considerable changes, particularly in the matter of representation. In a speech of some power, Mr. Randolph compared him to the captain, so famous in a celebrated novel, who fought on any side. The chief power of the speech was probably in weakening the courage of the gentleman, and in restraining him from the masterly defence he was capable of making in any respectable cause.

In the convention was a preacher, who had made some noise in the world. I was present when he rose to make his address, intended to be powerful. But Mr. Randolph, who was a great actor, drew many eyes to himself. At first he leaned forward, gazed as if with wonder and in awe.

For two or three minutes he looked and acted as if he expected something great. By degrees he seemed to lose interest in the speaker, and finally sunk back into his seat, with a strong expression of contempt on his countenance. He had not said a word, nor violated any parliamentary law. The acting was perfect. It had its effect. The speaker could not rally the courage of his party.

Yet near the close of the convention Mr. Randolph made a declaration of his good will towards every member of the body, but this came too late to relieve some very painful emotions in several minds.

The new constitution was submitted to the vote of the people in 1830. In April Mr. Randolph addressed the people who had elected him. I heard his speech at Charlotte Court-house. His appearance was impressive. He was tall and thin. His beardless face was pale, and full of small wrinkles. He was dressed like an old man, very neatly, but very simply. His eyes were as brilliant as they had ever been. His long bony forefinger seemed to have the power of a magician's wand. In five days from that time I could have repeated the whole speech.

And yet that speech disappointed some. A stranger, of some intelligence, came there expecting to be thrilled, or melted, or aroused to indignation. But Mr. Randolph, so far from being impassioned, was as calm as any man ever seems to be. He affected no humor. He was as simple as a little child. A few times his irony was cutting, his sarcasms biting, his rebuke terrible, but there seemed to be no passion in it all.

Mr. Randolph put his hearers in possession of his own thoughts. This was his aim. And his thoughts were indelibly impressed on the mind of every intelligent listener. My judgment to-day, at the distance of nearly forty-seven years is, that it was one of the most effective speeches I have ever heard. It was conclusive. No one asked any questions. The old men wept. Here is one entire paragraph: "Formerly tyrants and the authors of misrule used to slit the noses, crop the ears, and brand the skin of those under their hated power. But this course made it unpleasant to look at their subjects. Their faces were hideous. Afterwards they tried another plan. They hired out their subjects to fight for foreign potentates, in wars in which they had no concern. Many of these mercenaries never returned. This plan left their country filled with widows and orphans. At length this scheme was abandoned. But our modern wrong-doers in power have found a far better way of gaining their vile ends. They give to each man what they denominate a fee simple title to a piece of land, perhaps as much as he can cultivate. He calls it his own. His house is his castle. The law protects him in his possessions. He is encouraged to ply all the arts of industry, and to make all he can. Then the hated tyrants send around the tax-gatherer, three or four times a year, and take all he has made. This pays. Remember what I say. This one is to be the modern game."

Mr. Randolph never was married. He left a will, with codicils. This was virtually set aside, after long litigation, except so much as liberated his slaves. However much men may have hated or pitied Mr. Randolph, no man ever held him in contempt.

The following highly interesting article was clipped from the *National Intelligencer* of June 4, 1833:

JOHN RANDOLPH OF ROANOKE.—The following sketch of this distinguished orator, written thirty years ago, but never published, is furnished by a gentleman who had been in habits of intimacy with him ever since. It was written off-hand, after residing with him in the same hotel at Georgetown for some weeks, in a constant familiar intercourse which has continued at intervals until his decease. The writer bears his testimony that nothing in the life and conduct of Mr. Randolph, during all their subsequent acquaintance, gave him occasion to believe for a moment that his early impressions of his character were in the slightest degree erroneous.—*N. Y. Courier.*

Mr. Randolph is beyond comparison the most singular and striking person that I ever met with. As an orator he is unquestionably the first in the country, and yet there are few men who labor under so many physical disadvantages. He seems made up of contradictions. Though his person is exceedingly tall, thin and disproportioned, he is the most graceful man in the world; and with an almost feminine voice, he is more distinctly heard in the House than either Mr. D. or Roger—though the former is more noisy than a field preacher, and the latter more vociferous than a crier of oysters. When seated on the opposite side of the halls of Congress Mr. Randolph looks like a youth of sixteen, but when he rises to speak, there is an almost sublimity in the effect proceeding from the contrast in his height when seated or standing. In the former his shoulders are raised, his head depressed, his body bent; in the latter he is seen with his figure dilated in the attitude of inspiration, his head raised, his long thin finger pointing, and his dark, clear, chestnut eye flashing lightning at the object of his overwhelming sarcasm.

Mr. Randolph looks, acts, and speaks like no other man I have ever seen. He is original, unique in everything. His style of oratory is emphatically his own. Often diffusive and discursive in his subjects, his language is simple, brief and direct, and however he may seem to wander from the point occasionally, he never fails to return to it with a bound, illuminating it with flashes of wit or the happiest illustrations drawn from a retentive memory and a rich imagination. Though eccentric in his conduct in the ordinary affairs of life, and his intercourse with the world, there will be found more of what is called common sense in his speeches than in those of any other man in Congress. His illustrations are almost always drawn from familiar scenes, and no man is so happy in allusions to fables, proverbs and the ordinary incidents of human life, of which he has been a keen observer. His is not that fungus species of eloquence which expands itself into empty declamation, sacrificing strength, clearness and perspicuity, to the more popular charm of redundant metaphors and periods rounded with all the precision of the compass. Mr. Randolph is a man of wit, and wit deals in comparisons; yet his language is perfectly simple, and less figurative than that of any of our distinguished speakers. This I attribute to the clearness and vigor of his conceptions. When a man distinctly comprehends his subject, he will explain himself in a few words and without metaphor; but when he is incapable of giving it precise and definite form, his language becomes figurative, and his ideas, like objects seen through a mist, have neither outline nor dimensions. Nothing is of more easy comprehension than the ideas and language of the great orator of Virginia.

Though continually worried by the little terriers of the house, who seem to be sent there for no other purpose than to bark at him, Mr. Randolph never becomes loud or boisterous, but utters the most biting sarcasm with a manner the most irritatingly courteous, and a voice that resembles the music of the spheres. Such, indeed, is the wonderful clearness of his voice, and the perfection of his enunciation, that his lowest tones circulate like echoes through the hall of Congress, and are more distinctly understood than the roarings of M. L., the bellowings of R. N., or the bleatings of the rosy and stentorian Robert Ross. In all the requisites of a great orator he has no superior, and in the greatest of all, that of attracting, charming, riveting the attention of his hearers, no equal in this country, or perhaps in the world.

Mr. Randolph has fared, as most distinguished political leaders have done, in having his conduct misrepresented, his foibles exaggerated, and his peculiarities caricatured. The fault is in some measure his own. He spares no adversary, and he has no right to expect they will spare him. In this respect his example may well be a warning to inculcate among rival leaders the necessity of toleration in politics as well as religion. That he is irritable, capricious, and careless of the feelings of those for whom he has no particular respect or regard, no one will deny. That he is impatient in argument, and intolerant of opposition, is equally certain; and the whole world knows that he is little solicitous to disguise his contempt or dislike. But much of this peevish irritability may find its origin and excuse in his physical sufferings. Almost from his boyhood he has never known the blessings of health, nor ever enjoyed its anticipation. His constitution is irretrievably broken, and though he may live many years, they will, in all probability, be years of anxiety and suffering, embittered by ridicule, instead of being soothed by the sympathy of the world, which is ever apt to suppose that a man cannot be sick without dying. Men lingering under the slow consuming tyranny of a constitutional infirmity, and dying, not by inches, but the hundredth part of inches, seem to me among the most pitiable of the human race. The world, and even their friends, come at last to believe their malady imaginary, their complaints without cause. They grow tired of hearing a man always proclaiming himself a victim to disease, yet at the same time taking his share in the business, and apparently in the enjoyments of life, and living on like the rest of his fellow creatures. "They jest at scars that never felt a wound," and the very circumstances that should excite additional commiseration too often give occasion to cold neglect or flippant ridicule.

In this painful situation is Mr. Randolph at present, and it seems to me that an apology at least for his selfish disregard of the feelings of others may be found in his own hopeless sufferings and the want of sympathy. I know of no situation more calculated to make a man a misanthrope; and those who are foremost and loudest in their condemnation of Mr. Randolph would do well to look to their own hearts, place themselves in his situation, and then ask whether it does not naturally lead to, though it may not justify, occasional irritation, or even habitual ill temper. I here speak of this distinguished man as the world speaks of him. But so far as I saw him, and this was at all hours, he is full of benignity and kindness. His treatment of servants, and especially his own slaves, was that of the kindest master, and he always called his personal attendant "Johnny," a circumstance, to my mind, strongly indicative of habitual good will towards him. To me, from whose admiration or applause he could at that time at least anticipate neither honor or advantage, his behavior was uniformly kind, almost affectionate, and it will be very long before I lose the recollection of his conciliating smile, the music of his mellow voice, or the magic of his gentle manners. We passed our evenings together, or I may perhaps rather say a good portion of the night, for he loved to sit up late, because, as he was wont to say, the grave, not the bed, was the place of rest for him. On these occasions there was a charm in his conversation I never found in that of any other person.

Virginia was the goddess of his idolatry, and of her he delighted to talk. He loved her so much, and so dearly, that he sometimes almost forgot he was also a citizen of the United States. The glories and triumphs of the eloquence of Patrick Henry, and the ancient hospitality of the aristocracy of the Old Dominion, were also his favorite subjects, of which he never tired, and with which he never tired me. In short, the impression on my mind is never to be eradicated, that his heart was liberal, open and kind, and that his occasional ebullitions of spleen and impatience were the spontaneous, perhaps irrepressible, efforts of a suffering and debilitated frame, to relieve itself a moment from the eternal impression of its own unceasing worryings.

But, whatever may be the defects of Mr. Randolph's temper, no one can question his high and lofty independence of mind, or his unsullied integrity as a public agent or a private gentleman. In the former character, he has never abandoned his principles to suit any political crisis, and in the latter he may emphatically be called an honest man. His word and his bond are equally to be relied on, and as his country can never accuse him of sacrificing her interests to his own ambition, so no man can justly charge him with the breach of any private obligation. In both these respects, he stands an illustrious example to a country in which political talents are much more common then political integrity, and where it is too much the custom to forget the actions of a man in our admiration of his speeches.

It is with regret I add, that this brilliant man, who has already attracted attention, not only of his countrymen, but of the world, will, in all probability, survive but a few years. His health appears irretrievably lost, and his constitution irreparably injured. A premature decay seems gradually creeping upon all his vital powers, and an inevitable, unseen influence appears to be dragging him to the grave. At the age of thirty, with all the world in his grasp, wealth in his possession, and glory and power in perspective, he is, in constitution, an infirm old man, with light, glossy hair, parted over his forehead and tied loosely behind with a black riband; teeth white as ivory; an eye sparkling with intellect, and a countenance seamed with a thousand small wrinkles. At a distance of a hundred yards, he will be mistaken for an overgrown boy of premature growth; approach him, and at every step his appearance changes, and he becomes gradually metamorphosed into an old man. You will then see a face such as you never saw before, never will see again; if he likes you, a smile, such as you never beheld on the face of any other man; and when that smile passes away, a countenance bearing an expression of long continued anxiety and suffering that will make your heart ache.

Such is Mr. Randolph, as he appeared to me at the age of thirty years. He may be wayward, eccentric, self-willed and erratic. His opponents sometimes insinuate that he is mad; but this is nothing more than the whisperings of party malignity. Would to heaven there were more such madmen among our rulers and legislators to make folly silent and wickedness ashamed; to assert and defend the ancient principles of our revolution; to detect quack politicians, quack lawyers and quack divines, and to afford to his countrymen an example of inflexible integrity both in public and private life. But he is original and unique in this as in everything else; and when he departs this scene, in which he has suffered the martyrdom of sickness and detraction combined, if living, I will bear this testimony, that he will not leave behind any man that can claim superiority over him as a glorious orator, a sagacious, high-minded, independent patriot, and inflexibly honest man."

CHAPTER XIV.

Last Speech—Secession Resolutions—How He Managed to Force Them Down—Rare Scenes on the Political Stage.

AMONG the materials which we have collected for our "Home Reminiscences of John Randolph of Roanoke," is a manuscript report of the last speech, or "long talk," made by the great orator to the people of his adopted county, on the 4th of February, 1833, only four months and twenty days before his death. At that time he was quite an old man, his constitution a perfect wreck, tottering on the brink of the grave.

Court being in session, he sent word to the magistrates that he had a request to make of them; it might be the last he would ever make of them on earth. He desired to address the people, and wished the court to adjourn the moment he made his appearance in the court-house.

The reason assigned for making this unusual request was this: His mind, he stated, would only act for a short time, and then under the influence of artificial stimulant. The court, eager to hear what the dying man had to say, readily consented to his request.

He made his appearance, leaning upon two of his friends for support; and he had no sooner entered the house than it was filled with people. He commenced speaking from the chair, being too infirm to stand upon his feet. We are informed he began with three dress coats on, but that, before he concluded, he had on only one. His glass of toddy was sitting by his side, of which he drank freely from time to time. Though he spoke principally from the chair, ever and anon the "fire and motion of his soul" refused to be restrained by his feeble body, and at such times he would rise upon his feet.

But what was the meaning of this extraordinary proceeding? What mental stimulus was moving a mind prostrated by disease, causing him to forget for the moment the terrors of the unknown world to which he was hastening, and dragging along his withered body which his spirit could scarcely animate? Feeble as he was, he had ridden fifteen miles, on a winter's day, to address the people.

There was a scene for the moralist, the novelist and the painter. This is the conduct of a man whose mind was morbidly active, whose imagination was too much heated. Some might deem him mad, but such was not the case. He was only excited to the highest pitch by natural and artificial stimulants.

South Carolina had just passed her celebrated ordinance of secession, and General Jackson had issued his proclamation, and the whole country was thrown into the greatest excitement. Mr. Randolph began his political career upon the very spot where he was then standing in opposition to Patrick Henry and in defence of States Rights. General Jackson had assailed violently his favorite idea—the doctrine for which he had contended during a long life. This is what kindled the fire within his withered breast, rousing his palsied faculties, and causing his stagnant pulse its rapid play.

It has been objected to Mr. Randolph's patriotism that it was too limited—that it did not include the whole Union—that he did not have the prosperity of the entire country at heart. Mr. Baldwin has drawn an interesting parallel between Mr. Randolph and Mr. Clay, and in no respect does the contrast appear more striking than in this, viz: Mr. Clay knew no North, no South, no East, no West; Mr. Randolph knew only Virginia. Her glory was the pride of his life; her prosperity the end of his efforts. He was fully persuaded that these depended upon the doctrine of States Rights. Hence, as has been remarked by Mr. Baldwin, "Whenever he spoke, whatever he wrote, wherever he went, States Rights, States Rights, were the inexhaustless theme of his discourse."

It cannot be wondered at then that a man of his excitable nature, and devotion to an idea, when that idea was assailed by a powerful foe, should have shaken off the night-mare of death, to make a last spasmodic effort in its defence. His conduct on this occasion may be compared to the superhuman efforts of a man to rescue a friend from impending danger. The physical energy displayed was surprising to all who were acquainted with his bodily infirmities; but the mental energy exerted under the peculiar circumstances of his case was wonderful indeed.

Mr. Randolph said he desired to address the people. Could a man in his condition deliver a public address? It is a matter of curiosity to see what effect had age, disease, dissipation, stormy passions, intense mental, suffering upon that brilliant intellect and fearless spirit, which had the nerve in his youth to attack the gigantic powers of Patrick Henry.

He did speak, and a report of his speech is before us. Mr. William B. Green, in his "Recollections" of Mr. Randolph, informs us that the speaker was very anxious that his speech should be in whole, or at least in part reported. We quote from his manuscripts:

"Mr. Randolph drummed up for a stenographer. There happened to be present a schoolmaster by the name of Frost, who professed to be somewhat acquainted with the art, and Judge Beverly Tucker, who promised to assist Mr. Frost to the extent of his knowledge. The sequel, however, showed that neither of the gentlemen was very expert, for no part of the speech, so far as I know, was ever published, but simply the resolutions.

"The lecture, if I may so call it, which Mr. Randolph gave the stenographer, was exceedingly interesting, but I am unable to recall his express words, except in one or two sentences. He was anxious, as before remarked, to have the speech, which he was about to deliver, fully taken down; but, fearing that this might be impracticable, he insisted that the strong points, and the biting parts at least, should be preserved; and in conclusion said: 'When I say anything that *tickles under the tail*, be sure to put it down.'

"The speech was then commenced, and he spoke for a considerable time with overwhelming power and unsurpassed eloquence. The resolutions were then passed in the form in which you now find them.

"I never entertained a doubt that a majority of the committee were opposed to them, and that had they been offered and supported by any member of the committee, or indeed by any other person than Mr. Randolph, they would have been voted down. It was his address, management and eloquence alone, which caused their adoption. I have never ceased to regret that I had anything to do with the matter; and I may add, that I have always regarded the connection which I had with the subject as the meanest act of my political life.

"As an additional evidence of the power and influence which the speech exerted, not only upon the meeting, but also upon those who were casually present, I will mention a conversation which I had with a gentleman of Halifax county who was present.

"Mr. S., a very well educated and intelligent lawyer, called at my house the day after the meeting. He had seen and heard all. This gentleman acknowledged that it was the most eloquent speech he had ever heard, and that though he was a thorough administration Jackson man, yet, under the excitement of the moment, had he been a member of the committee, he would have voted for the resolutions."

Mr. Green was correct. No part of this speech was ever published. The report we have of it was not written by Mr. Frost, nor by Judge Tucker, but by a young man who happened to be present, and who afterwards rose to a high position in society. This speech and the famous secession resolutions which were passed at the same time, and the manner in which Mr. Randolph procured their passage, forms the most interesting chapter in the history of this remarkable man.

Mr. Randolph commenced by saying: "He should subject himself to the imputation of an overweaning arrogance in the attempt to address the good people of Charlotte; but the peculiar circumstances in which we are placed threw him unavoidably upon them. His being a public servant in their employment for thirty-five years, had given him some small claim to their confidence. It rested with them to accept or disapprove after they had heard. If the confidence which had been reposed in him were withdrawn, he would be the first to acquiesce and sanction the withdrawment? He was not what he had been. The prostration of his bodily powers was total, and if the destruction of mind had not kept pace with the body, they were almost abreast. Indeed it was hard for him to decide which rode the foremost horse.

"I see in this assembly some who would vouch for me, if

an endorsement were necessary, that I said I would give the best horse I possessed (and no small sum at that), for one-half hour's conversation with the President previous to writing his annual message. * * * * * *

"But after the annual message came to hand all was calmness and quietude. It acted like a charm, a quietus to my troubled breast. I was one of the happiest men living—in a perfect elysium. For, having some influence with the ruling party in South Carolina, I felt that that influence should be exerted to allay their rash and precipitate measures. Here I remark I am no NULLIFIER. The doctrine of nullification is sheer nonsense."

Further on he said:-

"I shall offer some resolutions to-day on this subject, not presuming to dictate to my old constituents, but endeavor to make it a subject of reference to a committee, a large, select committee, and I will further say, a committee of RANK, aristocratic as it may sound; yes, rank. By rank I mean age, ability and integrity; aye, and I will go further—I will say PROPERTY too. In such cases, he who has a stake in common with us, and a stake too which he cannot carry out of the State, is the man to whom I wish to entrust my affairs. You all know my principles have never been disguised. I would not disguise them if I could, and I could not if I would. I am fond of intrinsic worth—no overtoned, hypocritical cant, however admirable."

In the course of his remarks he gives us a little piece of human nature as follows:

"It is natural for us to prefer our barn to our neighbor's house. We will do it; we cannot subvert one of the strongest of nature's principles."

In the last "long talk" we find the following sentence, which breathes the spirit of misanthropy and misery:

"I would as lief die in my carriage, or on the road, at some of the wretched inns, between here and Washington, as anywhere."

To what a sad pass must his life have come! "Home, sweet home," had no charms for him.

"Those wretched inns!" He could never speak of them without indulging in unmerited censure, nor enter one without betraying his ungovernable temper.

But he continues:

"What is this breath? We may try with it to be honorable, or we may endeavor to be useful, but we hold it no longer than it is His pleasure who gave it. He still gives me a little. He will take it when He pleases, and I can only say, 'Blessed be His Holy name.'

"This is the only thing in the way of cant you shall hear from me. I will leave that for the work of enthusiasts or of fanatics, who live at the expense of our servants, and infest and eat up the houses of our neighbors.

"In my address at November court I meant to describe a certain class, which I entirely overlooked. I mean the Yazoo men, whose character has ever been odious to me. When they had much money at stake, I pledged my solemn word that they should find me opposing them in their iniquitous fraud. When I was a candidate for Congress in the last war, the men of this description (and there were not a few in this county, and Prince Edward, too) taking the advantage of the war clamor and my opposition to men and measures then, did everything they could to injure me. But these very men were here in October, after the war; yea, they went round to tow the ship back again—they had been bitter enemies, even when no cause existed. I well remember the day I spoke on the stile before the old court-house door, when I had a brush with Colonel Gideon Spencer, after which they left my opponent like the woman in the Scripture, who was taken in adultery; swarmed around me like a friend; and if the polls had been open then, I should have been elected by acclamation. But, the hunters were busy, and there are some voters who never throw away a shot, who never shoot at a dead duck. I was returned to be discharged from the confidence of my old constituents. When the polls were closed in Cumberland, I wrote to my friend James Garnet, and said to him, that the accounts between me and the district were fairly balanced. But ever since then, what is it that has bound me to my old district, with hooks of steel? Why did they stick to me even when the compensation law was passed, for which I voted. For that vote every man was turned out but myself and one other, and he, by basely turning, twisting, crouching and explaining, barely escaped being cashiered.

"He reminded me of the old man and woman who lived in the vinegar bottle. He, with the gaff and steel spur fitted to his leg, rode through, and, to use a common phrase, 'was whipped and cleared.' He is a man more mischievous, bringing more misery than any man in these United States, with one exception—I mean the present incumbent of the Presidential chair. The present incumbent will have been that exception, if his late doctrines are acted upon. I speak in the second future tense—will have been that exception. General Jackson heretofore has opposed the doctrines contained in that accursed proclamation; I know, up to the present time, for I have been acquainted with his sentiments. He knows it, and he knows that I am not to be swerved from an avowal of truth; for, in speaking of me in the presence of a respectable clergyman of this county lately, he remarked that he believed me to be invincibly honest.

"But now, if he speaks, it will be apparent that I shall

incur his deep resentment—he may change his opinion about my invincible honesty. But I will not anticipate, nor speak unguardedly; for, of his public services, I will speak in terms of respect.

"Now, life and death are before us. We are busy, we ought to be busy, and, in this bustle, we ought to pay but little deference to men—better attend to public benefit. I, for one, put to hazard all the power of public men, President and all, and take a firm, decided stand against the present course of the president.

"His message indeed charmed me; made me forget my miseries. But how long did I enjoy this enchantment? Here comes, in a few days, the proclamation, sweeping and blasting with death, like the simoons of Arabia or the whirlwinds of the Great Sahara.

"Theretofore, to use an expression of my friend P. P. Barbour—theretofore General Jackson professed to be friendly to the South, to Constitutional and State Rights. This proves that he has no share in the live or dead stock in the constitution? What is proof to the point? This proclamation is hailed with the loudest hosannas by the coalition and Clay party. If this is his former doctrine, how comes it about that every old States Rights man abominates it, and it meets so hearty a welcome by the Henry Clay party—the *ultra* tariff, *ultra* bank, *ultra* internal improvement parties— yes, and the whole mass of political heretics?· But real true believers will stand firm, even though they, like the devil, believe and tremble. All these combined make fearful odds; but, zeal in this cause, this true religion—political religion— is sure to triumph. Small as the minority may be, we are not too small to triumph, unless betrayed by those who are entrusted with the ark of the covenant. I was placed in a small minority before—a little proscribed minority, when I took a stand against the employment of standing armies—those mercenary troops, who are old John Adams's dogs of war. There was Virginia to be humbled in the dust and ashes. You frequently find me in despicable minorities.

"Who was General Washington—pure as he was—but a man? He had been prevailed upon to put himself at the head of the Federal party. If he had not died, we, the Republican party, could never have triumphed. But for the influence of Patrick Henry, General Washington wrote, saying to him that he was much needed; solicited him to come to the General Assembly. I was at March court '99, when Patrick Henry justified Adams and advocated the constitutionality of the sedition law. I was a stripling youth, called before the public by sheer accident, and was also elected by sheer accident. I spoke then and contended against the position, and have been contending ever since against it. But, Henry never lived to get to the House of Burgesses, and the resolution passed by seven votes, which, if he had gotten there, would have turned the scale. Patrick Henry was good for seven votes. Those who do not believe that he was good for seven votes, know very little about the character of that distinguished statesman. Even those who were Federalists, voted against the laws and for the resolutions, for fear of losing their popularity. Yes, but for this powerful struggle, Adams would have been reëlected; for Jefferson was elected by only four votes. We were interested, and we acted, and we triumphed.

"Now of one thing I am certain; of a fact I am convinced, and though I would I could not act differently; it is in the very nature of things. It is this, man always differs in proportion as interest is at stake. Self lies at the foundation of every effort. Notice the affairs of families. The overseer is not over the employer, but he will get all he can.

Whenever he can he will inch upon the employer, and whenever the employer can he will inch upon the overseer. How do they bargain? The general conditions are, you take my business, and I will give you so much meal, meat and money. If you change the condition, you change the proverb: 'What's sauce for the goose is sauce for the gander.' The overseer makes a fortune; he becomes an employer; he immediately gives you a different version of the * * * *

"But, again, suppose I, by my luxury or intemperance, or some other way, have reduced my family to poverty? If I am not an overseer myself, my sons are turned over to that employment. We change our tone, and take the version that decides in favor of the overseer.

"It is the essence of human nature to be guided by interest, and when we say that our worthy President is swayed and ruled in this way, we say no more of him than we say of one another. But he has sinned, and I for one will go to him, like Nathan, and say, 'Thou art the man,' though I may risk all like Nathan did with David.

"Mr. Randolph spoke of the Cabinet officers and their ladies, and stated that the proclamation was dictated by one of the grandest scoundrels, and put to paper by the best writer in the United States, one who fought with him side by side against the old bank. He said he was an intriguing partizan—dyed in the wool—one who came from the Empire State, from that city, worse than Paris.

"This party cabinet was also distinguished by another peculiar epithet; namely, the kitchen cabinet. And as the old adage is, 'no person can touch pitch without being defiled,' he did not choose to dirty his fingers by touching that dirty concern; but lest his hands, not too clean now, should be soiled in the dirty fat, he would throw all the grease on the kitchen fire.

"It is probable that General Jackson is obnoxious to this secret kitchen influence. He is charged with it; but for a moment we will suppose it false. Your enemies never charge you without having some failing in view, either supposed or real. They always therefore give just grounds for watchfulness. The public functionaries ought therefore to abstain or touch lightly when they are accused, for accusers will never pitch on anything but faults to blast us, because nothing else will do that thing.

"Not to resist this Cabinet counsel was Jackson's cowardice, though not naturally a coward. I well remember that in the worse speech I ever made, I told you that I chose General Jackson as the less of two evils. I still esteem him as a noble man, and he addressed me in so gentlemanly a way that I could not find it in my heart to desert him when I found he most needed help. I accepted the commission, but had not been in that frigid zone a week before my languished state of health recalled me. But still I fight under the banner against the Bank of the United States, that mischief-making machine. But I left St. Petersburg for the climate, which, of all others, most agrees with my shattered constitution, where I hope to eke out yet the last remains of my toilsome life. I could not stay at the Russian court. How could I go to the levees of the autocrat, and pretend familiarity with men and measures so repugnant to my views of liberty, or right and wrong? After Poland's blood was shed, not by Russian soldiers, but by Russian mercenaries, Russian gold and Russian paper, how could I withstand or palliate that deep feeling which naturally inspired my breast? If I had been writhing on the rack of the Spanish inquisition, it would have been a bed of roses in comparison of what my nature would have endured!

"But it has been alleged that I received the emolument

and did not perform the duty. But I had a right to the outfit, and did not receive that. With my own money I upheld my own credit, and the credit of the government too. I regarded the bill that came up before Congress, on my account, as intended to pick a quarrel with me, instead of advancing my pay; like a man or boy put at swing—you swing me and I'll swing you; or boys at play—you tickle me and I'll tickle you. My good friend S's bill very much grieved me. Who could listen at B. and other slanderers without seeing that they would cut both ways? V. was more honest than any, for he came out openly. How he has managed to prove my right you may decide.

"Suppose a case. I am agreeing for an overseer. I agree to pay any time he comes. Suppose, hypothetically, the delay of the law. I tell him, if he sues I will carry him through the miserable course of our law—ten years or more. I can fee a lawyer (he is not able); and thus deprive him of his just due. He might take his choice. Would this be an act of an honest man? No. This was the act of Government with reference to me. He may be bad, but I promise not to retaliate. Let it go with this passing tribute.

"But one thing is certain; the compensation law brought returning faith in me. (Here the reporter lost something about Yazoo, bank, Jackson, Adams, and their doing shabbily, and something about the dear county where Nat Price lives.)

"I am not the man that I would wish to be. I never could suffer to be imposed upon; I cannot permit a man to pull my nose or kick my backside. I am very far from being clear of the same faults that Jackson has. I would wish to turn the one cheek when the other was smitten, if I could; but I cannot, and I will not be hypocrite enough to pretend to it. For, if I did, there would soon be occasion to expose my hypocrisy. I cannot dissemble.

"Now I don't wish that anybody should rely on my assertion. I will read something which comes from the heads of the church. It comes from Mr. Walsh. (Reads—no note of what was read.)

"Mr. Randolph remarked, that as regarded the proclamation, A. Hamilton did not go half as far; he, Hamilton, was too honest a man. After reading, he made some remarks about a letter from Governor Hayne and his opinion of the politics of Calhoun—his decided opposition to Calhoun. But he was not disposed to set the house on fire to get rid of the rats, or a worse enemy, the chinches.

"He then introduced a letter from Governor Hamilton, reluctantly, he said, because so complimentary; but it was the partial effusion of a friend. They were friends indeed. Perhaps one cause of friendship was the attachment of their mothers, who went together through the toils of the Revolution. He well knew her, Mrs. Hamilton, the S. & P. of all the chivalry of the State. But, partial as the evidence was, it was evidence that would be admitted in any court of record, especially in this court, where presumptive evidence was well received. (Reads.) After which he produced what he himself styled his bald and disjointed resolutions. After the resolutions were read, he began again:

"I told you, if not, I intended to tell you, that how much soever I might despise nullification, yet I am of the same land with the South Carolinians, the same to me as to Hamilton; and however it may come to issue, I could not desert those whose interests were identical with mine. Lord Gray said once in Parliament, 'I must stand by my order.' I have no idea of seeing them humbled at the feet of their task-masters. I would as soon expect a real honest man among the Henry Clay men, a Pole to join the autocrat to fight for liberty, as to expect liberty in the South and join the present dominant party. When do you meet with any from the North who neglect to write down our customs? Were we to listen to their religion, we would liberate our slaves, cure no more tobacco; but all with them would become natural abettors to tyranny. I profess a reverence for true religion; but I declare to you, I have as little faith in priests as any man living—and none in priestcraft. Their creed is, I must labor and they will swallow. Some of their tenets and allowed practices would place the South in the condition of San Domingo—in flames, and those flames would be quenched by the blood of the inhabitants.

"There is a meeting-house in this village, built by a respectable denomination. I never was in it; though, like myself, it is mouldering away. The pulpit of that meeting-house was polluted by permitting a black African to preach in it. If I had been there, I would have taken the uncircumcised dog by the throat, led him before a magistrate and committed him to jail. I told the ladies, they, sweet souls, who dressed their beds with their whitest sheets, and uncorked for him their best wine, were not far from having mulatto children.

"I am no prophet, but I then predicted the insurrection. The insurrection came; was ever such a panic? Dismay was spread through the country. I despised it when it was here. To despise distant danger is not true courage, but to despise it when you have done all you could to avoid it, and it has and would come, is true courage. Look at the conduct of our last General Assembly. The speeches that were made there were little dreamed of. What kind of doctrine was preached on the floor of the House of Burgesses? If I had been there I should have moved that the first orator who took the liberty to advance that doctrine, should be arrested and prosecuted by the State's attorney."

He concluded by saying he "envied B. W. Leigh; that he was completely discomfited; had only raised one laugh on so important a matter."

The following is a copy of Mr. Randolph's resolutions, taken from the manuscript report of the proceedings of the meeting, in the well known handwriting of the secretary, Winslow Robinson, Esq.:

1. *Resolved*, That while we retain a grateful sense of the many services rendered by Andrew Jackson, Esq., to the United States, we owe it to our country and to our posterity to make our solemn protest against many of the doctrines of his late proclamation.

2. *Resolved*, That Virginia "is, and of right ought to be, a free, sovereign and independent State;" that she became so by her own separate act, which has been since recognized by all the civilized world, and has never been disavowed, retracted, or in any wise impaired or weakened by any subsequent act of hers.

3. *Resolved*, That when, for purposes of common defence and common welfare, Virginia entered into a strict league of amity and alliance with the other twelve colonies of British North America, she parted with no portion of her sovereignty, although, from the necessity of the case, the authority to enforce obedience thereto was, in certain cases and for certain purposes, delegated to the common agents of the whole confederacy.

4. *Resolved*, That Virginia has never parted with the right to recall the authority so delegated for good and sufficient cause, and to secede from the confederacy whenever she shall find the benefits of union exceeded by its evils, union being the means of securing liberty and happiness, and not the end to which these should be sacrificed.

5. *Resolved*, That the ALLEGIANCE of the people of Virginia is due to HER; that to her their obedience is due, while to them she owes protection against all the consequences of such obedience.

6. *Resolved*, That we have seen with deep regret that Andrew Jackson, Esq., President of the United States, has been influenced by designing counselers, to subserve the purposes of their own guilty ambition, to dis-

avow the principles to which he owed his election to the chief magistracy of the government of the United States, and to transfer his real friends and supporters, bound hand and foot, to the tender mercies of his and their bitterest enemies—the *ultra*-federalists, *ultra*-bank, *ultra*-internal improvement, and Hartford convention men—the habitual scoffers at States Rights—and to their instrument—the venal and prostituted press— by which they have endeavored, and but too successfully, to influence and mislead public opinion.

7. *Resolved,* That Virginia will be found her own worst enemy whenever she consents to number among her friends those who are never true to themselves, but when they are false to their country.

8. *Resolved,* That we owe it to justice, while denouncing the portentous combination between General Jackson and the late unhallowed coalition of his and our enemies, to acquit THEM of any dereliction of principle, and to acknowledge that they have but acted in their vocation.

9. *Resolved,* That we cannot consent to adopt principles which we have always disavowed, merely because they have been adopted by the President; and although we believe that we shall be in a lean and proscribed minority, we are prepared again to take up our cross, confident of success under that banner, so long as we keep the faith and can have access to the public ear.

10. *Resolved,* That while we utterly reprobate the doctrine of nullification, as equally weak and mischievous, we cannot for that reason give our countenance to principles equally unfounded, and in the highest degree dangerous to the liberties of the people.

11. *Resolved,* That we highly approve of the mission of Benjamin Watkins Leigh, not only as in itself expedient and judicious, but as uniting upon the man the best qualified, whether for abilities, integrity and principles, moral and political, beyond all others in the commonwealth or in the United States, for the high, arduous and delicate task which has been devolved upon him by the unanimous suffrage of the assembly, and as we believe of the people, and which he alone is perhaps capable from all these considerations, united in his person, of discharging with success, and restoring this confederate republic to its former harmony and union.'"

(Signed) JOHN RANDOLPH, *of Roanoke,*

Chairman.

The following is a copy of the official report of the proceedings of the meeting, signed by the secretary, and marked, "For Capt. Wm. M. Watkins:"

CHARLOTTE COURT-HOUSE, Feb. 4th, 1833.

There was an unusually numerous collection of people at Charlotte Court-house to-day, it being expected that the subject of the proclamation would be taken into consideration, and hoped that Mr. Randolph might be there. Though in a state of the most extreme feebleness, he made his appearance last night, and to day at twelve o'clock was lifted to his seat on the bench. He rose and spoke a few minutes, but soon sat down exhausted, and continued to speak sitting, though sometimes for a moment the excitement of his feelings brought him to his feet. He ended his speech by moving a set of resolutions, of which a copy is subjoined.

On motion, these resolutions were referred to a committee consisting of the following gentlemen:

Colonel Clement Carrington, Captain Thomas Pettus, Henry A. Watkins, William M. Watkins, Robert Morton, Samuel D. Morton, John Coleman, B. W. Lester, George Hannah, John Marshall, John Thomas, John H. Thomas, Henry Madison, Dr. Isaac Read, William B. Green, Joseph Friend, Edward B. Fowlkes, Mathew J. Williams, Samuel Venable, William Bacon, John Booth, Francis Barnes, William H. Dennis, Richard Venable, Jr., Joseph M. Daniel, Thomas F. Spencer, Paul Carrington, John Daniel, Charles Raine, Benjamin Marshall, Colonel Marshall, J. H. Marshall, Cornelius Barnes, Dr. Hoge, Dr. Bouldin, Elisha Hundley, Dr. Patillo, Dr. Edwin Price, Dr. Garden, Samuel Daniel, Winslow Robinson, Nicholas Edmunds, Major Gaines, R. I. Gaines, Henry Carrington, Edward W. Henry, Thomas T. Bouldin, James W. Bouldin, William B. Watkins, Anderson Morton, John Morton, Thomas A. Morton, Martin Hancock, D. B. Hancock, Clement Hancock, Colonel H. Spencer, G. C. Friend, Jacob Morton, Wyatt Cardwell, William Smith, Colonel Thomas Read, Thomas Read, Archibald A. Davidson, William T. Scott, Major Thomas Nelson, Isham Harvey, Dr. Joel Watkins, T. E. Watkins, Major Samuel Baldwin, Robert Carrington, and John Randolph of Roanoke.

Colonel Clement Carrington having declined serving, and the committee being called, Captain Thomas Pettus, J. Coleman, J. Thomas, J. H.

Thomas, Joseph Friend, E. B. Fowlkes, William Bacon, Colonel Marshall, J. H. Marshall, Cornelius Barnes, Dr. Pattillo, Dr. Garden, Nicholas Edmunds, Henry Carrington, Edward W. Henry, Thomas T. Bouldin, Thomas A. Morton, Martin Hancock, D. Hancock, G. C. Friend, William Smith, Major T. Nelson, Colonel J. Harvey, Joel Watkins, T. E. Watkins and Samuel Baldwin, were found to be not present.

The members present then formed themselves into a committee, Captain Henry A. Watkins in the chair, and Winslow Robinson acting as secretary. Captain William M. Watkins then moved that the meeting be adjourned to some future day, which was lost; whereupon, Captain William M. Watkins withdrew from the committee.

The committee then proceeded to take the resolutions into consideration. The first four resolutions were adopted unanimously; the fifth with one dissentient voice—Mr. Green.

On the sixth resolution there were five dissentient voices, Mr. Paul Carrington, Mr. Lester, Mr. Madison, Mr. John Daniel, and Mr. Isham Harvey.

The seventh resolution was carried unanimously. The eighth also was carried, Mr. Paul Carrington alone dissenting; and the ninth, tenth and eleventh were adopted unanimously.

The committee then rose and reported the resolutions, which were adopted by the meeting with only two dissentient voices—Colonel Clement Carrington and Mr. R. W. Gaines.

On motion of Mr. John Marshall, it was then

Resolved, That copies of the proceedings of this meeting be sent for publication to the different presses in Richmond, Petersburg, Norfolk, Lynchburg and Fredericksburg; and that copies be also sent to Mr. Bouldin, our representative in Congress and his colleagues, to our Senators, to the President of the United States, to Benjamin Watkins Leigh, Esq., to the Governor of South Carolina, and to Major General James Hamilton, commander of the State troops of South Carolina in Charleston.

On motion of Mr. Whitfield Read,

Resolved, unanimously, That the thanks of this meeting be given to Mr. Randolph for his open and decided support of the rights of the states, and his strenuous and efficient opposition to the odious consolidating doctrine of the President's late proclamation.

Mr. Randolph then expressed his thanks in a speech of considerable length, in the course of which all the warmest sympathies, which have so long united him to his old constituents, seemed to be awakened, and on the breaking up of the meeting they parted with feelings such as no man besides ever excited.

WINSLOW ROBINSON, *Secretary.*

We thought proper to publish a full list of the names of the gentlemen composing Mr. Randolph's "committee of rank," if for no other reason, to let the rising generation see who were at that day some of the leading and most substantial citizens of the county of Charlotte.

As soon as the speaker concluded "his long talk," he commenced to procure the passage of his resolutions. In his speech he had stated that he would not presume to dictate to his old constituents. The public are well acquainted with Mr. Randolph's manner of doing things in the halls of Congress, and it may gratify a laudable curiosity to be informed how he carried on among his constituents *at home.*

Captain —— was chairman of the meeting, but, we are assured that Mr. Randolph named every member of the committee. When he stated that he would not presume to dictate to his old constituents, he was at that very time preparing a dose which he alone could administer.

Here is a specimen of what they had to swallow—a bitter pill, we are informed, to some:

"*Resolved*, That we have seen with deep regret that Andrew Jackson, Esq., President of the United States, has been influenced by designing counsellors, to subserve the purposes of their guilty ambition, to disavow the principles to which he owed his elevation to the chief magistracy of the government, and to transfer his real friends and supporters, bound hand and foot, to the tender mercies of his and their bitterest enemies— the *ultra*-Federalist, *ultra*-tariff, *ultra*-bank, *ultra*-improvement, Hartford convention men—the habitual scoffers at States Rights."

This is the sentiment which bank, tariff, internal improvement, Jackson men were required to endorse.

Mr. Randolph preferred the driving process, but he occasionally flattered very adroitly. Sometimes, however, he encountered a man who could neither be seduced by his flattery nor intimidated by his threats.

When he was getting up his committee, he said:

"Call Colonel Clem. Carrington—the man who shed his blood at Eutaw—none of your drunken stagger-weeds of the court-yard."

Colonel Carrington soon made his appearance, with hat in hand; but, when requested to endorse the resolutions, he promptly said:

"I am for Jackson and the Union, sir," and disappeared.

Knowing that Mr. William B. Green had always been an *anti*-Jackson man, Mr. Randolph approached him thus:

"Mr. Green, I know you are dead shot against Jackson, and I appoint you one of the committee."

Mr. Green replied:

"I am also dead shot against nullification."

He then commenced making explanations, saying that nullification was not intended, and that all would be right if South Carolina took the ground intended by the resolutions.

Two or three of the gentlemen named on the committee, who had made objections, consented to serve, Mr. Green himself being one of them.

Mr. G., a young gentleman of promise, and who might well have aspired to political preferment, suggested an alteration in one of the resolutions. Mr. Randolph asked him if every word stated in the resolution was not true.

Mr. G. replied, that the facts might all be true, but he did not like the tone of the resolution—perhaps, the facts were put forth in rather too strong a light.

"You are right, Mr. G.," said Mr. Randolph in his peculiar manner, "I have lost much in my life by telling the truth. If I were young, I would pea-vine it, too. I owe Mr. G. something," said he, "alter the resolution to suit him."

When the amendment was made, he pronounced the resolution "a little stronger than it was before."

The following breathes the very essence of the intellectual tyrant. Mr. Henry Madison declined to endorse some of his resolutions. Mr. Randolph darted a piercing glance upon him, but made no open attack, as Mr. Madison expected. But still the presumption to differ with him weighed upon his mind. For that night, at supper with a friend, he expressed his surprise that Mr. Madison refused to endorse one of his resolutions—said he could not understand it. The gentleman who differed with him on this occasion was a man of fine sense and considerable influence. The fact that it was a matter of surprise to him that Mr. Randolph did not make an instantaneous direct attack upon him is evidence of what everybody expected who had the temerity to oppose him. If he came off with whole bones he was more than satisfied. If he escaped unscathed it was a subject of self-gratulation all the days of his life. Mr. Randolph was conscious of his mental superiority, and he had no scruples in asserting his power. He used various means of maintaining his dominion. He could melt to tears, provoke to rashness, or drive to desperation. And there was another weapon which he used with great effect—"severe repartees and sayings, creating great mirth at the expense of others." His favorite weapon was the whip and the spur. He might have it in his power to conciliate, still, if possible, he preferred to ram the pill down the throats of his opponents.

When Captain William M. Watkins was spoken to, he

positively and promptly refused to act. Mr. Randolph was very indignant, and made use of harsh language.

Up to that time Mr. Randolph had been a Jackson man. Mr. Watkins was also a Jackson man; nor did he desert him after the issue of the proclamation. Indeed he expressed himself publicly as highly pleased with it, and full of admiration for it. He went to Mr. Cardwell's, where Mr. Randolph was staying at the time, and asked Mr. Randolph what he thought of it. The latter declined to express his opinion, but went home to prepare his resolutions, and to plan an attack upon his friend.

At the meeting, while the resolutions were under consideration, Mr. Randolph took occasion to say, addressing himself to Captain Watkins, he did "not expect an old Yazoo speculator to approve of them."

Captain Watkins rose and made a statement denying the charge. Mr. Randolph looked him steadily in the face, and pointing his long bony finger at him, said:

"You are a Yazoo man, Mr. Watkins!"

Mr. Watkins rose again, agitated and embarrassed, and made some explanatory remarks.

Mr. Randolph, with the same deliberation, simply repeated:

"You are a Yazoo man, Mr. Watkins!"

Mr. Watkins rose a third time, completely overcome with mortification and chagrin. As he rose, his savage foe plunged the same dagger into his breast.

"You are a Yazoo man," said he, when Mr. Watkins left the room, completely vanquished by the single word "Yazoo."

This scene reminds us forcibly of the description given of Mr. Randolph in the "Recollections" of the Honorable James W. Bouldin, who states "that he had all the deliberation and self-possession and outward calmness that would belong to a man who was cool, and he was guarded, but his mind and passions were roused to the highest pitch of excitement within." He compares him to "an enraged tiger, whose eye burns and flashes with fiery vengeance, but who prepares to make his spring with the greatest deliberation."

This inward boiling and outward coolness is forcibly illustrated in his conduct with regard to Captain Watkins. Besides, Mr. Randolph on this occasion displayed a very bad quality of the heart. The gentleman against whom the charge of being concerned in the great Yazoo fraud was made was entirely innocent. He was a high-toned gentleman, of the strictest integrity, and in solid abilities had no superior in the county of Charlotte.

With regard to the charge made against Captain Watkins by Mr. Randolph, Mr. William B. Green in his recollections says:

"It was but the repetition of a similar charge made many years before, during the administration of Mr. Madison, when Captain Watkins took ground in favor of that administration, and voted for Eppes against Mr. Randolph in the Congressional election in 1809 or 1810. I have never been able to learn the precise nature of these speculations, but have understood in a general way that there were two classes of speculators—one, a party who had combined and associated themselves together for the purpose of corrupting and bribing the legislature; the other, individuals who proposed to purchase land on their own accounts.

"Captain Watkins, it was understood, belonged to the latter class, and consequently was an innocent purchaser, if, indeed, he made any purchase. All that I know with regard to the matter is simply this: From a very early period (1807) I had free access to all the books, papers and accounts of Captain Watkins, without having seen the least trace or vestige of anything relative to the subject. And, moreover, Mr. Randolph was at all times (except at the time when he had fallen out with Captain Watkins on account of the vote given against him for Eppes) on friendly, social and intimate terms with him, which I think would not have been the case had Mr. Randolph really thought that these so-called speculations were derogatory to the character and standing of Captain Watkins. I have thought it due to the memory of my old friend and partner to say thus much on this subject."

The same gentleman, Mr. Henry Madison, to whom we referred above, as having refused to endorse one of Mr. Randolph's resolutions, related to us a little incident which shows at once what sway he held in his own county.

Mr. Madison and his friend were riding together in a buggy to Lynchburg, discussing, all the way, General Jackson's proclamation, which had just come out. Mr. Madison was pointing out its consolidating doctrines, and highly disapproving of them. His friend was defending them.

A few days afterwards, they were both standing together in the committee room, considering Mr. Randolph's resolutions. Presently they came to one which was too strong for Mr. Madison even to endorse.

Said he, to his friend, who was swallowing each resolution whole as they came to it: "You can't go that, can you, after all you stated to me going to Lynchburg?"

"Yes," replied his friend, "let's *swallow it all!*"

Mr. Madison was admonished by another friend that Mr. Randolph would "kill him off" completely for presuming to differ with him even in one particular.

"No," replied Mr. Madison, "I am a plain farmer; not conspicuous at all; he will not disturb me. But you, who are an aspirant for political promotion, are the one who has cause to fear."

We have thus given the reader the recollections of the old people of Charlotte with regard to the most extraordinary meeting of the kind, we dare say, which ever occurred in this or any other country. We obtained the facts from gentlemen who were eye-witnesses of the scene, and whose statements may be implicitly relied on. As to the accuracy of their memories, there is little room to doubt, when it is borne in mind that the most impressive man that ever lived was the chief actor in the scene.

Considering Mr. Randolph's really "dying" condition, the reader no doubt was astonished at the able manner in which the resolutions were drawn; and there are some striking passages in his speech: for instance, where he describes the proclamation as coming "sweeping and blasting with death, like the simoons of Arabia, or the whirlwinds of the Great Sahara." No less striking is the passage in which he speaks of his mind and body being in a whipping race to destruction, and it being hard to tell which rode the foremost horse.

When we came to these remarkable expressions in the manuscript report of his speech, we recognized them as exactly the same that the Hon. James W. Bouldin repeated to us when a boy, and which we knew by heart.

These and other parts of the speech, which we had learned in the same way, satisfied us of the general accuracy of the report.

The following is another remark, which was indelibly impressed *verbatim* upon the minds of many, for long before we saw the report of the speech we had heard several gentlemen repeat it:

"If I had been there I would have taken the uncircumcised dog by the throat, led him before a magistrate, and committed him to jail. I told the ladies, they, sweet souls, who dressed their beds with their whitest sheets, and uncorked for him their best wine, were not far from having mulatto children."

The allusion made by Mr. Randolph to the position taken by Patrick Henry, with regard to the Alien and Sedition law, reminds us of the written statements of three of the leading citizens of Charlotte in their day, viz: the Rev. Clement Read, Colonel Robert Morton and Colonel Clement Carrington, all of whom were present and heard the speech referred to by Mr. Randolph. From the certificates now before us, of the above named gentlemen, we gather the true position of the great orator of the revolution. Declining to give any opinion of the Alien and Sedition laws, he neither approved nor disapproved of them, his only object being to quiet the minds of the people and to prevent them from resorting to unreasonable methods to remove any grievances that they thought they then labored under. He decidedly condemned the Virginia resolutions as tending to civil war. During his speech, Colonel Carrington states that he used this language: "Let us all go together, right or wrong. If we go into civil war, your Washington will lead the government armies, and who, I ask, is willing to point a bayonet against his breast?"

The Rev. Clement Read closes his certificate by saying, he "believed Mr. Henry lived and died a true Republican."

Colonel Morton states that it was the *last* time that Mr. Henry appeared in public, and the *first* time that Mr. Randolph appeared in public before the people of Charlotte. Colonel Carrington says the latter "was not much attended to."

No doubt a portion of the audience left the stand in disgust, that such a young and inexperienced speaker should rise in reply to the great orator of the revolution; but it is nevertheless true, that some of the crowd listened to Mr. Randolph, and may have been captivated by his eloquence. It was honor enough, however, for the young orator that they listened to him at all. It was Mr. Randolph's moral courage which is most to be admired on this occasion; there is not a braver act of the kind on record.

But to return to Mr. Randolph's last speech: In four months and twenty days from the time that he delivered it he breathed his last. And this was his last political battle. In the language of Mr. Baldwin: "His political life terminated where it began, in a contest for States Rights. It began by lifting his lance against Patrick Henry, and ended by turning its point against Andrew Jackson."

CHAPTER XV.

MR. RANDOLPH'S WILL.

AFTER the death of John Randolph, it was ascertained that he had left several wills. One in the possession of Dr. John Brockenbrough, written in 1819; another without date, though written in 1821, with four codicils dated respectively on the 5th of December, 1821, the 31st of January, 1826, the 6th of May, 1828, and the 26th of August, 1831; and yet another will, dated the 1st of January, 1832. The first, for some cause, was not admitted to probate, and the last was set aside, because he was not considered of sound mind at the time. The will of 1821, however, after a long contest, was finally established.

As a matter of curiosity, we give it in full to our readers, copied literally from Grattan's Reports:

In the name of God, Amen.

I, John Randolph, of Roanoke, do ordain this my last will and testament, hereby revoking all other wills whatsoever.

1. I give and bequeath all my slaves their freedom, heartily regretting that I have ever been the owner of one.

2. I give to my ex'or a sum not exceeding eight thousand dollars, or so much thereof as may be necessary to transport and settle said slaves to and in some other State or territory of the U. S., giving to all above the age of forty not less than ten acres of land each.

To my old and faithful servants, *Essex* and his wife *Hetty*, who, I trust, may be suffered to remain in the State, I give and bequeath three-and-a-half barrels of corn, two hundred weight of pork, a pair of strong shoes, a suit of clothes, and a blanket each, to be paid them annually;

also, an annual hat to Essex, and ten pounds of coffee, and twenty of brown sugar.

To my woman servant *Nancy*, the like allowance as to her mother. To *Juba* (*alias* Jupiter) the same; to Queen the same; to Johnny, my body servant, the same, during their respective lives.

I confirm to my brother Beverly the slaves I gave him, and for which I have a reconveyance.

I bequeath to John Randolph Clay four hundred dollars annually to complete his education, until he shall have arrived at the age of twenty-four years, earnestly exhorting him never to eat the bread of idleness or dependence.

I bequeath to my namesake, John Randolph Bryan, my gold watch, chain and seals, and the choice of my horses.

I bequeath to his brother Thomas the choice of two of my horses.

To William Leigh, of Halifax, I bequeath to him and his heirs forever all the land on which I live, lying between the Owen's ferry road and Carrington's, Cooke's, Lipscomb's and Morton's lines. Also, the books, plate, linen, household and kitchen furniture, liquors, stock, tools, and everything as it now stands, hereby appointing him my sole executor. And I do desire that he may not be required to give security, or to make any inventory of anything here; that is, at my mansion-house or the middle-quarter.

(Cut out in the original.) B. Dudley, all the interest I have under the will of Mrs. Martha Corran.

My interest, under the will of Mrs. Judith Randolph, I desire my executor to sell if he shall see fit, but not otherwise.

The land above the Owen's ferry road and the lower quarter, and the land I bought of the Reads, to be sold at my said executor's discretion, and whatever m (cut out in the original) y debts I give and bequeath to Francis Scott Key and the Rev. Wm. Meade, to be disposed of towards bettering the condition of my manumitted slaves.

I have not included my mother's descendants in my will, because her husband, besides the whole profits of my father's estate during the minority of my brother and myself, has contrived to get to himself the slaves given by my grandfather Bland, as her marriage portion when my father married her, which slaves were inventoried at my father's death as part of his estate, and were as much his as any that he had. One-half of them,

OF JOHN RANDOLPH. 205

now scattered from Maryland to Mississippi, were entitled to freedom at my brother Richard's death, as the other would have been at mine.

Witness my hand and seal.

The name (cut out in the original.) [SEAL.]

In the presence of

RICHARD RANDOLPH, JR.

Codicil to this my will, made the 5th day of December, 1821. I revoke the bequest to T. B. Dudley, and bequeath the same to my executor, to whom also I give in fee simple all my lots and houses in Farmville, and every other species of property whatever that I die possessed of, saving the aforesaid specifications in my will.

(The name cut out of the original.)

AMELIA COUNTY.

The reason of the above revocation I have communicated to Wm. J. Barksdale, Esq.

The codicil of 1826.

In the name of God, Amen. I, John Randolph, of Roanoke, being of sound mind and memory, but of infirm health, do ordain this codicil to my last will and testament, now in the possession of Wm. Leigh, Esquire, of Halifax county, Virginia, executor thereof, which said appointment I do hereby confirm, with all the bequests made to him therein, and bequests to or for the benefit of all, each and every of my slaves, whether by name or otherwise, and all bequests to him and them which may be contained in my codicil to my last will. I make the same provision for my body servant *John* that I made in my will for his father *Essex*, and the same provision for the said John's wife Betsy that I made for *Hetty*, the wife of Essex aforesaid, and similar provision for my man servant *Juba*, and his wife *Celia*, and the same for mulatto *Nancey* at the Lower Quarter, *Archer's* wife. And I humbly request the General Assembly (the only request that I ever preferred to them) to let the above named, and such other of my old and faithful slaves as desire it, to remain in Virginia, recommending them, each and all, to the care of my said ex'or, who I know is too wise, just and humane, to send them to Liberia, or any other place in Africa, or the West Indies.

I revoke all and every bequest in my said will, or in any former codicil thereto (except as aforesaid, to my executor William Leigh, and my slaves, whether by name or otherwise), of every description whatsoever, whether of my own proper estate, or in expectancy or reversion from the Bland and Bizarre estate, or from any other contingency or source whatsoever. These reversions or remainders, or executor's devises, or whatsoever the law chooses to call them, I bequeath to my said executor, as a fund to be used at his discretion for the benefit of my slaves aforesaid, the surplus, if any, to be his own.

I also give and bequeath to the said William Leigh, my executor, the land that I bought of Pleasant Lipscomb's estate, to him and his heirs forever.

I also give and bequeath to my said executor and his heirs forever the lot of fifty-three acres of land lying at the deep gut on Staunton river, in Halifax county, that I bought of William Sims Daniel, and I request my said executor not to sell or lease the same, but to work it in three shifts, and to enable him to do so, I give and bequeath to him the lot of one hundred and seventy-five acres of land in Halifax county, which I also bought of William Sims Daniel, to have and to hold during his natural life, and at his decease to that one of his children to whom he shall bequeath the aforesaid lot of fifty-three acres at the deep gut.

I give and bequeath to my friend, Thomas H. Benton, all that part of the tract of land that I bought of Jonathan Read's heirs, that lies on the south-eastern side of Little Roanoke, containing about six hundred acres, as a mark of my regard to one whose friendship towards me was not expressed merely in words. I also give him my large pistols, made by Woydon & Burton.

To my friend, Dr. John Brokenbrough, I leave all my plate made by Rundle, Bridge & Rundle, viz: 1 tea pot, one coffee pot, 1 sugar dish and tongs, two tureens, 4 sauce dishes. All the rest and residue of my plate, furniture of every sort, plantation utsensils, &c., I give to my said executor, Wm. Leigh, and all my books, maps, charts, pictures, prints, &c., except three folio manuscript volumes, bound in parchment, which I bequeath to the master and fellows (and their successors) of Trinity College, Cambridge, old England, the first college of the first University of the world.

To my friend William J. Barksdale, of Haw Branch, Esquire, I bequeath my new English saddle and bridle, my silver spurs, my new English boots and shoes, two pair each, my gold watch made by Baiwese, with the chain and seals, except the oldest seal with the Randolph arms and motto *nil admirari*, which I leave to R. Kidder Randolph, of Rhode Island.

I also leave to the said W. J. Barksdale the choice of any of my mares or fillies.

I leave to Edmond Irby, of Nottoway, the next choice of my mares or fillies, and any one of my horses or colts, to be selected by himself; also, my double barrel gun.

To Peyton Randolph, of Buck river, Prince Edward, I leave my small cockney gun by Mortimer.

All the rest and residue of my estate, real or personal, I leave to my executor, Wm. Leigh, hereby directing that no inventory or appraisement be made of my estate, and that no security shall be required of my said executor for the faithful discharge of the trust reposed in him—his own character being the best security, and where that is wanting, all other is unavailing.

In witness whereof I have hereunto set my hand and affixed my seal (the following interlineations and expungings being first made: in the second paragraph the word "Essex" interlined; in the third paragraph the word "former" interlined, and the word "or" expunged; and in the 7th paragraph the words, "and tongs" interlined) this thirty-first day of January, one thousand eight hundred and twenty-six (the whole of this codicil being written in my own hand).

JOHN RANDOLPH, *of Roanoke*, [SEAL.]

In presence of
    M. ALEXANDER,
    NATH. MACON.

MEMORANDUM.—The folio volumes of MS. bound in parchment, containing the records, &c., of the old London company.

The Codicil of 1828.

Being in great extremity, but in my perfect senses, I write this codicil to my will in the possession of my friend Wm. Leigh, of Halifax county, Esquire, to declare that will is my sole last will and testament, and that if any other be found of subsequent date, whether will or codicil, I do hereby revoke the same.

Witness my hand and seal.

JOHN RANDOLPH, *of Roanoke*, [SEAL.]
May 6, 1828.

Witness,
    EDMUND MORGAN,
    JO. M. DANIEL,
    ROBERT CARRINGTON.

N. B.—When I was about to embark for Europe, in 1822, I did write a codicil on board the steamboat that was carrying me to the packet ship Amity, which codicil, by my direction, Mr. Leigh destroyed.

Since writing the above, it has occurred to me that the will referred to, as being in Mr. Leigh's possession, makes no disposition of the land that I purchased of Walter Coles and Letty his wife; also the land I bought of ―― Daniel, consisting of two small tracts in Halifax; also, of the land purchased of Pleasant Lipscomb's heirs. Now this writing witnesseth, that I give and bequeath the whole of the above recited lands, purchased since the date of my will aforesaid, to William Leigh, Esquire, my faithful friend, who has given me aid and comfort, not with words only, but by deeds.

I also give and bequeath to him and his heirs forever, not each and every of the aforesaid tracts of land, but all the property of every description and kind whatsoever that I may have acquired since the date of that will aforesaid.

Witness my hand and seal this same sixth day of May, 1828.

JOHN RANDOLPH, *of Roanoke*, [SEAL.]

    EDMUND MORGAN,
    JO. M. DANIEL,
    ROBT. CARRINGTON.

In the will above recited, I give to my said ex'or, Wm. Leigh, the refusal of the land above Owen's (now Clark's) ferry road, at a price that I then thought very moderate, but which a change in the times has rendered too high to answer my friendly intentions towards my said executor in giving him that refusal. I do, therefore, so far, but so far only, modify my said will as to reduce that price 50 per cent.; in other words, one-half, at which he may take all the land above the ferry road that I inherited from my father, all that I bought of the late John Daniel, deceased, and of Tom Beaseley, Charles Beaseley, and others of that name and family, this last being the land that Gabriel Beaseley used to have in possession, and whereon Beverley Tucker lived, and which I hold by deed from him and his wife, of record in Charlotte county court.

Witness my hand and seal —— day and year aforesaid.

JOHN RANDOLPH, *of Roanoke*, [SEAL.]

(The words, "but so far only," and the word "from" in the preceding page, first interlined.)

Witness,
    EDMUND MORGAN,
    JO. M. DANIEL,
    ROBT. CARRINGTON.

As lawyers and courts of law are extremely addicted to making wills for dead men, which they never made when living, it is my will and desire that no person who shall set aside, or attempt to set aside, the will above referred to, shall ever inherit, possess or enjoy any part of my estate, real or personal.

JOHN RANDOLPH, *of Roanoke*, [SEAL.]

Teste,
    ROBT. CARRINGTON,
    EDMUND MORGAN,
    JO. M. DANIEL.

Codicil of 1831.

On the eve of embarking for the U. S., considering my very feeble health, to say nothing of the dangers of the seas, I add this codicil to my last will and testament and the codicils thereto, affirming them all, except so far as they may be inconsistent with the following disposition of my estate:

1. It is my will and desire that my dear niece, Elizabeth Tucker Bryan, shall have my lower quarter, with the lands purchased of Coles and wife and of Allen Gilliam's estate, with the mill; and I do hereby bequeath the same to her and her heirs forever.

2. To my brother, Henry St. George Tucker, I give and bequeath all my Bushy Forrest estate, on both sides of Little Roanoke, bought of the Reads, and all my interest in the estate of Mrs. Martha Corran, and my lots and houses in Farmville.

3. I have upwards of two thousand pounds sterling in the hands of Barring Brothers & Co., of London, and upwards of one thousand pounds of like money in the hands of Gowane Marx; this money I leave to my ex'r, Wm. Leigh, as a fund for carrying into execution my will respecting my slaves. And in addition to the provision which I have made for my faithful servant *John*, sometimes called *John White*, I charge my whole estate with an annuity to him during his life of fifty dollars; and, as the only favor that I ever asked of any government, I do entreat the Assembly of Virginia to permit the said John and his family to remain in Virginia; and I do earnestly recommend him and them to my executor aforesaid and to my dear brother and niece aforesaid.

4. My plate and library I leave to my dear niece, E. T. Bryan.

Witness my hand, in Warwick street, Charing Cross, London, this twenty-ninth day of August, one thousand eight hundred and thirty-two, to which I have also appended my seal.

JOHN RANDOLPH, *of Roanoke.* [L. S.]

(Endorsement on the envelope) J. R., of R.

In case of accident, to be sent to the U. S.

The will of January 31st. 1832.

In the name of God, Amen. I, John Randolph, of Roanoke, in the county of Charlotte and Commonwealth of Virginia, do ordain and appoint this my last will and testament, hereby revoking all other wills and .. testaments and codicils whatsoever, in the manner and form following, that is to say: On this first day of January, one thousand eight hundred and thirty two, to which I have set my hand and affixed my seal, binding my heirs and assigns forever:

I give and bequeath all my estate, real and personal, in possession or action, reversion or remainder, to John C. Bryan, only son of John Randolph Bryan and Elizabeth Coalter his wife, daughter of my dear sister Fanny, for and during the life of the said John C. Bryan, with remainder to his eldest son in fee simple, to him and his heirs forever: and in defect of such issue, then to the son of Henry St. George Tucker, called John Randolph after me, for and during his natural life, with remainder to his eldest son; and in defect of any such issue, then to Tudor Tucker, brother of the aforesaid Randolph Tucker, for and during his natural life, with remainder to his eldest son.

And I do hereby appoint my friends, Wm. Leigh, of Halifax, and my brother, Henry St. George Tucker, president of the Court of Appeals, executors of this my last will and testament; requiring them to sell all the slaves and other perishable or personal property, and vest the proceeds in bank stock of the bank of the United States; and in default of there being no such bank (which may God grant for the safety of our liberties), in the *English* three per cent. consols; and in case of there being no such stocks (which also may God grant for the safety of old *England*), then in the United States three per cent. stock; or in defect of such stock, in mortgages on land in England.

From the sale of my perishable property I except my library, books, maps, charts and engravings included, my pictures, plate, household linen, and the furniture of my bed chamber in the old house, and all the furniture in the new house, wines, together with such other articles as my said ex'ors may deem proper to keep for the benefit of the heirs. And my will and desire is, that my said executors may select from among my slaves a number not exceeding one hundred for the use of the heir; the remainder to be sold. I also desire that my Bushy Forest tract of land may be sold and made chargeable with such debts and legacies as hereafter I may see fit to give when I shall have more leisure to make my will; this being made in consequence of having cancelled a former will this night in presence of Wm. Leigh aforesaid, the sole executor under that will, and joint executor under this will, which I make to guard against the possibility of dying intestate.

I have in the bank of Virginia upwards of 20,000 dollars; of which sum I desire payment to be made for the land purchased by me the day before yesterday of Elisha E. Hundley; and I bequeath the remainder to be equally divided between my said executors, Wm. Leigh and H. S. G. Tucker, Esquires: and I farther charge my Bushy Forest estate with a farther legacy to John Randolph Leigh, youngest son of Wm. Leigh aforesaid, of five thousand dollars.

And it is my will and desire that no inventory be taken of my estate, except of my slaves and horses, and that no security be given by or required of my said executors, having full faith in their honor; neither shall they be held to account to any court or person whatsoever for their discharge of this trust so confided by me in them.

To Dr. John Brokenbrough I leave all my French plate now in Richmond at J. P. Taylor's, also my chariot and harness and the horses called John Bull and Jonathan, alias John W.

To John Wickham, Esquire, my best of friends, without making any professions of friendship for me, and the best and wisest man I ever knew except Mr. Macon, I bequeath my mare Flora and my stallion Gascoigne; together with two old-fashioned, double-handled silver cups, and two tankards unengraved—the cups are here, and the tankards or cans in Richmond—and I desire that he will have his arms engraved upon them, and at the bottom these words: "From J. R., of Roanoke, to John Wickham, Esquire, as a token of the respect and gratitude which he never ceased to feel for unparalleled kindness, courtesy and services."

To Nathaniel Macon I give and bequeath my oldest high silver candlesticks, my silver punch ladle with whalebone handle, a pair of silver cans with handles and my crest engraved thereon, my hard metal dishes that have my crest and J. R. in old English letters engraved thereon, also the plates with the same engraving, the choice of four of my best young mares and geldings, and the gold watch by Roskell that was Tudor's with the gold chain: and may every blessing attend him—the best, purest and wisest man that I ever knew. To my brother Henry Tucker, my gold watch, by Bauwise. The chronometer by Arnold, and knives and forks &c., from Rogers, to go to the heir. To Wm. Leigh, all duplicates of my books, and my brood mare's last chance, and Amy. To H. Tucker, young Whalebone and young Never Tire, also Topaz and Janus and Camilla and Marcella.

JOHN RANDOLPH, *of Roanoke.* [ ]

CHAPTER XVI.

MR. RANDOLPH'S SANITY DISCUSSED.

IN his Biography of John Randolph of Roanoke, Mr. Sawyer has this observation: "It might be expected of him to decide the important question of Mr. Randolph's sanity." We must confess that we, at least, expected this of him. Nor are our expectations, we think, unreasonable. A writer who devotes more than a hundred pages to a particular subject should certainly inform his readers whether his hero be in his senses. But Mr. Sawyer, we are sorry to say, confesses himself incompetent to judge. But, he adds, "on the main point, that on which the happiness of our whole lives in this world depends, the promotion of his self-interest and pecuniary independence, if perfect success is the test of sanity, he must stand acquitted on the charge of insanity." Mr. Bouldin, it appears, agrees with Mr. Sawyer that Mr. Randolph's practical skill and judgment in business ought to be made a test. For, we remember, when Mr. Wickham remarked that he thought "there was always a vein of madness in him," he asked him, "how he accounted for his paying off those mortgages and interest and buying as much more property during thirty years, with negroes and overseers only."

"Some," says Mr. Baldwin, "set Mr. Randolph down as a madman, whose sagacity was only the cunning of a lunatic, and his brilliancy only the occasional gleamings of light which are fitfully emitted from the darkness of a mad-house.

But that others viewed him as a man eccentric indeed, but whose acuteness of thought, deep insight into the motives of men and the affairs of government, and whose perspicuity and prudence were nearly miraculous."

The Hon. James W. Bouldin, from whose manuscript we have so often quoted, says he once asked Rev. John Robinson: How is it that you all have found out at last that Mr. Randolph is a fool? He replied: "I am ashamed of that; I know some of us say so; I wish he had less sense; he never makes one of his great speeches but it shakes the whole continent—every man, woman and child can repeat some of it. Some of his conceptions, however, though vast and powerful, are such, I think, as no mind entirely sane would have."

The learned judges to whom was referred the question of his sanity, after the most thorough and patient investigation of the whole subject, decided that he was of sound and disposing mind when he wrote his will in 1821, but insane when he wrote the will of 1832. The reader will remember the testimony of Mr. Daniel, one of the witnesses in that celebrated cause. He represents Mr. Randolph as acting on some occasions, in the most singular manner; but frequently making use of the most striking language, full of meaning and consistent. When asked the direct question, did he think he was in a fit state of mind to make the acknowledgments to his will, he replied: "He was excited by drinking, but capable, in his estimation, of transacting business." This truthful witness had the very best opportunity of forming a correct opinion, as he lived very near him and had a great deal to do with him.

Mr. Benton said, "his opinion was fixed of occasional temporary aberrations of mind; and during such periods he would do and say strange things, but always in his own way—not only method, but genius in his fantasies; nothing to bespeak a bad heart; only exaltation and excitement." "The most brilliant talks," continued he, "that I ever heard from him came forth on such occasions—a flow for hours (at one time seven hours) of copious wit and classic allusion—a perfect scattering of the diamonds of the mind."

He tells us that he once sounded Mr. Randolph to discover what he thought of his own case. He heard him repeating those lines of Johnson on "Senility and Imbecility."

"In life's last scenes what prodigies surprise,
Fears of the brave and follies of the wise;
From Marlborough's eyes the streams of dotage flow,
And Swift expires, a driveller and a show."

"Mr. Randolph," said Mr. Benton, "I have several times heard you repeat those lines, as if they could have an application to yourself, while no person can have less reason to fear the fate of Swift." "I have lived in dread of insanity," replied Mr. Randolph.

Many a man with fewer mental troubles and mental diseases than Mr. Randolph has lived in dread of the same thing, but whose apprehensions were never realized. We are not at all surprised that a man of peculiar genius, especially one who looks narrowly into the machinery of his own mind, should live in dread of insanity. It is no wonder that those who think "long and darkly," whose feelings are morbidly active, who are so constituted as to dwell upon a particular subject with intense interest, should be fearful of the effects of overaction.

Mr. Baldwin thought him insane at times. Mr. Garland, on the contrary, speaking of his conduct on the occasion of the funeral of Commodore Decatur, says: "The cold and heartless world, that is unconscious of anything else but a selfish motive, and the ignorant multitude that followed the funeral pageant with gaping mouth, agreed on a common explanation of his extravagance by proclaiming, 'the man is mad.'"

There seems to be a great difference of opinion both as to Mr. Randolph's sanity and his habit of drinking to excess. Mr. Benton says, he "never saw him affected by wine." The reader will remember what the Hon. James W. Bouldin said on this subject. He emphatically states, that from the first time he ever saw him to the last, say from 1808 or '9 till his death, he drank very hard, great quantities of intoxicating drink."

The reader will also remember the manner in which Mr. Bouldin attempts to account for the fact that it was not generally believed that Mr. Randolph drank to excess. He said: "Although he drank much in public, he drank still more in private; and although the public and private drinking was known to so many, yet it is a matter of great surprise to nine-tenths of persons to be told that he drank to excess. He had the power of fascination and charm to such an extent on most men that, though he drank much, they thought it had no effect on him." Mr. Bouldin was of a different opinion, however.

The testimony of Mr. Benton and Mr. Bouldin differs; both may be true. But if the question were submitted to a judge on the bench upon the evidence of these two witnesses, he would be bound to decide, according to settled principles of law, that the fact of drunkenness was proved.

He was in a drunken, prostrate condition when he made Mr. R. B. put the paper in the box and seal it with the sign of the cross; when he unconsciously bid the same person adieu.

He was intoxicated when he took that cold ride in his

carriage from his house to Watkins's store—the time he offered his friend the bottle of hot water, and put his cloak over one of his horses. He was inflamed by drink when he stormed and raged at his servant Queen about the bank note—the time he raised himself up in his bed with the pantaloons in his hands and swore they had been boiled. Nor was he at all sober when he displayed the clothes he wore before the Emperor of Russia, when he said, they were rich but not gaudy, and thereupon commenced to read a volume of Skakespeare, saying he would read the whole story; and he was in a drunken stupor when he pressed the hand of his friend, and closing his eyes, whispered, "I am dying."

He was surely drunk when he did a thousand things which some attributed to madness. True, they had seen other men drinking vast quantities of intoxicating liquors, and then acting strangely and talking strangely; and they had no hesitation in pronouncing such, not mad, but drunk. But when they saw Mr. Randolph drinking to the same extent, and talking and acting strangely, they could not believe it was drunkenness, but madness.

The main question now comes up for decision—was Mr. Randolph a sane man?

There are some who attribute, in a great measure, those strange things, of which so much has been said, in the life of Mr. Randolph, to his intemperate habits. Of this number is one of our most reliable witnesses. If the reader will recollect, in a conversation upon this very subject with Mr. Wickham, Mr. Bouldin said, "he was drunk." Mr. Wickham replied, "he did not know whether the intoxication came first, or the madness came first, but they came together."

We have no doubt that this is the correct opinion. He

was no more mad than some other men under the influence of ardent spirits. He lost his senses from the same cause, and to no greater extent.

If he were living, he might so fascinate and charm us that we might not believe he was intemperate; or we might be afraid to say so, as thousands were. But, now that he is dead, and has been for some time, we think we can form an unprejudiced opinion, and may safely express it.

There is not a shadow of a doubt resting upon our mind, of Mr. Randolph's sanity. We repeat, his nerves were of the finest texture of any man almost that ever lived, and his brain had become morbid from inordinate exercise upon particular subjects.

> . " He had thought
> Too long and darkly, till his brain became,
> In its own eddy boiling and o'erwrought.
>
> And thus, untaught in youth his heart to tame,
> His springs of life were poisoned."

His nerves were strained to the highest pitch, but he was not mad. To a state of high natural excitement was added artificial excitement, and it was while under the combined influence of both, that he said and did those strange things which induced the belief in many, that he was mad.

CHAPTER XVII.

LETTERS.

WE have a small collection of Mr. Randolph's letters, which have never been published. They were written at various periods of his life, from youth to old age. The first, which we propose to lay before our readers, was written when he was at school and only fifteen years of age. It is said that Dryden, Swift, Goldsmith, Sir Walter Scott, Gibbon and Napoleon, were all dull scholars; this letter of Mr. Randolph's shows conclusively that he was not of that class. It moreover reveals his early taste for politics.

NEW YORK, Dec. 25, 1788.

I received my dear papa's affectionate epistle, and was sorry to find that he thought himself neglected. I assure you, my dear sir, that there has scarcely a fortnight elapsed since uncle's absence without my writing to you, and I would have paid dearly for you to have received them. I sent them by the post, and indeed no other opportunity except by Capt. Crozier, and I did not neglect that. Be well assured, my dear sir, our expenses since our arrival here have been enormous and by far greater than our estate, especially loaded as it is with debt, can bear; however, I flatter myself, my dear papa, that upon looking over the accounts you will find that my share is, by comparison trifling, and hope that by the wise admonitions of so affectionate a parent, and one who has our welfare and interest so much at heart, we may be able to shun the rock of prodigality, upon which so many people continually split, and by which the unhappy victim is reduced, not only to poverty, but also to despair and all the horrors attending it.

Brother R. writes you, that I am lazy. I assure you, dear papa, he has been egregiously mistaken. I attend every lecture that the class does. Not one of the professors have ever found me dull with my business or even said that I was irregular. All my leisure time I devote to the study of ———, and then read the poets from five o'clock in the morning till twelve. I am constantly reading in my ———. The rest of my time is allotted to College duty. If brother Richard had written you that I did nothing all the vacation he would have been much in the dark—neither was it possible for me. We lived in this large building without a soul in it but ourselves, and it was so desolate and dreary that I could not bear to be in it. I always was afraid that some robber, of which we have a plenty [as you will see by the enclosed paper] was coming to kill me after they made a draught on the house.

Be so good, my dear sir, when it is convenient, to send me the debate of the Convention of our State. My love to the families of Butler, ———, Cawsons. My love to Mr. Tucker, Jr., Miss Maria, and the children. Tell them I wish them a Merry Christmas. That you, my ever dear papa, may enjoy many happy ones, is the sincere wish of your ever affectionate son,

JOHN RANDOLPH, Jun'r.

P. S. My best love to Aunt Betty Carlos. Capt. Henry of Bermuda says that cousin F. Tucker of the Hermitage is to be married to young Jack Tucker.

St. Geo. Tucker, Esq., Petersburg.

Superscribed,
The Hon'ble St. George Tucker, Esq.,
Williamsburg, Va.
Franked, Thos. Fred. Tucker.

The following two were written when Mr. Randolph was twenty-one years of age, and reflect credit upon his matured understanding:

PHILADELPHIA, 26TH JANUARY, 1794.
MY DEAR FATHER:

I received last night your letter of the 17th instant, covering a draft on the treasury for $104.27, for which accept my hearty thanks. I wish I could thank you also for your news concerning the conjectured "marriage between a reverend divine and one who has been long considered among the immaculate votaries of Diana." I can easily guess at the name of the former; but there are really so many ancient maids in your town, of desperate expectations in the matrimonial lottery, that it is no easy task to tell what person in particular comes under the above denomination.

You may depend on my contracting no debts. I have known the sweets of that situation too well again to plunge into the same gulph of extreme misery for a long time by dint of extreme parsimony, extricating myself from that most horrid of all calamities.

You have not, I perceive, received some of my letters, for immediately on the late change in our ministry, as 'tis styled by the countrymen here, I wrote to you informing you minutely of the circumstance. I have wished to send you several important publications; our executive's correspondence with the ministers of France and Britain, &c., but I had no mode of conveying them to you. Mr. Madison's resolutions, respecting the restrictions of commerce in regard to those nations not in alliance with us, are now before the House of Representatives, and will be, I am afraid, thrown out, from the circumstance of two of our southern men being absent—Mr. Page and Mercer. It is an unpardonable thing for men to offer themselves as candidates who cannot punctually attend. Mr. Madison's sentiments, and those of Columbus, are in perfect unison.

I will now, my dear, sir, touch upon that part of your letter dated New Year's day, which relates to my studying in Williamsburg. I have found my conduct and character, during my residence in that place, canvassed in so ungenerous and malicious a manner, that were it not the residence of yourself, and your beloved family, I never would set foot in it again, but if you wish me to return, I will conquer my aversion to the place. I ought to have said its inhabitants, as far as 'tis in my power, and endeavor to avail myself of every advantage which it may afford.

Dr. Tucker is expected in town every minute. I need not say how happy I shall be to see him. I am extremely unwell, owing to the amazing vicissitude of weather which we have experienced. For some days we have the air so immoderately warm that we are obliged to open our windows and extinguish the fire, and in the course of five hours we experience the utmost severity of winter.

Present my best love to all the family, particularly Mrs. Tucker and Fanny. Why does not the latter write? Believe me, my dear sir, with the most ardent love and sincere esteem your affectionate son and friend,

JOHN RANDOLPH.

No news of my trunk. Colonel Cole, of Virginia, has lost his youngest child, a girl of about fifteen months old, with the small pox.

30th January, Wednesday.

I have been so unwell as to be incapable of carrying this to the post office until to-day. Yesterday we had a most violent snow storm, which lasted from 10 o'clock A. M. till two this morning, during which time it snowed incessantly. Uncle T. is not come. No news of my trunk, at which I am very uneasy. I wrote to Mr. Campbell by Capt. Dangerfield to learn by what vessel it was sent, but have received no answer. There is no such thing in this city as Blackstone in 4to. The house has come, as yet, to no determination respecting Mr. Madison's resolutions. They will not pass, thanks to our absent delegates; nay, were they to go through the H. of R. the S. would reject them, as there is *no senator* from Maryland and but one from Georgia. Thus are the interests of the Southern States basely betrayed by the indolence of some and the villainy of others of her statesmen,—Messrs. G—r, H—n and L—e generally voting with the paper men.

Pray write at least once a week, and not such short letters as you sometimes do. I wish very much you would indulge me with a watch. I can get a very good gold one for 50 Dolls: and will not *sell it* I assure you. Once more, dear father, adieu.

Yours ever,

J. RANDOLPH.

Wednesday evening, 9 o'clock.

I was mistaken, my dear sir, when I said Uncle Tucker had not arrived in town. He got here the day before yesterday, and did not know where to find me. In my way to the post office this morning, I was told of his arrival, and flew to see him. He looks as well as I ever saw him, and was quite cheerful—made a number of affectionate enquiries concerning you and your family, my brother and his wife and little boy. He cannot go through Virginia in his way to Charleston. I pressed him very warmly to do it, but you know his resolutions when once taken are unalterable. I gave you in a former letter a full account of our friends in Bermuda. My uncle says that they complain much of your neglecting to write to them. He seemed much hurt at the circumstance. You cannot think how rejoiced I was to see him look so well and cheerful. It has quite revived my spirits. He stays in this city a week or ten days, when he returns to New York, where he will remain five or six weeks before he goes to Charleston. If you write him, which I suppose you will unquestionably do, you had better direct to New York. I shall write next post, till then, my dearest father, adieu. I must not forget to tell you that Dr. Bartlett, the spermaceti doctor, as Mr. Tudor used to call him, has turned privateersman, and commands a vessel out of Bermuda. Miss Betsy Gilchrist is to be married to a Lieut. Hicks of the British army, and Mr. Fibb, it is reported, is also to be married to another officer whose name I do not recollect.

J. R.

St. Geo. Tucker, Esq.,
          Williamsburg,
Mail.   *Virginia.*

PHILADELPHIA, MARCH 1, 1794.
MY DEAR FATHER:
    I see that you begin again to cease writing to me; and I hope that you will be so good as to send me a letter at least once a week, as you are so shortly to set out on your circuit, when I cannot expect to hear from you as often as when you are at home. The enclosed letter I wrote some time ago. I have every day been expecting an opportunity by which I could send it without subjecting you to the expense of postage, which perhaps I too often do. As the subject is an important one, I hope you will answer it as soon as you conveniently can.

Yesterday the important question, whether Mr. Gallatin, a senator from this State, was entitled to a seat in the Senate or not, was determined against him.

AYES.	NOES.
Langdon, N. H.	Livermore, N. H.
Bradley, } Verm.	Cabol, } Massachusetts.
Robinson, }	Strong, }
Burr, N. Y.	Bradford, } R. Island.
Monroe, } Virg.	Foster, }
Taylor, }	Ellsworth, } Conn.
Brown, } Kent.	Mitchell, }
Edwards, }	King, N. York.
Martin, N. C.	Frelinghuysen, N. Jersey.
Butler, S. C.	Morris, Penn.
Jackson, } Geor.	Vining, Delaware.
Gunn, }	Potts, Maryland.
	Hawkins, N. C.
	Irrard, S. C.

12   14

The Republican party are much hurt at this decision, since in abilities and principles, he was inferior to none in that body. So said Mr. Taylor, from Virginia. Altho' he came here in 1780, took up arms in our defence, bought lands and settled, yet, nine years not having elapsed between the time of his taking the oaths of allegiance and his election, he was declared not qualified according to the constitution. It was agreed that by art. 2, sect. 1, clause 4, a resident of 14 years standing might take the oaths of citizenship one day and be elected the next to the presidential chair; and therefore it was apprehended that the constitution of the U. S. was not more vigilant with respect to the election of senators than presidents. Certainly, if a man be not a citizen of the United States at the time of the adoption of the Federal constitution, he is not eligible to the office of president: however, Mr. Gallatin had been nine years a *citizen* and thirteen an inhabitant when he took his seat. Query, can a man be a senator until he qualifies as is prescribed by art. 6, clause 3, and informed by c. 1, 2d sess. 1st congress? I wish you would inform me what your opinion is on the subject.

My uncle is still in town. I saw him the day before yesterday. He desires me to tell you that he will write you when he arrives in New York. He is very well.

In almost every one of my letters I have made enquiries concerning my trunk. Pray, my dear sir, inform me, if you can, where it is. Do you know by what vessel it was sent? I am *sans chemise* and *sans culottes* in every sense of the word. Toulon is certainly retaken. The English are apprehensive of a descent on their coast. The vessels in ——— exterminated. My best love to Mrs. T. & Co.

Yours ever,

JOHN RANDOLPH, Jun'r.

When do you set off upon your circuit? What districts do you visit?

JACK LACONIC.

Superscribed,

St. George Tucker, Esq.,

Williamsburg, Virginia.

Care of James Brown, Esq., who will be so obliging as to forward it by the first good conveyance.

The first letter in this chapter was written when Mr. Randolph was a school boy; the second just as he reached

maturity; we will now lay before the reader one written
when he was fifty-three years of age. He was noted for his
love of fine horses and opens upon that subject; but he
touches upon several other points, and, altogether, this letter
is not only characteristic, but highly interesting:

WASHINGTON, January 16, 1828.
DEAR SIR:

Your welcome letter of the 13th from Petersburg reached me yesterday.
I waited for its receipt, that I might acknowledge that of its predecessor
at the same time. I am sorry that I did so, for I wanted to know whether I could advantageously place my horse, Roanoke, in your neighborhood? I am sorry that you can't take filly; but I *pledge*, as the boys say,
a place for her in your training stables next autumn, and another if you
have it to spare. Could I get Bolling Graves, think you, to train for me?
I mean next autumn of course, for his spring engagements are no doubt
complete. There is some mistake about that rifle. It was never sent
home. The last time I saw it it was in J. M. & D.'s compting room.
Have I any other article there except the fir pole from Mont Blanc?
Uncle Nat.* is greatly mended, and I am satisfied that if the "wicked
world cease from troubling," which they will not do in this world, I wish
they may in the next, he would be well. He made a remark to me the
other day, that forcibly reminded me of Gay's Shepherd and Philosopher—the best of all his fables, except "the Hare and many friends." It
will not require your sagacity to make the application. "All animals,"
said he, "provide for their own offspring, and there the thing stops. The
birds rear their young by their joint cares and labours. The cow suckles
and takes care of her own calf, but she does not nurse or provide for that
calf's calf." "The birds do not build nests for their young one's eggs, nor
hatch them, nor feed the nestlings."

I return the good wishes and "best regards of *all* your family to one
and all. But I must particularly name the matron mother of them all, and
Virginia. Edward I see is married. Being now aged, and having his
full weight to carry, he will I trust "*plumb the track*," as I have heard
old racers say. To George I am indebted for a very kind letter. John I

---

* Honorable Nathaniel Macon.

am satisfied, with proper training and exercise, which last depends upon himself, will make a fine fellow, but he must bear in mind that no nag can run just taken off the grass, and that with the best management he must sometime *muzzle*. The younger boys, in which members I include your grandson, I need not advise to diligently mind their work, which, at their age, is *play*. This they will do without aid from any quarter.

Mr. Macon's kindness to me on all occasions, but particularly last winter and this, cannot be requited by any return that I can make. But for him last winter I don't know what I should have done. But if you were to hear him, you would suppose that *he*, and not *I*, was the obliged party. We have had but one fair day this month (New Year's day), and but four in December. It has been very warm and damp—the worst possible weather for preserving meat. I wish that you may have "saved your bacon." If practicable, I am sure that it has been done by Mrs. J.'s management, who, in her department, I will back against any that can be named; and now you are fairly tired of a letter of two closely written pages. So farewell, and God bless you all.

Yours, truly,

J. R., *of R.*

I send George the *Advocate* every week.

(Private and particular.) Yesterday our friend* and your representative made a speech, which although, in some respects, the best I ever heard from him, yet was (as is too often the case with him) more injurious to us than to the enemy. It was on the slave question.

Superscribed,

William R. Johnson, Esq.,
Wilkinsonville, Chesterfield county, Virginia.

free, J. RANDOLPH.

The following letter, addressed to his personal friend and business manager, Thomas A. Morton, Esq., of Prince Edward, was written at the time that he was minister to Russia. Knowing that he was buried at Roanoke by his direction,

---

*Honorable Wm. S. Archer.

we were surprised to see a desire expressed to lie by the side of his father and mother, at Matoax. We have heard no reason assigned for his change of feelings in this respect.

LONDON, Warwick St. Charing Cross.
Dec. 6, 1830. Monday.

MY DEAR SIR:

Since the sailing of the last packet from Liverpool, I received *via* St. Petersburg your letter of the 21st of August—the only one that I have had the pleasure to get from you.

It is with no small difficulty that I summon strength to thank you for it; for I am as low as I can be to be able to write at all.

In case that you shall not have contracted for the house at Bizarre, I wish to countermand the request. I intended it for a purpose that now can never be.

My expectations from the tobacco were very small; but I had hoped it would not turn out quite so badly. Meanwhile, I have no supply from Government. Congress and the Virginia Assembly both meet this day, and I pray God to send us, the people, a safe deliverance.

It will be very unlucky in case of a general war in Europe, which some look forward to, that we shall have eaten all our wheat, for I learn that there is a total destruction of Indian corn.

I must refer you to the newspapers for European politics. Nothing will preserve peace but the dread of the "Great Powers," lest their subjects should catch the French and Belgic disease (for such they deem it). If they touch Belgium, France will strike. This country is in a deplorable condition of splendid misery. A great discovery has been made on the Continent, far surpassing any of Archimedes or Newton. The people have discovered the secret of their strength; and the military have found out that *they* are the people. The teeth and nails of despotism are from that day drawn and pared.

Commend me earnestly to all my old friends and constituents. I shall be among them (dead or alive) next Summer. I have provided for a leaden coffin, feeling as I do an inexpressible desire to lie by the side of my dear mother and honored father at old Matoax.

Remember me to the old servants—particularly Syphax, Louisa, Sam and Phil, and be assured, my dear sir, that I set the highest value on the good opinion with which you have honored me, and I fully reciprocate it.

Most sincerely and faithfully,

J. R. *of Roanoke.*

John, my servant, is quite well; he has not been otherwise since we left the U. S.; and is a perfect treasure to me. He desires his remembrance to Syphax, &c., &c.

To
  Thos. A. Morton, Esq.

Pray let Mr. Leigh know of the receipt and date of this letter.

The following letter was written about eighteen months before his death. He speaks of "thankless heirs," and complains of having been deserted in his old age. We have, moreover, a picture of a man on the brink of the grave, whose thoughts were eager for the acquisition of wealth, and he seems to have intended it as a picture of himself. The letter is short, but it "unmasks man's heart," and enables the reader to "view the hell that's there."

ROANOKE, Dec. 6, 1831.

MY DEAR FRIEND:

This is no common-place address, for without profession or pretension such you have quietly and modestly proved yourself to be, while, like Darius, I have been

"Deserted in my utmost need,
By those my former bounty fed."

All this is only acting according to your character, and you can hardly help it now, second nature being superadded to the first. In the whole course of my unprofitable life I never received a letter *from a man* that affected me so deeply as yours of the 3d.

If I can I will be with you on the 14th (the day before the sale.) I will bring with me the original blotter of the sale, which Creed Taylor can verify, if he be not *civiliter mortuus*, as I greatly fear he is. There is no body else left, unless it be our old friend Bedford. * * *

But my dear friend, what are, or what ought to be, the cares of a man about property that believes himself to be dying? and almost, but not "altogether," hopes it. I am now as much worse than when you saw me on my way to Buckingham November court, as then I was worse than when I left London.

I wish to sell the lots next the warehouse at cost, and interest if to be had, or exchange them for others, adjoining the lots I got from your father and of Wathell, or those on the branch; or I could sell all, or improve for the benefit of thankless heirs.

"He turns with anxious care and crippled hands
His bonds of debt and mortgages of lands."

A long credit to me is the same as a short one; I shan't outlive a bank discount.

Caught like Bonaparte by an Arctic winter, setting in on November (Prince Edward) court, but not like him in latitude 50-55, I am in 37° 30 north, a little south of Algiers. I am tied here until the March and April winds and MAY frosts are over, if I live so long.

Most truly yours,

J. R., *of Roanoke.*

To
Thos. A. Morton, Esq.

The last letter which we shall place before the reader is one written for Mr. Elisha E. Hundley, formerly of Charlotte county, Virginia, but now a citizen of Chicago—a letter of introduction to John Rowan, Esquire, of Kentucky, one of the most distinguished men of his day. It is as follows:

ROANOKE, August 15, 1832.
MY DEAR SIR:

This will be presented to you by my neighbor, Elisha E. Hundley, whose affairs take him to what, in old times, we used to call the *Bear Grass Country.*

The estate of his relative, which Mr. Hundley goes out to settle up, lies within six miles of Louisville, and he may stand in need of advice. As there is no man in Kentucky, or out of it, more capable of aiding him in this behalf than yourself, I have given him this letter; but not so much on that account, as to recommend him to your good offices as a man every way worthy of them. Mr. Hundley is a plain, industrious, quiet man, who minds his own affairs and does not meddle with other people's business. He is also a pious member of the Wesleyan Methodist Church. I have purchased his land next to my own, and thereby deprived myself of an excellent neighbour—but he was resolved to sell.

My old acquaintances, the Maupins, whom we called Maupanes, Richard especially, will oblige me by any attentions they may show Mr. H.

I am in the most wretched health that can be conceived or endured.

With the highest respect, D'r Sir, your faithful serv't,

J. R. *of Roanoke.*

To
John Rowan, Esquire,
Louisville.

Mr. Hundley in his letter enclosing Mr. Randolph's to us, and kindly granting us the use of it, writes that it was presented to him "without being asked for," and adds, "I never leave home on a trip of business without it, as it has ever proved a never-failing passport to me where I was not known." It was written, as the reader will observe, only ten months before his death; but it shows no signs of mental decay, and is as much like its author as anything that ever came from him. No other person, in the short space of a single page of manuscript, and that a letter of introduction, would have presented such a variety of subjects, nor should we expect to find anywhere else such a remark as he makes about the Maupins. It is a little singular, that while he signs himself "of Roanoke," he writes—John Rowan, Esquire—the *Esquire* in full. The distinguished gentleman to whom this letter was addressed, it would seem, should have had the prefix "Hon." to his name since he had occupied the high position of senator in Congress from 1825 to 1831.

It appears that when he was at college Mr. Randolph signed his name John Randolph; a few years afterwards it was John Randolph, of Roanoke. In the sharpest correspondence we ever read between Mr. Randolph and his cousin Nancy, who married Gouverneur Morris, that brilliant lady severely rasps her distinguished relative for taking upon himself the title of John Randolph, of Roanoke.

But the letter served more than its purpose; never having been delivered to the gentleman to whom it was addressed, it was used on sundry occasions by Mr. Hundley in his extensive travels in this country and in Europe.. Indeed, he prized it so highly, that he had a hundred lithographic copies taken of it, to hand down to his children and grandchildren, as a precious memorial of his distinguished friend and neighbor.

We have thus exhausted our fund of letters. Our collection, though not large, presents a pleasing variety, and every page of this short chapter is a valuable index to the character of our distinguished subject. The reader, who is curious to peruse other letters of Mr. Randolph, will find a great number in Garland's life of him. Our object was not to repeat what has been already published, but to furnish fresh food, to satisfy the appetite of the public, who, it has seemed to us, have devoured with more than ordinary interest everything concerning John Randolph, of Roanoke.

CHAPTER XVIII.

JOHN RANDOLPH AS AN ORATOR.

WHATEVER doubt may exist as to whether Mr. Randolph was a great man, a consistent statesman, a profound thinker, a logical debater, there can be none as to his being a great *orator*.

In criticising oratory, we must be careful not to confound the orator with the mere logical reasoner or debater. There is a wide difference between them. The object of the two classes of speakers is different, the effect is different, and the criterion, by which their respective merits are estimated, is different.

The logician may be able to accomplish more in the end, particularly in this country, where so many facilities are afforded for publishing speeches; and he certainly furnishes an agreeable exercise for the mental faculties; but the orator *proper* exhibits the highest order of talent, and dancing to the most fascinating music, is not more delightful than the stimulus of hearing him speak.

The object of the mere debater, at least in the halls of Congress, is the remote and permanent effect. There, nine-tenths of the speakers address themselves mainly to the reporters. They do not care so much for the *immediate* effect upon their hearers, as the *lasting* impression upon their constituents particularly, and the public generally.

The facility afforded by the press for having speeches reported and disseminated all over the nation, within a few hours after delivery, has a great tendency to decrease the cultivation of real oratorical talents. But occasionally there appears a sudden and bright light, who stirs every feeling of the human breast, who may, indeed, be reported, and with considerable effect, but whose object is *immediate* conviction and persuasion, and whose glory is to electrify his audience.

Such was John Randolph.

We doubt whether there ever lived a more eloquent man than Mr. Randolph.

Some are eloquent in the pulpit or at the bar, but dull and uninteresting around the social circle. Others are gifted with great colloquial powers, but are unable to deliver a public address. But Mr. Randolph was eloquent, both in his speeches and in his conversations. Thousands, who never had the good fortune to hear him address a public assembly, have felt his power of fascination in private, when he chose to exert it, with wonder and admiration.

But, in our humble opinion, we should be wide of the mark, if, being called upon for the evidences of his great oratorical powers, we should point to his reported speeches.

His speech, in answer to Mr. Everett, of Massachusetts, is all that Mr. Garland claims for it. It is a specimen of his "large acquaintance with history, profound knowledge of human character, his copiousness of illustration, and the rapidity, beauty, strength and purity of his style."

But however much we admire the beauty of the composition, or the profundity of the views expressed, there is nothing in that speech which entitles its author to be styled a great orator. We cannot tell from the length of David's sling, or the weight of Francisco's sword, how they wielded these instruments of death. We are convinced that Randolph and Clay were orators, but not from *reading* their speeches. We might admit they were great masters of composition, logical reasoners—wise men; but we should not be justified in pronouncing them great orators from *reading* their speeches.

Mr. Randolph was an orator *proper*. He possessed the faculty of producing an instantaneous and powerful effect upon his auditors; and his speeches lose half their charm when they appear in print. Sheridan was well aware of this pecularity of the orator when he refused to permit his great speech, in the case of Warren Hastings, to be reported.

If called upon to select the passage which we most admire of all that we have seen from the great Virginia orator, we should point to a sentence in his speech made at Charlotte Court-house, at the time he excused himself, on the ground of ill health, for declining a reëlection to Congress. The reader will remember we gave it among the recollections of the Honorable James W. Bouldin; but, for the better illustration of our subject, we repeat it. He said:

I am going across the sea, to patch up and preserve a shattered frame—a frame worn out in your service, and to lengthen out, yet a little longer, hitherto certainly, not a very happy existence, for, excepting the one upbraided by a guilty conscience, no life can be more unhappy than that, the days of which are spent in pain and sickness, and the nights in travail and sorrow.

This passage *written* reads very well, but of its force and beauty, *as pronounced by Mr. Randolph*, we have no adequate conception. We are told that while he was speaking, every bosom swelled with sympathy for the fate of the unhappy exile, who was going to a foreign land to "eke out the last remains of his toilsome life."

But we repeat the words used on that occasion, and admire them with scarcely a sigh. The harp is before us, with all its strings in tune, but in vain we attempt as he played to play.

Still, after all, this sentence may have been spoken by a tongue *by no means eloquent.*

In the trial of a case of murder, in which Patrick Henry defended the prisoner at the bar, he made use of the following language:

> You have been told, gentlemen, that the prisoner was bound by every obligation to avoid the supposed necessity of firing, by leaping behind a house near by which he stood at that moment. Had he been attacked with a club, or with stones, the argument would have been unanswerable, and I should find myself compelled to give up the defence in despair. But surely, I need not tell you, gentlemen, how wide is the difference between sticks or stones and double triggered loaded rifles cocked at your breast.

These were the instruments employed by the speaker to convey to the jury the terrible image which was in his own mind. But there appears nothing in his words which enables us to rank him one of the greatest orators the world has produced. And yet, we are informed, that when he uttered this sentence, it produced "*paroxysms of emotion in every breast.*"

What is there in the expression, "If we are wrong, let us all go wrong together?" Yet such was the effect when spoken by Henry with the appropriate action, that the whole auditory moved unconsciously with the speaker.

If we were to take our seat by the side of some beautiful woman and listen to a piece of music which charmed our souls, and afterwards were to show the notes to a friend, what a faint idea he could form of the treat we had really enjoyed. So, if we had the good fortune of hearing a great orator speak, and were to adduce, as proof of it, an accurate report of the words which he used, how very far short we should fall of conveying an adequate conception of the spell that bound us?

If we wanted to convey a just idea of the tumultuous rage of a great battle we had witnessed, we should not, when it was all over—the dead removed, and silence restored to the scene, point to the fell instruments which were used, the swords of the veteran warriors, the quality of the ammunition which was belched from the mouths of the cannon; nor can they be taken as the proofs of a successful battle. The genius of the warrior consists in the *use* he makes of his instruments of death, and the manner in which they are handled; and the criterion of his merit is the *actual effect*.

The speech of Mr. Randolph, so highly spoken of by Mr. Garland, is not a complete evidence of his oratorical powers. There we read the strategic plans of the author; are enabled to conceive of his wonderful facility in gathering materials for crushing the feelings of his adversaries; behold the dreadful weapons he employed; but the *action* is wanting. We cannot witness the running through with the long bony finger, the rage of his eyes, which flashed from side to side, nor the awful contractions of the muscles of his face. We cannot tell how he bore himself upon the field of battle, when the cry was, "*delenda est Carthago*," nor how the victims of his displeasure writhed and agonized with pain.

A book of military tactics affords about as much evidence of the genius of the *warrior* as the speeches of Mr. Randolph afford of his genius as an *orator*.

The evidence, we repeat, of the oratorical powers of any man is not to be found in his reported speeches. The orations of Demosthenes and Cicero are perhaps the most perfect models of composition of their kind which the world ever saw, yet from them we can gather naught to convince us that they were orators of the first magnitude. If the speeches of Patrick Henry were ten times more logical than they really are; if those of Mr. Randolph were really more brilliant, the language more chaste and harmonious, still, from the perusal of them, we could form but a very imperfect estimate of the oratorical powers of these wonderful men.

We said the object of oratory is to sway the crowd; to produce an *immediate* effect. Orators are fully aware of the advantages they possess over the historian or novelist. As we read the pages of the one, we pause to weigh the testimony; to consider the truth and accuracy of the statements, and the representations of the other must still be held up to nature, to determine whether they be drawn to life. But, when a great orator is speaking we are filled with electricity; it passes from him to us, and from us to him; we catch the passions which burn and flash within his animated breast; are hurried along from point to point, and have no time for sifting arguments; we are transported with the scenes he describes; our imagination is filled with glowing pictures; we are charmed, fascinated, and often our reason is led captive by a *single expression*.

In illustration of the last idea, we will mention the effect which the Rev. Dr. Speece says a single expression had upon him. He was at the trial, in one of our district courts, of a man charged with murder. After briefly stating the case, he remarks:

A great mass of testimony was delivered. This was commented upon with considerable ability by the lawyer for the commonwealth, and by another lawyer engaged by the friends of the deceased for the prosecution. The prisoner was also defended in elaborate speeches by two respectable advocates. These proceedings brought the day to a close. The general whisper through a crowded house was, that the man was guilty, and could not be saved.

About dark candles were brought in, and *Henry* rose. His manner was exactly that which the British Spy describes with so much felicity, plain, simple, and entirely unassuming. "Gentlemen of the jury," said he, "I dare say that we are all very fatigued with this tedious trial. The prisoner at the bar has been well defended already, but it is my duty to offer you some further observations in favor of this unfortunate man. I shall aim at brevity. But should I take up more of your time than you expect, I hope you will hear me with patience when you consider that *blood is concerned.*

I cannot admit the possibility that any who never heard Henry speak should be made fully to conceive the force of impression which he gave to these few words, "blood is concerned." I had been on my feet through the day, pushed about in the crowd, and was excessively weary. I was strongly of the opinion, too, notwithstanding all the previous defensive pleadings, that the prisoner was guilty of murder, and I felt anxious to know how the matter would terminate, yet when Henry had uttered these words my feelings underwent an instantaneous change.

There is something almost superhuman in the gift which moves a crowd to tears by the utterance of a simple sentence, as Flechier did in his funeral oration on Turenne, when he said: "Here I am almost forced to interrupt my discourse. I am troubled, Messieurs! *Turenne dies!*" and when his audience, which had been held breathless, at that passage, burst forth into tears and cries.

One reason why no description can convey to another the impression produced by eloquence, is because of the impossibility of reproducing the circumstances which gave effect to the original utterance. Of this there is a striking illustration in the life of Whitfield.

Once, when he had an appointment to preach in London, before the hour came, the brightness of the morning was eclipsed by ominous and lurid clouds. His text was, "Strive to enter in at the strait gate."

"See," said he, pointing to a shadow that was flitting across the floor—"see that emblem of human life." "See there," as a flash of lightning lit up the deepening gloom of the house. "It is a glance from the angry eye of Jehovah!"

Raising his finger in a listening attitude, as the thunder, gradually growing louder, burst in one tremendous crash over the building, he continued the instant it ceased: "It was the voice of God proclaiming his wrath."

Then, as the sound died away, he knelt in the pulpit, and covered his face with his hands in silent adoration.

The audience that day was under his spell, and he swayed them at pleasure. This induced Dr. Campbell, in his sketch of Whitfield, to say of that discourse, that it was easy to print it, but the thunder and lightning could not be struck off by the press.

Neither the surrounding circumstances, nor the magnetic currents which pass from the speaker to his hearers, can ever be reproduced by the narrator, and therefore the written and the reported speeches of an orator give little idea of his power.

The intoxicating effect of eloquence is, indeed, delightful. The excitement of reading a good speech is agreeable, that of reading a good novel still more so, but it is nothing compared to the stimulant of hearing a great orator *speak*. The effect of a sudden flash from the brain of genius is a striking illustration of the direct influence of the mind over the physical system. As he becomes more and more excited, the speaker himself is almost transfigured, his eyes kindle and brighten, and his cheeks grow rosy, and the wrinkles on his withered face disappear, and the hollow and meagre features of old age become beautiful objects to behold.

Such, we have seen, was the appearance of John Randolph, on one occasion, as he walked across the floor and saw the people gather round the stand. But if the speaker is transfigured, the auditors are intoxicated with intense excitement; every heart beats rapidly, and every bosom swells with emotion.

Now, to be able to stir these absorbing passions of the mind, to find one in a calm, cool state, unexcited by any strong feeling, and in a few moments to cause him to blaze all over, requires the most extraordinary endowments which the Creator bestows upon the creature. The mere dialectician cannot begin to excite those thoughts, which exert such intense influence over an audience. Like a caterpillar, he crawls along, laying down his premises, step by step, perfectly satisfied that his auditors are following him through his laborious journey, while the orator, with a few rapid strides, gains in an instant an object, which the other never can attain.

The instantaneous change which the feelings of his auditors underwent when Henry uttered the words, "blood is concerned;" the paroxysms of emotion produced on the other occasion, when he spoke of "double-triggered loaded rifles cocked at your breast," shows the powerful and mysterious effect of a single thought. But to be able to conceive, and clothe, and speak that single thought, as Henry spoke, is, perhaps, to be endowed with all the finest qualities of the mind, united with great physical advantages, and adorned by all the embellishments of art. A look or a tone may at first seem accomplishments of easy attainment, but when they produce these extraordinary impressions upon others, they are themselves the result of the highest mental and physical development. All the noblest qualities of the entire structure of man—body, mind and soul—may be required to produce them. It is deep feeling which makes the sound that melts tears, and to give the expression to the eye which kindles fire within the human breast, may require the habitual indulgence for years in the most ennobling thoughts. An ignorant, uncultivated man, with none of the rare natural gifts of his Creator, cannot look like Patrick Henry when his arms seemed to cover the whole house; nor like John Randolph when he was describing Napoleon Bonaparte's strides to universal dominion.

The following incident shows the susceptibility of Mr. Randolph to oratorical excellence, at the same time it affords a striking proof of the oratorical powers of the immortal Henry.

We quote from the manuscripts of the Honorable James W. Bouldin:

Mr. Randolph, in speaking of Patrick Henry, said " he was profoundly wise," and that " in *eloquence* his deceit was deeper than the bottom of the sea."

He then told me "that when a lad he witnessed the trial of the case of the British debts, in which Henry appeared against the payment of the debts. When the case was about to come on he (Randolph) got near the judges by the favor of some one, and retained his position during the trial for that day. A dispute arose in a low tone between the judges (Iredell and Chase, I think) as to whether Henry was a great man and an orator. Chase said he was; Iredell that he was not. The dispute became so warm that they determined to decide the question immediately. So when John Marshall, afterwards Chief Justice of the United States, had finished speaking, they called on Henry next, though they knew that he was to speak last on that side."

Mr. Henry was sitting with his head resting on the bar, wrapped up, and appeared to be old and infirm, and with unaffected surprise raised his head and said: "They had arranged for others to speak before him, that he was not prepared to go on." The court insisted, but Henry urged his age and debility as a reason for not taking the laboring oar. The court insisted still, when at last Henry yielded.

After some short time he commenced to raise himself up to an erect position in order to speak. Mr. Randolph said he "impressed him with

16

the feeling that the court were the most cruel creatures; but he would reflect that this was all put on."

Henry complained before he had gotten fairly erect, that "an old man, trembling on the brink of the grave, had been made to take the laboring oar in that great cause in preference to young men in the prime of life, and much more able than he in his best days—he who had been in his best days but feeble."

Mr. Randolph said that he knew this was all deceit, but still his feelings of sympathy would return, and he would think the court guilty of the most wanton cruelty.

Mr. Randolph then gave an outline of his progress, and compared him to the practicing of a four-mile horse—sometimes displaying his full powers for a few leaps, and then taking up. At last he got up to full speed, and took a rapid view of what England had done when she had been unfortunate in arms, and of the condition of the people during the war, and what would have been their fate had England been successful, and having arrived at the highest point of elevation, he made one of his solemn pauses, and raised up his hands. Mr. Randolph said they seemed to cover the whole house. While the color would come and go in the face of Judge Chase, Iredell sat with his mouth wide open, and at this pause exclaimed: "*By G—! he is an orator.*"

There was a general burst of applause through the house, which produced confusion. After a little time Henry looked out at the window where there were some horses on exhibition prancing about and neighing. He remarked: "It was only some horses out that had produced a little confusion," and went on apparently unconscious of what had occasioned the interruption.

Here the speaker had not uttered a dozen sentences before he displayed the oratorical faculty, producing a powerful illusion upon the imagination of Mr. Randolph, and we presume of the auditors generally. But the words used by the speaker on that occasion might well have been employed by one who had no pretentions to oratory.

What was it which impressed Mr. Randolph with the feeling, in spite of his judgment, that the judges were the most cruel creatures for insisting on Henry's speaking first, and that, too, when he knew that he was far more able to take the laboring oar, feeble as he represented himself to be, than any of the learned counsel who were arranged to precede him? It was something which cannot be transmitted to paper; it was precisely that which made him preëminently an orator.

Mr. Randolph was a great actor. The reader, we dare say, well remembers a passage in the recollections of Mr. James M. Whittle, which for the better illustration of our subject, we repeat. He says:

His words were only a part of the performance; the uttering of but few of these showed that he was an *actor*. They were few. So were his gestures. But his gestures were as expressive as his words. I had studied some of the orations of Cicero, and had read of Roscius; but I could not understand the power of the latter over his spectators until that day. Had Mr. Randolph lived when pantomime was in vogue, it is not unlikely that he could have communicated his thoughts and feelings effectually, though he spake never a word. As he proceeded, the impression was, there is Cicero and Roscius combined—two men in one—Cicero within, Roscius without. The auditors, of course, yielded themselves prompt and willing captives. This combination required deliberation for its display; otherwise, it cannot be conceived how so much time was consumed in uttering so few words, without any apparent impatience of his hearers, or that throbbing twitter which is felt when expectation is excited and held too long in suspense.

After reading the above, we were not surprised at the following, which the reader found in the sketch of Mr. Randolph by Dr. W. S. Plumer. He says:

In the Virginia Convention of 1829 was a preacher (Alexander Campbell, we suppose), who had made some noise in the world. I was present when he rose to make his address—intended to be powerful. But Mr. Randolph, who was a great *actor*, drew many eyes to himself. At first he leaned forward, gazed as if in wonder and in awe. For two or three moments he looked and acted as if he expected something great. By degrees he seemed to lose interest in the speaker, and finally sank back into his seat with a strong expression of contempt on his countenance. He had said not a word nor violated any parliamentary law. The acting was perfect. It had its effect. The speaker could not rally the courage of his party.

Nor did he practice his art in public only; he carried it into every-day life. In the dramatic scene at the granary described by Mr. Henry Carrington, Mr. Randolph's *acting* is pronounced "inimitable." His extraordinary conduct at the time that the Hon. Thomas S. Flournoy, when a boy, with his father visited Mr. Randolph, was, in our opinion, *acting*. For the whole programme—his pretending that he was dying, his warming up with his subject and surprising his guests with a speech, his request to have his name withdrawn as a candidate for the Convention, bidding them adieu as if he never expected to see them again, and afterwards mounting his horse and overtaking them on the road, and going to Halifax court next day and making a public speech—all flashed across his mind the moment that his servant announced that Mr. John James Flournoy and his son were at the door.

The actor uses arts which are totally inadmissible in the debater. The latter expects to be reported, and hopes his speech will be carefully perused by those who have time to weigh every argument. Hence he is exceedingly particular about his process of reasoning, the accuracy of his statements, and the style of composition. He labors to give it exquisite finish and to enhance its value by all the arts of the logician. But the orator is not so mindful of these things. If he carries the crowd with him, he is satisfied. The demonstrations of the multitude do not make Poe a poet or Prescott a historian; but they do make Henry and Randolph *orators*.

It matters not whether the statements of the orator proper are true or false; whether he covers the whole ground, or jumps to conclusions, or touches the subject directly at all. He may not be logical, may not be consistent; yet, if he sways the multitude, he is an orator.

Therefore, he who should undertake to assign Mr. Randolph his proper rank as an orator must not sit down to the task with a volume of his speeches, but with a record of the instantaneous effects of those speeches.

Of the actual effects produced by the speeches of Mr. Randolph we have the most ample and satisfactory proof. There are still many living witnesses. True, it has been a long time since the spell was broken; but they can testify as clearly as if it were but yesterday they felt his mental power.

The reader has not forgotten the interesting reminiscences of an address delivered at Charlotte Court-house soon after the adjournment of the Virginia Convention of 1829. In this address Mr. Randolph was giving an account of his stewardship and the proceedings of said convention. It is important that we should repeat a few words uttered by the speaker on that occasion. He said:

"I appear here to take my leave of you for the last time. What shall I say? Twenty-eight years ago you took me by the hand, when a beardless boy, and handed me to Congress. I have served you in a public capacity ever since. That I have committed errors I readily believe, being a descendant of Adam, and full of bruises and putrifying sores from the crown of my head to the soles of my feet. People of Charlotte, which of you is without sin?"

A voice in the crowd exclaimed, "Gracious God, what preaching!"

Speaking of the trust committed to him by his constituents, the duties of which he had so long discharged, he made use of the following expression:

"Take it back, take it back," at the same time moving his hand forward towards the multitude.

Mr. H. says he instinctively shrank back, feeling as if the speaker was about to roll a tremendous stone upon him. Just as the orator concluded, and while still under the intoxicating effects of his eloquence, a gentleman standing near turned to him and exclaimed; "He is almost a god."

In the recollections of Dr. C. H. Jordan, the reader comes across this remarkable passage:

"Here he drew a striking and vivid picture of the ship of state, sailing amongst the breakers, and with extended arms and eyes raised to heaven, he threw his body forward, as if to catch her, crying as he did so, in a half-imploring, half-confident tone, 'God save the old ship.'

"It was the most solemn, the most impressive gesture I ever saw from any human being; and so powerful was the impression made that the whole multitude, many with extended arms, seemed to move involuntarily forward, as if to save the 'old ship.'"

It has been said that Mr. Randolph's greatest efforts in speaking were made on the hustings, during his canvass with Mr. Eppes, in which he was beaten. Mr. Bouldin heard many of them. The greatest speech he ever made, in his opinion, was the one at Prince Edward Court-house, in the Fall preceding the election.

His effort at Charlotte Court-house is characterized as being of the "satirical order." Severe repartees and sayings creating great mirth at the expense of others, are said to have "overshadowed in a measure the able and eloquent view he took of the politics of the day;" but the address delivered at Prince Edward Court-house was "sublime."

"He spoke," says Mr. Bouldin, "for an hour, perhaps, and, when he concluded, I found myself musing and walking without any aim or object, and, looking around, found the crowd gradually dispersing in the same mood. The Rev. Moses Hoge was sitting in a chair opposite him, and remained till I observed him, still with his mouth open and looking steadily in the same direction. Said he, to Parson Lyle, who was standing by him, 'I never heard the like before, and I never expect to hear the like again.'"

Mr. Bouldin, who had heard all the distinguished orators of that day, states that he never heard the like before or since, nor did he ever expect to hear the like again.

Mr. Sawyer, his first biographer, speaks of Mr. Randolph's sallies of wit, his biting sarcasm, his happy retorts and home-thrusts, his satiric turn or his playful humor, which rendered him a more agreeable and popular speaker than others who were more severe and elaborate.

"If ridicule," says he, "be the test of truth, he had the most effectual way of drawing her into the light of all the orators of his day. With this powerful lever," he continues, "he could shake, if not move from its foundations, any administration. That it contributed in no small degree to subvert that of the second Adams no man can doubt, who witnessed his repeated and dexterous attacks and observed the effects of his peculiar mode of warfare."

This is high and just praise of his powers of ridicule; but he does not mention his wonderful powers of pathos. Mr. Baldwin, too, we think, underrates his capacity in this respect.

It is not strange that those who only heard him in Congress, should labor under the impression that Mr. Randolph had no pathos; but the reader will remember that Mr. John Robinson, one of his old constituents, who had heard all the distinguished orators of the day, from Patrick Henry down, gave it as his opinion that "Mr. Randolph was the most *pathetic* speaker he ever heard open his lips."

In the halls of Congress, we presume, he seldom, or never, indulged in that strain; but, we are informed that when he declined to run for Congress, expecting to visit Europe, he delivered several addresses of a character wholly different from any made by him on any other occasion. While riding around his district, taking leave of his constituents, he was placed under very different circumstances from those which called forth his mighty powers of ridicule and satire in the halls of Congress. He was in a situation to counterfeit tenderness and a generous forgiveness, if they did not spring from the heart, and to make appeals to the sympathies of his constituents for having to decline their service, after their long and continued confidence in him, on the ground of ill health.

These addresses, we are informed, were filled with grave and solemn advices and the most pathetic appeals, without the least allusion to party or feud, and did more to strengthen his popularity, which, during the war, had been a little shaken, than anything else he ever did. They soothed, softened and set aside much of the bitterness which had been engendered during those bitter party conflicts. Mr. Bouldin says: "I certainly saw tears roll down the cheeks of those who hated him then, and would curse his memory now if he were named in their presence."

The deep and dark impression which he was capable of making is only less wonderful than the power of genius to wipe it out.

The language of the witness is strong, but all of Mr. Randolph's acquaintances knew how he could make a man hate him. His talents in this respect were wonderful. Let the reader turn to his speech on Retrenchment and Reform, note D, in the appendix, and there see his attack upon Mr. C., and tell us, if ever a man had, to such a degree, the faculty of raking up, condensing, and bringing into a speech materials to make a man hate him. And let the reader say if an individual thus treated—and there were many such— was much to blame for cursing his memory even after he was buried.

Nor was it a sudden ebullition of passion with Mr. Randolph, soon over and forgotten. All his life he pursued his opponents, whose presence was hateful to him and all they possessed.

Now, when he had retired from the victorious field, where he had stirred up the most violent feelings, and had left so many foes chafing under the wounds which he had inflicted, to have chosen "a mournful muse, soft pity to infuse," and to have persuaded his old constituents that "the heat and collision produced by the necessary differences of opinion among men, during a period of fourteen years, had passed off with him—that he was not conscious of having an enemy among them; that, certainly, he did not feel enmity to any himself;" and to have expressed himself on this occasion in such a manner as to have hushed in a moment the jarring strings, and by a few words of tenderness to have blotted out a hundred bitter recollections, and melted hearts which had been steeled against him, changed the current of long years of adverse feeling, and forced unwilling tears down the cheeks of *hatred* itself, was the highest effort of genius; and those tears will be received by the sentinels, who guard the temple of Fame, as an offering, which entitles the author to take his position as an orator by the side of the immortal Henry.

Mr. Sawyer, who was an associate with Mr. Randolph for

sixteen years in Congress, and who, as we have before stated, wrote a biographical sketch of him, expresses the opinion that he "wanted the profound views of a great statesman; wanted consistency of political conduct." He says: "His fame is founded entirely upon his talents as an orator." But he does not speak in unqualified praise even of his oratory. He characterizes it as "more splendid than solid. He was listened to," he says, "with undivided attention;" but, according to his view, the mind was "fascinated by the ease, the grace, the fluency, and the pleasing emphatic delivery of the speaker, not chained and carried captive in the triumphant march of a gigantic intellect, by the depth of research and the force of reasoning."

We do not now propose to discuss Mr. Randolph's claims to statesmanship, but we feel compelled to differ with the biographer with regard to his oratory.

After enumerating the bad qualities of his heart, and expressing the opinion that there were no redeeming virtues, except "some of a negative" kind, we could but be disappointed when he spoke disparagingly of the noble qualities of his head.

We were highly gratified at the manner in which Mr. Baldwin speaks of our distinguished countryman, when he says he was "not only a consistent statesman, but a great man." But we are confident that even Mr. Baldwin fails to do the great Virginia orator justice when he expresses the opinion that "Henry Clay was the more eloquent of the two."

The reason which he assigns for this opinion is this: He claims that Mr. Clay "spoke with more enthusiasm, with more loftiness, with better adaptation to the hearts of men; and this he says is the most effective office of eloquence. It takes more than brains to make a man. To convince the judgment, you must often do more than show it a good reason. You must enlist the heart, for it sways the brains."

From all the information which we can gather, we are forced to differ from the learned critic. Mr. Randolph was a most enthusiastic man. His deep feeling and highly excitable imagination was a marked feature of his intellectual constitution. It is difficult to conceive how an individual of his temperament could fail to speak with the greatest enthusiasm. But, to speak with enthusiasm, we submit, it is not necessary to indulge in "sudden bursts of passionate emotion," in an "unpruned luxuriance of gesticulation."

An orator may be enthusiastic, and still pronounce his words "trippingly on the tongue, not sawing the air too much with his hands, but using all gently; for in the very torrent, tempest, and, as we may say, whirlwind of the passions, you must acquire and beget a temperance that may give it smoothness."

This is precisely the character which has been given to Mr. Randolph's oratory. He spoke so clearly, and with such perfect pronunciation, that as far as his voice could be heard his words could be distinguished. "An accurate ear could discern, as he went along, commas, semi-colons, colons, periods, exclamation and interrogation points, all in their proper places." One of the gentlemen who has furnished us with interesting *data* upon this subject, states that "his manner was deliberate, beyond that of any speaker he had ever heard, not only every word and syllable, but it seemed that every letter of every syllable in every word was distinctly sounded."

And still we contend he spoke with enthusiasm, with a warm imagination and feelings wrought up to the highest pitch of excitement. The last speech he ever made to the people of Charlotte was the effect of the most enthusiastic and unheard of devotion to an idea. Nothing else could have roused his palsied faculties and set his worn-out frame in motion.

Mr. Clay had the art of making men in love with his views and with himself. Mr. Randolph may not have had the same talent to an equal degree, but that does not affect the question whether he spoke with as much enthusiasm.

As to "loftiness," we should not suppose that the "grave and sublime" address delivered at Prince Edward by Mr. Randolph, in which he took such "an able and eloquent view of the politics of that day," was ever surpassed by Mr. Clay. This was the opinion of some who had heard both, and would be, we imagine, the opinion of a majority.

As to "enlisting the heart, and thereby swaying the brains," after all the evidence we have adduced of the ability of Mr. Randolph to excite the tender sensibilities of his audience, it is hardly necessary to enlarge. We think we have shown him equal to Henry in pathos, and that is sufficient. We must be permitted, however, to observe that it would be difficult to persuade those enemies of Mr. Randolph, who shed tears of sympathy for him, that Mr. Clay, or any other man, could have so drowned their senses, so intoxicated their brains.

It does not alter the case that Mr. Randolph did not choose to speak *often* in that strain. A few instances are sufficient to establish his capacity; as to how often he exerted it, it is immaterial.

"In particular passages," continues the gifted writer, last quoted, "he was brilliant as Curran and Grattan; in all, he was interesting, enchaining attention, gratifying an exquisite taste, imparting instruction, and frequently moulding conviction; but the *permanent* impression left was not so strong."

Now, as we have argued, this "permanent" impression is

not the criterion of eloquence. When we are comparing the eloquence of two great orators, the question is not the *permanent* impression, but the *instantaneous* impression. As in the case of Mr. Henry, one of our witnesses, of whom we have already spoken, we do not inquire whether the speaker advanced arguments which stood the test of his sober reason a month afterwards; but did the orator overpower his reason for the moment, and seize upon his imagination with such force as to make him actually feel that he was rolling a great weight upon him?

In the case of the jury, which Mr. Henry addressed, they acquitted the prisoner at the bar, under the *immediate* effects of his speech. It is useless to inquire how strong was the impression of innocence a few days afterwards. The work of the orator was done. Mr. Bouldin, another of our witnesses, does not inform us how strong was the *permanent* impression made upon him and others by the great speech of Mr. Randolph at Prince Edward Court-house; but it is sufficient that he states, when he concluded, he found himself walking and musing without any aim or object—an evidence that all his senses had been completely absorbed, and that he had been wholly under the mental influence of another. We are not informed whether Mr. Hoge's judgment was so well addressed by arguments that he voted for Mr. Randolph at the polls; but we are told that while listening to his speech he sat with his mouth wide open, and remained in that state for several minutes after the speaker had retired from the stand. The individual, who thought the orator "almost a god" at the moment, may have taken him for a devil the next day; but still the powerful illusion created at the time is proof of eloquence of the highest degree. The feeling of sympathy which came over Mr. Randolph himself, while Henry was speaking, was momentary, and yet it is adduced as a proof that "Henry's deceit in eloquence was deeper than the bottom of the sea."

But is it entirely certain that Mr. Clay surpassed Mr. Randolph in the "permanent impression?" If one of his old constituents were interrogated on this point, he would say, Mr. Randolph's eloquence, at a distance of thirty years, still haunts his mind; and if he chanced to be one of the victims of his eloquence of scorn, when brought to the confessional he would be forced to acknowledge that his wounds were still bleeding, that his memory, in reviewing the dark passages of his life, would forget the bitter words of all inferior men, and dwell with hopeless persistency upon the inflictions of that long, bony finger.

When Mr. Sawyer states that, as an orator, Mr. Randolph was more "splendid than solid," we confess we do not know his precise meaning. *Solidity* is not the criterion of eloquence. If he had said that as a logician he was "more splendid than solid, we should not be at a loss to understand him. We suspect that Mr. Sawyer was criticising Mr. Randolph's printed speeches instead of his oratory. But, even on this hypothesis, in our humble opinion, he is mistaken. His speeches are more "solid" than "splendid." As an orator he was perfect; but the most of the splendor vanished the moment his words were printed. We look upon them as we would the instrument of some celebrated musician who had departed this life. The keys are in place and strings in repair, but the *music* is wanting.

Though we can form very little idea of Mr. Randolph's splendor as an orator, the solid part of the performance remains. We should like to be informed whose speeches were more "solid" than Mr. Randolph's. Mr. Baldwin tells us truly, that "most largely developed of all his faculties, probably, was his quick, clear and deep comprehension." One of our own witnesses states, that he "thought more philosophically and profoundly than any man he ever saw;" another, that "his conceptions were vast and powerful;" and still another, that he took an "able view of the politics. of the day;" and yet another will come forward and testify, that "the speeches of this remarkable man were characterized by all that is conclusive in argument, original in conception, felicitous in illustration, forcible in language, and faultless in delivery."

We have expressed the opinion that a speaker is not obliged to be argumentative in order to be solid. In his public addresses or his private conversations he may be deep and mould conviction too, and still not go through the form of a single argument. Mr. Randolph's speeches are filled with as much good, sound sense as any man's we ever read, and contain as many ideas in a single page. For, while some consume much time in laying down premises and advancing to conclusions step by step, he arrived at his conclusion at once, and condensed a long argument into a few words.

If Mr. Sawyer meant to say that Mr. Randolph was too scattering, that he wanted connection and continuity, we refer him to the fable of the caterpillar and the horseman. The critic speaks as if he had a book of his orations in his hands and was reading them at leisure. The man who reads a speech with a view of estimating oratorical excellence forgets that he cannot be hurried along with the speaker as his auditors were, that he cannot assume the same state of feeling which the orator addressed.

But if he has no better means of estimating the genius of the orator than his printed speeches, the effect produced by the first rapid perusal is the surest test. "It requires repeated perusal and reflection," says Mr. Macaulay, "to decide rightly on any other portion of literature. But with respect to the works of which the merit depends on their instantaneous effect, the most hasty judgment is likely to be the best."

This being the case, we should do the orator an injustice if we go back to correct an argument or exaggerated statement, or to expose sophistry, or to exclude extraneous matter; because fallacies of that description are supposed to have been overlooked by the hearers in the bustle of the mental faculties, which are hurried along from point to point by the new scenes presented in the kaleidoscope-world of the orator.

There is no record of more powerful effects produced upon an audience by any man than those we have mentioned in the case of Mr. Randolph. If, therefore, we be correct in stating that the merit of oratory consists in its immediate effect, if he who sways the multitude at the time be an orator, then we have no hesitation in pronouncing John Randolph as great an orator as ever lived.

CHAPTER XIX.

Death Bed Scene—Visit to His Grave by Capt. Harrison Robertson—
, Closing Reflections.

A FEW months before his death, Mr. Randolph determined again to visit England, the climate of which he thought, above all others, most agreed with his shattered constitution, where, to use his own language, he "hoped to eke out yet, the last remains of his toilsome life." His intention was to go to Philadelphia to be in time for the packet which would sail from the Delaware in the latter part of the month of April. When he arrived in Washington, he proceeded at once to the Senate Chamber and took his seat in rear of Mr. Clay. That gentleman happened at the time to be on his feet, addressing the Senate. "Raise me up," said Mr. Randolph, "I want to hear that voice again." When Mr. Clay had concluded his remarks he turned round to see from what quarter that singular voice proceeded. Seeing Mr. Randolph, and that he was in a dying condition, he left his place and went to speak to him; as he approached, Mr. Randolph said to the gentleman with him, "Raise me up." As Mr. Clay offered his hand, he said, "Mr. Randolph I hope you are better, sir." "No, sir," replied Mr. Randolph, "I am a dying man, and I came here expressly to have this interview with you." They clasped hands and parted never to meet again. He hurried on to Philadelphia, where he was taken very ill.

For the following highly interesting account of the closing scene we are indebted to Mr. Garland:

Dr. Joseph Parish, a Quaker physician, was sent for. As he entered the room, the patient said, "I am acquainted with you, sir, by character. I know you through Giles." He then told the doctor that he had attended several courses on anatomy, and described his symptoms with medical accuracy, declaring he must die if he could not discharge the puriform matter.

"How long have you been sick, Mr. Randolph?"

"Don't ask me that question; I have been sick all my life. I have been affected with my present disease, however, for three years. It was greatly aggravated by my voyage to Russia. That killed me, sir. This Russian expedition has been Pultowa, a Beresina to me."

The doctor now felt his pulse. "You can form no judgment by my pulse; it is so peculiar."

"You have been so long an invalid Mr. Randolph, you must have acquired an accurate knowledge of the general course of practice adapted to your case."

"Certainly, sir; at forty, a fool or a physician you know."

"There are idiosyncracies," said the doctor, "in many constitutions. I wish to ascertain what is peculiar about you."

"I have been an idiosyncrasy all my life. All the preparations of camphor invariably injure me. As to ether, it will blow me up. Not so with opium; I can take opium like a Turk, and have been in the habitual use of it in one shape or another for some time."

Before the doctor retired, Mr. Randolph's conversation became curiously diversified. He introduced the subject of the Quakers; complimented them in his peculiar manner, for neatness and economy, order, comfort—in everything. "Right," said he, "in everything except politics—there always twistical." He then repeated a portion of the Litany of the Episcopal church with apparent fervor. The following morning the doctor was sent for very early. He was called from bed. Mr. Randolph apologized very handsomely for disturbing him. Something was proposed for his relief. He petulantly and positively refused compliance. The doctor paused and addressed a few words to him. He apologized and was as submissive as an infant. One evening a medical consultation was proposed; he promptly objected. "In a multitude of counsel," he said, "there is confusion; it leads to weakness and indecision; the patient may die while the doctors are staring at each other." Whenever Dr. Parish parted from him, especially at night, he would receive the kindest acknowledgments, in the most affectionate tones. "God bless you; he does bless you, and he will bless you."

The night preceding his death, the doctor passed about two hours in his chamber. In a plaintive tone he said, "My poor John, sir, is worn down with fatigue, and has been compelled to go to bed. A most attentive substitute supplies his place, but neither he nor you, sir, are like John; he knows where to place his hand on anything in a large quantity of baggage prepared for a European voyage." The patient was greatly distressed in breathing, in consequence of difficult expectoration. He requested the doctor at his next visit to bring instruments for performing the operation of bronchotomy, for he could not live unless relieved. He then directed a certain newspaper to be brought to him. He put on his spectacles as he sat propped up in bed, turned over the paper several times, and examined it carefully, then placing his finger on a part he had selected, handed it to the doctor with a request that he would read it. It was headed "Cherokee." In the course of reading, the doctor came to the word "omnipotence" and pronounced it with a full sound on the penultimate—omni*p*otence. Mr. Randolph checked him and pronounced the word according to Walker. The doctor attempted to give a reason for his pronunciation. "Pass on," was the quick reply. The word impetus was then pronounced with the *e* long, imp*e*tus. He was instantly corrected. The doctor hesitated on the criticism. "There can be no doubt of it, sir." An immediate acknowledgment of the reader that he stood corrected, appeared to satisfy the critic, and the piece was concluded. The doctor observed that there was a great deal of sublimity in the composition. He directly referred to the Mosaic account of the creation, and repeated, "Let there be light and there was light." There is sublimity.

Next morning (the day on which he died), Dr. Parish received an early and urgent message to visit him. Several persons were in the room, but soon left it, except John, who was much affected at the sight of his dying master. The doctor remarked to him, "I have seen your master very low before and he revived; and perhaps he will again! "John knows better than that, sir." He then looked at the doctor with great intensity, and said in an earnest and distinct manner, "I confirm every disposition in my will, especially that respecting my slaves, whom I have manumitted, and for whom I have made provision."

"I am rejoiced to hear such a declaration from you, sir," replied the doctor, and soon after proposed to leave him for a short time, to attend to another patient. "You must not go" was the reply; "you cannot, you shall not leave me. *John*, take care that the doctor does not leave the room." John soon locked the door, and reported, "Master, I have locked the door and got the key in my pocket, the doctor can't go now."

He seemed excited and said, "if you do go, you need not return." The doctor appealed to him as to the propriety of such an order, inasmuch as he was only desirous of discharging his duty to another patient. His manner instantly changed, and he said, "I retract that expression." Some time afterwards, turning an expressive look, he said again, "I retract that expression."

The doctor now said that he understood the subject of his communication, and presumed the will would explain itself fully. He replied in his peculiar way, "No you don't understand it; I know you don't. Our laws are extremely particular on the subject of slaves. A will may manumit them, but provision for their subsequent support, requires that a declaration be made in the presence of a white witness; and it is requisite that the witness, after hearing the declaration, should continue with the party, and never lose sight of him, until he is gone or dead. You are a good witness for John. You see the propriety and importance of your remaining with me; your patients must make allowance for your situation. John told me this morning, "Master, you are dying."

The doctor spoke with entire candor and replied, that it was a matter of surprise that he had lasted so long. He now made his preparations to die. He directed John to bring him his father's breast button; he then directed him to place it in the bosom of his shirt. It was an old-fashioned large-sized gold stud. John placed it in the bosom hole of his shirt-bosom—but to fix it completely required a hole on the opposite side. "Get a knife," said he, "and cut one." A napkin was called for, and placed by John over his breast. For a short time he lay perfectly quiet, with his eyes closed. He suddenly roused up and exclaimed, "Remorse! Remorse!" It was thrice repeated, the last time at the top of his voice, with great agitation. He cried out, "Let me see the word. Get a dictionary, let me see the word." "There is none in the room, sir." "Write it down then—let me see the word." The doctor picked up one of his cards, " Randolph of Roanoke "—"shall I write it on this card?" "Yes, nothing more proper." The word *remorse* was then written in pencil. He took the card in a hurried manner and fastened his eyes on it with great intensity. " Write it on the back," he exclaimed. It was done so and handed him again. He was extremely agitated. " Remorse! you have no idea what it is; you can form no idea of it, whatever; it has contributed to bring me to my present situation; but I have looked to the Lord Jesus Christ, and I hope I have obtained pardon. Now, let John take your pencil and draw a line under the word," which was accordingly done. " What am I to do with the card?" inquired the doctor. " Put it in your pocket; take care of it; when I am dead, look at it."

The doctor now introduced the subject of calling in some additional witnesses to his declarations, and suggested sending down stairs for Edmund Badger. He replied, " I have already communicated that to him." The doctor then said, " With your concurrence, sir, I will send for two young physicians, who shall remain and never lose sight of you until you are dead; to whom you can make your declarations—my son, Dr. Isaac Parish, and my young friend and late pupil, Dr. Francis West, a brother of Capt. West."

He quickly asked, " Capt West of the packet?" " Yes, sir, the same." " Send for him—he is the man—I'll have him."

Before the door was unlocked he pointed toward a bureau and requested the doctor to take from it a remuneration for his services. To this the doctor promptly replied, that he would feel as though he were acting indelicately to comply. He then waived the subject by saying, " In England it is customary."

The witnesses were now sent for, and soon arrived. The dying man was propped up in the bed with pillows, nearly erect. Being extremely sensitive to cold he had a blanket over his head and shoulders; and he directed John to place his hat on, over the blanket, which aided in keeping it close to his head. With a countenance full of sorrow, John stood close by the side of his dying master. The four witnesses—Edmund Badger, Francis West, Isaac Parish, and Joseph Parish, were placed in a semi-circle in full view. He rallied all the expiring energies of mind and body, to this last effort. " His whole soul," says Dr. Parish, "seemed concentrated in the act. His eyes flashed feeling and intelligence. Pointing toward us, with his long index finger, he addressed us."

" I confirm all the directions in my will, respecting my slaves, and direct them to be enforced, particularly in regard to a provision for their support." And then raising his arm as high as he could, he brought it down with his open hand, on the shoulder of his favorite, John, and added these words, "especially for this man." He then asked each of the witnesses whether they understood him. Dr. Joseph Parish explained to them what Mr. Randolph had said in regard to the laws of Virginia, on the subject of manumission, and then appealed to the dying man to know whether he had stated it correctly. "Yes," said he, and gracefully waving his hand as a token of dismission, he said, "The young gentlemen will remain with me."

The scene was now changed. Having disposed of that subject most deeply impressed on his heart, his keen penetrating eye lost its expression, his powerful mind gave way, and his fading imagination began to wander amid scenes and with friends that he had left behind. In two hours the spirit took its flight, and all that was mortal of John Randolph of Roanoke was hushed in death. At a quarter before twelve o'clock, on the 24th day of June, 1833, aged sixty years, he breathed his last."

For the following interesting sketch we are indebted to Capt. Harrison Robertson, of Danville, Va:

In 1839, he says, being a student at Hampden Sidney College, I visited, in company with several fellow students, the residence of John Randolph, of Roanoke. His will being at that time the subject of litigation, his estate appeared to be in a condition of neglect. The grounds surrounding the dwelling were entirely destitute of ornament. The negro, John, who had been Mr. Randolph's body-servant and constant attendant for many years, received us and showed us the objects of interest connected with the place.

There were two buildings, one a log house with two rooms, the floor raised but a foot or two above the ground, of a style and material the rudest, and such as belonged to the poorest class of white persons in the rural districts of Virginia. The single door opened into the sitting room, which communicated by an inner door with his bed room. The other building was a small framed house which stood about twenty yards off, with large, well-glazed windows, containing two rooms on the ground floor, raised a few feet above the ground, evidently built long after the log house, of better material and more civilized style of finish. John called this his master's "Summer House;" the log house his "Winter House."

Entering the log house we found every article of furniture remaining exactly (John assured us) as it had been left by Mr. Randolph at the time of his departure for Philadelphia on his last journey.

At this distance of time, many particulars which then interested me have escaped my recollection. The furniture, with the exception of a few articles, was very plain. I recollect his fowling pieces, pistols, etc., of exquisite manufacture; also his fair top boots of the best materials and finish. But that which I recollect with most distinctness, in regard to this sitting room, was a small, old fashioned mahogany stand, upon which laid a plain leather portfolio, a candlestick, and a half-consumed candle, and one or two books. John informed us that this stand and what was upon it, remained as it was left by his master when he ceased reading and went to bed, the night before he started for Philadelphia. One of the books was open and laid upon the open pages, the back upwards, as if it had just been put down by the reader. It was a thin duodecimo volume, bound in discolored sheepskin. On examination, I was surprised to find this book was McNish on Drunkenness. I opened the portfolio and found writing paper, some blank and some manuscripts in Mr. Randolph's own hand writing. I recollect particularly a sheet of foolscap which had not been folded, with the caption, "A LIST OF MY PRINCIPAL FRIENDS," followed by a list of names, numbered 1, 2, 3, 4, &c., the numbers (if my memory be correct) running as high as 20. The list covered two or three pages. On the right hand side of the pages, opposite to each name, or to many of the names, were remarks indicating Mr. Randolph's estimate of the character of the persons named, or some special circumstance of his history or friendship. Among the first, if not the first, was the name of Thomas H. Benton. Near the middle or latter part of the list was the name of Robert Carrington, with the remark opposite—Mr. Randolph "admired him for his courage, honor, and manliness," or words to that effect. I learned at the time and afterwards that this Mr. Carrington had emigrated from Virginia to Arkansas, with his family, after having lived many years on a plantation adjoining Mr. Randolph's, and that they had been at dagger's draw for years, and that no reconciliation had ever taken place between them.

In the bed room we found the furniture generally of the same simple description. The garments and personal apparel were in some instances costly and elegant. The room was ill-lighted and must have been badly ventilated from the small size of the windows, unless the cracks in the log walls aided in ventilation. On the wall above the bed, hung a portrait of Mr. Randolph (in oil.) I have forgotten the name of the artist, but the painting was well done. I distinctly recollect the beardless boyish appearance of the face. In the "Summer House" we found a library of perhaps more than a thousand volumes, embracing many of the standard authors of pure "English undefiled," of choice editions and binding; also a number of fine engravings (without frames) and books and prints of art and science. I saw no musical instruments. There were many manuscript letters, notes and cards, invitations to dinners, &c., which had been received by Mr. Randolph—some of them from persons of the highest distinction both in England and America. Doubtless, many of the like kind had disappeared before our visit; for John made no objection, but rather encouraged us, to take away some of the notes, invitations, cards, etc., as souvenirs of our visit.

The grave of Mr. Randolph was near his dwelling house, at the foot of a tall pine tree, the shadows of which together with the unfriendly soil, prevented the growth of grass upon it. It was marked by no monument save a large unshapely stone, placed at the head. We were told by John that his master caused the rock to be hauled from another part of the plantation with considerable labor and difficulty, and commanded that it should be placed at his grave at his death, and that there should be no other monument, and no inscription or epitaph.

The reader is now in possession of all the facts. He has doubtless formed his own opinion. It was our plan for him to do so. Our views are merely given as a connecting link to hold our materials together. The facts, anecdotes, and incidents, which we have recorded, are so pointed and characteristic, that, apart from the office above indicated, our deductions can be of no possible use, except perhaps to save some indolent mind the trouble of thinking.

It has been said that men are neither devils nor angels. To every character there is a bright side and a dark side.

There is a spot of sin upon every face, but always some redeeming feature.

We have recorded many circumstances tending to prove that Mr. Randolph was proud, dictatorial, overbearing, violent, unforgiving, void of pity, full of subtlety, of gall and wormwood; and as some go about hunting wild beasts for sport, he hunted mankind. But, on the other hand, we have introduced some testimony in addition to what has been published by others, to show that he was capable at times of conferring acts of the greatest generosity, and in the most acceptable manner; that his *mind* was not debauched, his sentiments being pure, whatever his frail body might do; that he was bold and fearless; that when he was not excited by passion, or irritated by disease, he was gentle and kind. The tone of his general character was so high, so singularly free from abjectness, servility, or meanness of any description, that nothwithstanding all his faults, we cannot say he was a bad man, in the sense in which that term is ordinarily used. Possessed of no qualities to inspire our love and affection, still he was free from all which excites the feeling of contempt. And he was endowed with all the noblest qualities of the head. He possessed a most extraordinary memory, a memory which seemed never to forget anything; and yet it was not an unnatural development. But such a memory, if other qualities had not been developed in an equal degree, would, in all probability, have induced him to draw altogether upon the resources of others; his opinions upon matters of state, would have been mere collations of authorities; when his views upon a subject were solicited, he would have cited to a book. Such was not the case however. His speeches are filled with apt quotations; but they are not the efforts of a retentive memory alone, but of a great mind drawing its own conclusions, using the learning of others only to illustrate and adorn. It has been said he had the imagination of Byron, the wit of Sheridan, and that his powers of sarcasm were unsurpassed. Indeed we should say that the latter quality was the distinctive feature of his mind. If an important measure were before Congress, and we in search of the ablest debater we could find, we should select perhaps a Webster. But when we were driven off from all our positions of defence, and had to rely upon thrusting as well as parrying, we should undoubtedly prefer a Randolph. Webster might beat him in the argument, but without exaggeration, when he fell back upon his stronghold of sarcasm and ridicule, when the war must be carried into Africa, there was no man in Europe or America that could equal him.

But where so many features are prominent, it is hard to tell which is most so. We have already fully discussed his wonderful powers of elocution.

When we consider Mr. Randolph's genius we are possessed of the same feeling with Mr. Macaulay, who said: He "could almost forgive all the faults of Bacon's life for one singularly graceful and dignified passage." But our enthusiasm for the abilities of a great man should not induce us to neglect the lessons of warning which his life is calculated to teach.

It does not require any considerable stretch of the imagination to conceive the character of the reflections indulged by one of the sons of toil as he stands over the solitary grave of his illustrious countryman. He may well spare himself the pangs of envy. He had rather dwell in obscurity all the days of his life, "his mind upon the furrow, and diligent to give the kine fodder;" he had rather "sit by the anvil and consider the iron work, fighting with the heat of the furnace, the fire wasting his flesh," than to be John Randolph. True, he can never enjoy the applause of the multitude, nor "sit high in the congregation," "nor in the judge's seat;" he has to "trust solely to his hands," and is "wise only in his work;" but he is more than compensated by not having mental troubles, "corroding joy and youth;" not having ascended to "mountain tops," he is not "forced to look down on the hate of those below." He is not devoured by discontent, nor rendered miserable by remorse. He would not exchange one hour's joy of his cottage home, blessed with the comforts which his wife spreads before him, his little ones playing around him, for all the pleasures which Mr. Randolph experienced during a long life of "golden sorrow."

Nor is it difficult to imagine the nature of the thoughts which pass through the mind of the man of genius as he stands by the solitary pine over the grave of John Randolph. He is conscious of possessing himself more than ordinary abilities, but he is reminded that in order to be ensured of happiness here and a glorious immortality, his abilities must be properly directed. Possibly he may be endowed with ardent feelings; these must be controlled, else his life must be one of "splendid misery." Like the illustrious personage, whose life he contemplates, he may be formed with intense sensibility; this, he feels, may prove a blessing or a curse, according to his training. The life of John Randolph, he is convinced, is full of useful warning. He sees the penalty of failing to school the affections, of cherishing the love of the misery of others, of giving way to a violent temper, of midnight draughts. He is confident that to be eminently miserable must be the lot of all such eminent men. But he does not admit that it was genius which rendered its possessor miserable. He is loth to believe that the most coveted gift of heaven is bestowed for any such purpose.

We will not say that Mr. Randolph was not a Christian;

he was evidently not what he should have been; but who can tell what he would have been but for the faith which was given him.

> "What's done we partly may compute,
> But never what's resisted."

We are disposed to make a great many allowances for this truly unfortunate man. He was born with a most ungovernable temper; he suffered all his days from bodily disease, and he had a secret sorrow, as deep as that which "the fabled Hebrew wanderer bore."

For his religious impressions he acknowledges himself indebted to his mother. But for her training, like Byron, he might have defied the powers of heaven as well as earth.

The example of Mr. Randolph affords a lesson of encouragement to every mother, upon whom rests the responsibility of training up a child in the way he should go. No matter how wicked that child may be, no matter how violent his passions, she need not despair. Let her reflect that it was the influence of a gentle mother, which shed a ray of light through the dark recess of Mr. Randolph's remorseful heart, and enabled him, upon his dying bed, to look to the Lord Jesus Christ, and hope he had obtained pardon.

APPENDIX.

APPENDIX.

SPEECH ON RETRENCHMENT AND REFORM.

AS we proposed to publish a volume of *Home Reminiscences*, it could not be expected that we should swell our pages with the numerous speeches made by Mr. Randolph while he was in Congress. We have selected one as a specimen of his style of composition, and as a literary curiosity—the one on Retrenchment and Reform, delivered in February, 1828, in answer to Mr. Everett of Massachusetts. It was carefully revised by its author, dedicated to his constituents, and published in pamphlet form.

The reader will remember that the Presidential election of 1824 resulted in the return of Crawford, Jackson and Adams to the House; no choice having been made by the people. Mr. Adams was elected through the influence of Mr. Clay. Mr. Randolph was the leader of the opposition party, and his speech on Retrenchment and Reform was a blow at the administration.

Mr. RANDOLPH rose and said:

I cannot make the promise which the gentleman who has just taken his seat (Mr. Everett) made at the outset of his address, but I will make a promise of a different nature, and one which I trust it will be in my power to perform—I shall not say with more good faith than the gentleman from Massachusetts, but more to the letter—ay, sir, and more to the spirit too. I shall not, as the gentleman said he would do, act in mere self-defence. I shall carry the war into Africa. *Delenda est Carthago!* I shall not be content with merely parrying; no, sir, if I can, so help me God, I will thrust also, because my right arm is nerved by the cause of the people and of my country. I listened to the gentleman with pleasure—I mean to the general course of his remarks, with a single exception, and to that part of his speech I listened with the utmost loathing and disgust. But disgust is too feeble a term. I heard him with horror introduce the case of the Queen of France*—and in answer to what? To a handbill, a placard, an electioneering firebrand. And in the presence of whom? Of those who never ought to be present in a theatre where men contend for victory and empire. Sir, they have no more business there than they have in a field of battle of another sort. Women, indeed, are wanted in the camp; but women of a very different description. What maiden, nay, what matron, could hear the gentleman without covering her face with her hands, and rushing out of the House? But for some of the remarks of the gentleman from Massachusetts, in allusion to newspaper publications, I should have begun in at least as low a key and as temperate a mood as he did. To that key I will now pitch my voice.

I have been absent from the House for several days. I requested my colleague (Mr. Alexander) to state the cause of that absence, which he did. Yet even this could not be reported correctly. As this may be the last act of public duty which I shall be able to perform, at least during the present session, and as I have given up myself a sacrifice to its performance, I respectfully ask the House to give their attention to what I have now to say. I understand that during my absence I have been replied to by various gentlemen (some of whom I have not the honor to know by person) on different sides of the House in a manner which I do not doubt was perfectly satisfactory, at least to the speakers themselves. I certainly do not wish to disturb their self-complacency—*de minimis non curat*—whether of persons or of things. The gentleman from Ohio (Mr. Vance), with that blunt plainness and candor which I am told belong to him, and which I admire in proportion as they are rare qualities in these time-serving days—I like him the better for his surly honesty—I hope he will take no offence at the term, for I can assure him that none is intended—charged me in my absence (so my friends have informed me) with what I believe he would not hesitate to have charged to my face, and to which I have no objection, but I must except to the authority on which he relied, for I protest against any gentleman's producing—as proof of what I have at any time said—a newspaper, or anything purporting to be

---

* " The Devil himself will not eat a woman."—SHAKSPEARE.

a register of debates, unless I endorse it, and become answerable for it, and more especially remarks drawn from the debates of another body, which, in regard to me, are particularly unfaithful. I shall show to the House not such matter as the gentleman from Massachusetts stirred, to the offence of every moral sense, of every moral being. I do not pretend to impose my standard of delicacy and propriety upon the gentleman, who will no doubt measure by his own—*de gustibus non est disputandum*—and it is not for me to interfere with the gentleman's tastes, whether in literature, morals or religion. I shall refer to a matter of recent notoriety, that will test the correctness of these reports. In the debate on the motion of the gentleman from South Carolina (Mr. Hamilton), respecting a picture of the battle of New Orleans, I did state, as distinctly as I could articulate, that I had seen a monument erected to the memory of Andrè, the British spy, in Westminster Abbey; that it was mutilated, the head of General Washington, and arm (I think) of Andrè having been broken off, the General's, most probably, by some Tory boy, from the neighboring school of Westminster, and that of Andrè probably by some Whig boy in retaliation. The name of Hamilton did not escape my lips. I thought, indeed, of Hamilton, but it was of a living Hamilton—the gentleman from South Carolina. But then parliamentary usage does not permit us to speak of one another by name. Now, sir, I can show you, on the same authority, which was relied on by the gentleman from Ohio—although I acknowledge that the reports of that paper, so far at least as I am concerned, have generally been more accurate this year than I have for a long time known them to be before—that I am represented as saying that the monuments in Westminster Abbey were mutilated in the same manner as the *tombs* of Hamilton and Washington had been mutilated here. The word *tomb* never escaped my lips on that occasion. This would have been a palpable falsehood. Where is the tomb of Washington? There is no such thing in this country, nor have I ever heard that a tomb has been erected to the memory of Hamilton; but I suppose that the next thing we shall hear will be, that the Quarterly, or some other impartial Review, comes out and observes with a sneer, that as Roger Sherman said the vote was the monument, so a gentleman from Virginia had by a speech in Congress built up a tomb for Washington—a "constructive" tomb—that existed nowhere but in his eccentric imagination. Sir, the tombs of Washington and of Hamilton might stand anywhere in this country unenclosed; they might, indeed, be liable to injury from the beasts of the field, or from some invidious foreigner, but the hand of no American would ever mutilate them. In the course of another debate, it seems that I rendered to a gentleman from New York (Mr. Storrs) the homage which his abilities deserved; and God forbid that the time should ever arrive when I refuse to do justice to an adversary, when I shall disparage any merit because it is found in the person of an opponent. When that time shall arrive, may I never receive mercy from that fountain of it, to which alone we all must look if we hope for forgiveness hereafter. I said that I would not, *like him*, pronounce a palinodia, neither am I now going to pronounce a palinodia in respect to the gentleman from New York. I shall not take back one jot of praise bestowed upon him. With whatever views he introduced it, the doctrine has always been mine—the strict subordination of the military to the civil authority—Scripture is Scripture, by whom, or for whatever purpose it may be quoted. I know nothing of the private habits of that gentleman (Mr. Storrs), but I know that he has too much good taste not to agree with me that time may be much better spent than in reading the documents piled up here. Yet in the report of that debate, I was represented as saying that, like the gentleman from New York, I did not—what? pronounce a palinodia? No, not at all; but that, like him, I did not read the documents. Sir, nobody reads the documents, for this plain reason, that no man can read them, and, if he could, he could hardly be worse employed. Sir, with a few exceptions, the documents are printed that they may be printed, not that they may be read.

And now, sir, comes another charge about the miserable oppressed inhabitants of Ireland. This subject has been mentioned to me by no gentleman on the other side, except a member from Maryland, from the Eastern Shore of Maryland (Mr. Kerr), who is not only by the courtesy of this House, but in fact a gentleman. He, in Committee on the Rules and Orders of the House, expressed to me his astonishment, that what I said on that occasion could have been so much misunderstood and misrepresented, that he heard me most distinctly. I now call on any member, who understood me differently at the time, to rise in his place and say so. [Here Mr. Randolph paused for a reply. None being given, and some friends having said across the seats that no member could or would say that he had understood Mr. Randolph as he had been misrepresented, Mr. Randolph went on.] Without meaning to plead to; that is, without meaning to admit, the jurisdiction of the press in the extent which it arrogates to itself, I am perfectly sensible that no man is above public opinion. God forbid that any man in this country shall ever be able to brave it. This is what our great adversary has, with characteristic audacity, attempted to do, sorely to his cost and that of his less bold compeer—now braving, now truckling to it—bullying and backing out—all in character.* I regret that any one should have supposed me capable of uttering such sentiments. So far from it, I have been the steady, firm, constant and strenuous advocate to the best of my poor ability of the oppressed people of Ireland. And why? For the reason I stated on a former occasion: They fought our battles, sir. I have known and esteemed many of them. Some of them have been—they are dead—others are now living among my warmest friends and best neighbors. In the course of a not uneventful life I have seen many things, but I have yet to see that *rara avis in terris* (I have seen a black swan) an Irish Tory. I have known Tories of every description; yes, sir, some even in Virginia—even we had a few of them during the Revolution, but too few to give us any trouble or alarm—but I never have yet seen an Irish Tory, or the man who had seen one. .

Sir, I don't read the newspapers—I don't read gentlemen's speeches, and then come here to answer them. But I am extremely pleased, nay, flattered, in the highest degree, at being told by my friends that the gentleman from Ohio attributed in his speech so much to my efforts in bringing the administration to its present lank and lean condition. The gentleman could not have pleased me better—I only fear that with all his bluntness and frankness the gentleman was not quite sincere, and was only adorning me with fillets and garlands, like the priests of the sacrifice of yore, previous to knocking me, and with me the party whom he strives to wound through my sides, on the head. He was pleased to place me at the head of what has been denominated the opposition party in this House; but at its head, or that of any other party in this House, he will never find me, for reasons which I could state, but which are wholly unnecessary. Times are, indeed, changed with the gentleman and his friends when they hold this language concerning me. But a little while ago, and the friends of the administration, nay, the members of the administration, affected to consider me as one of their firmest props. They could not, indeed, vote for me—they were men too nice in their principles for that; but consider-

---

* The *pledge*, written and published under Mr. Clay's own proper signature, to call out any member of Congress who should prove to be the author of the letter avowed by Mr. Kremer, is yet unredeemed.

ing the great benefit which they derived from my opposition, they could not (except for the honor of the country) regret my reëlection. Amiable and excellent men! But they now sing to a very different gamut.

If any gentleman will bring against me any allegation, from a clean and reputable source, I will do one of two things—I will either deny it, or admit and defend it upon my views and principles. Sir, it seems I committed a great offence in not voting for the admission of the new States into the Union, and especially of Ohio. Yet, if the thing were to do over again, I should act precisely in the same manner, and past experience would teach me I was right. What were the new States? Vast deserts of woods, inhabited by the Aborigines, to whom, if we come to the question of right, they did of right belong; and it was a question whether sound policy would dictate that we ought, by creating these States, to encourage sparse settlements, and thereby to weaken our frontier. I thought this was bad policy. Not that I am in favor of a very dense population. I am against the rabble of your great cities, but I am equally opposed to having a land without inhabitants. But, sir, I had other reasons—*graviora manent*. Does the gentleman from Ohio, with all his laudable prejudice and partiality towards his own State, think that I, as a Virginian, feeling at least equal prejudice and partiality to my native land with that which he feels for his State, would lend my sanction to an act on the part of Virginia, which beggars every instance of fatuity and folly extant in the history of nations? Why, sir, the Knight of La Mancha himself, or poor old Lear in the play, never was guilty of a grosser act of fatuity than was the State of Virginia when she committed that suicidal deed—the surrendering of her immense territory beyond the river Ohio, upon the express condition of excluding her own citizens from its benefit, when the country (yielded for the common good of the confederacy) should come to be settled. Yes, sir, it was an act of suicide—of political suicide—the effects of which she has felt, and will continue to feel, so long as she has any political existence at all. This was one of the most amiable and philanthropic acts of legislation, which, however good in point of intention, lead to the most disastrous and ruinous consequences. Can the gentleman from Ohio conceive that I, a Virginian, could further this cut-throat policy? I thought the Ohio a well defined natural boundary, and that we ought not to weaken by extending our frontier. The late war verified my foresight. Whom have I injured? The native savages and the trees, or the States that have been drained of their population to fill out Ohio? I

APPENDIX. 277

offered no wrong to the people of Ohio, for there were then none to injure. They have gone there, or have been born since. This was the "head and front of my offending;" and if the gentleman has his apparatus ready, I am prepared to undergo any form of execution which his humanity will allow him to inflict, or which even his justice may award.

Smarting under the injurious election of a President against the will of the people, by the votes of Louisiana and Missouri balancing those of Pennsylvania and Virginia in this House, I spoke of ourselves as the only people so overwise as to acquire provinces, not that we might govern them, but that they might give law to us.

And, sir, I have always held, and shall forever hold it to be the height of injustice (and of folly, too, on the part of the old States), that thirty or forty thousand persons, who so long as they remained in Pennsylvania or Virginia, were represented in the Senate, only as the rest of the Pennsylvanians and Virginians should, by emigrating to one of the geographical diagrams beyond the Ohio or the Mississippi, acquire, *ipso facto*, an equipollent vote in the other House of Congress with the millions that they left behind at home. In case of the old States, necessity gave this privilege to Rhode Island, &c.; they were coördinate States—free, sovereign and independent—and as such, *ex vi termini*, equal to the largest; but here it was a gratuitous boon, at the expense of the original members of the confederacy—not called for by justice or equity.

Sir, do not understand me as wishing to establish injurious or degrading distinctions between the old and the new States, to the disadvantage of these last. Some such already exist, which I would willingly do away. No, sir, my objection was to the admission of such States (whether south or north of the Ohio, east or west of the Mississippi) into the Union, and, by consequence, to a full participation of power in the Senate with the oldest and largest members of the confederacy, before they had acquired a sufficient population that might entitle them to it, and before that population had settled down into that degree of consistency and assimilation which is necessary to the formation of a body politic. The rapidity with which these new States fill up, would have retarded their full participation in the power of their co-states but a very short time. And in that short interval the safety of the other States (witness the vote of Missouri for President) required such a precaution on their part. If I had been an emigrant myself to one of these new States—and I have near and dear connexions in some of them—I could not have murmured against the denial to forty or fifty thousand new settlers (although I had been one of them) of a voice in the Senate, potential as New York's, with a million and a half of people.

The gentleman from Massachusetts cannot expect that I shall follow him through his elaborate detail of the diplomatic expenses of this government with which he came prepared. The House, however, will permit me to observe that there was a hiatus—*valde deflendus*, I do not doubt, but certainly not deeply lamented by me—a *hiatus* which embraces the whole period of the administration of Mr. Jefferson. I am not going into the question of these expenses; I will stir no such matter—demands which have dogged the doors of the treasury so long, and so perseveringly, as that they have been at length allowed, some from motives of policy, others to get rid of importunate and sturdy beggars, although they were disallowed under Mr. Jefferson's administration. But, sir, if every claim that gets through this House, or is allowed by this government, after years of importunity (some of them of thirty years standing), is for that reason considered by the gentleman as a just claim, and fit to be drawn into precedent, my notions of justice and of sound precedent differ greatly from his. I, too, am as much opposed as he can be to what is truly called the prodigality of parsimony. The gentleman thinks that the salaries of our foreign ministers are too low, and therefore they must be eked out by these allowances from the contingent fund—out of what is called the secret service money. The gentleman is right as to the existence of such a fund. It was appointed, and perhaps properly, for Washington was to be the first charged with its disbursement. But our early Presidents always made it a point of honor to return this fund untouched. They said to the nation, you trusted me with your purse—I have had no occasion to use it—here it is—count the money—there is as much by tale and as much by weight as I received from you. But was it ever dreamed that such a fund was to be put into the hands of a President of the United States, to furnish him with the means of rewarding his favorites? No, sir; it was to pay those waiters and chambermaids, and eaves-droppers, and parasites, and panders, that the gentleman told us of on the other side of the water—and there it might be all very right and proper—but not here, because we flatter ourselves that the state of morals in this country is such as to save us from any such necessity. No gentleman would understand him as speaking of the sums which had been placed at the disposal of different Presidents, to a vast amount, for the purpose of negotiating with the Barbary Powers, &c.,

but of that amount set apart and generally known as *secret service money*. Mr. Jefferson used a small portion of this fund one year, the last of his administration, to pay some expense in relation to Burr's conspiracy, which was not allowed at the treasury.

With regard to the old billiard table, which is said to have cost some fifty dollars, it is a subject that I should never have mentioned. I consider that game as a healthy, manly, rational mode of exercise, when the weather is such as to confine us within doors. I shall certainly never join in any cant or clamor against it. I look upon it as a suitable piece of furniture in the house of any gentleman who can afford it, where it is allowed by law, as it is here and throughout the State of Maryland, as well as many other States. It is a fit subject for taxation, but I should be sorry if we were to proscribe that manly and innocent amusement.* If I have any objection to that item, it is that such a pitiful article should have been bought. I would have given him one that cost five hundred dollars, and I would have voted the appropriation with cheerfulness. My objection to such a charge is, that it is a shabby affair, and looks too much like a sneaking attempt to propitiate, by the cheapness of the thing, popular displeasure. The attempt to keep the thing out of sight only makes the matter still worse. I do not charge the gentleman from North Carolina with any such intention, but this seems to me to be too small a matter. I would strike at higher game.

The gentleman from Massachusetts says that Franklin received a higher compensation than Mr. Adams did, and other ministers of these times. He did, sir, and what was the answer which that shrewd and sensible man gave (for poor Richard had always an eye to the main chance) when his accounts were scrutinized into, and his receipts were deemed exorbitant! It was this, sir: "Thou shalt not muzzle the ox that treadeth out the corn." The very answer that I myself gave in Morrison's hotel, in Dublin, to a *squireen* and an *agent*. For a description of these varieties of the plagues of Ireland see Miss Edgeworth—delightful, ingenious, charming, sensible, witty, inimitable, though not unimitated Miss Edgeworth. When describing the misery of the South and West of Ireland, that I had lately traveled over, I was asked, "And what would you do, pray, sir, for the relief of Ireland?" with an air that none but Miss Edgeworth can describe, and that no one that has not been in Ireland can conceive. My

---

*See Appendix—Note A.

reply was, "I would unmuzzle the ox that treadeth out the corn;" and I had like to have got myself into a sad scrape by it, as any one who has been in Ireland will readily understand. Yes, sir, I was disposed to give to the houseless, naked, shivering, half-starved Irish laborer something like a fair portion of the product of his toil, of the produce of the land on which he breathes, but does not live; to put victuals into his stomach, clothes upon his back, and something like a house over his head, instead of the wretched pig-sty that is now his only habitation—shelter, it is none; and this was just the last remedy that an Irish agent, or middle man, or tythe-proctor, or absentee, would prescribe or submit to.

But to return. "These salaries are too small." I cannot agree with the gentleman. There is one touchstone of such a question—it is the avidity with which those situations are sought—I will not say by members of this House—we are hardly deemed of sufficient rank to fill them. A receivership or inspectorship of the LAND OFFICE must do for us; ay, even for such of us as, by our single vote, have made a President. Sir, the generous steed by whose voice the son of Hystaspes was elevated to the throne of Persia, was better recompensed, as he deserved to be, than the venal asses whose braying has given a ruler to seven millions of freemen, and to a domain far surpassing in power as well as extent that of the GREAT KING—the GRAND MONARQUE of antiquity! So long as these foreign missions are sought with avidity—so long as members of Congress, and not of this House only, or chiefly, will bow, and cringe, and duck, and fawn, and get out of the way at a pinching vote, or lend a helping hand at a pinching vote, to obtain these places, I never will consent to enlarge the salary attached to them. Small as the gentleman tells us those salaries are, I will take it on me to say, that they are three times as great as they are now managed, as the net proceeds of his estate, made by any planter on the Roanoke. But then we are told that they live at St. Petersburgh and London, and that living there is very expensive. Well, sir, who sent them there? Who pressed them to go there? Were they impressed there like D' Auterive's slave? Were they taken, like a free-born Englishman, by a press-gang, on Tower hill, knocked down, handcuffed, chucked on board of a tender, and told that they must take the pay and rations which his Majesty was pleased to allow? No such thing, sir. I will now quit this subject, and say only this, that our minister (Mr. Adams) was paid for a *constructive* journey—that, I think, is the phrase, which means neither more nor less than a journey, which was never performed.

[Here Mr. Everett made a gesture of dissent.]

The gentleman shakes his head. Sir, we shall see more of this hereafter, but I will reason only hypothetically. If the gentleman in question, while he remained at St. Petersburgh, could make the journey imputed to him, it beats the famous journey from Mexico to Tacubaya, as far as some distance, however small, exceeds no distance whatsoever. If a gentleman from Washington goes to Georgetown or to Alexandria; yes, sir, to Bladensburg, I will acknowledge that he performs, at least in some sense, a sort of journey. But not if he remains in this city, and never stirs out of it. However, I will not now press this matter farther—others will do more justice to it—*de minimis non curat.*

Paulo majora canamus: There was one remark which I took down while the gentleman was speaking, and which I cannot pass over. Who that gentleman was, described by the member from Massachusetts, who proposed to him that if he would move to raise these salaries that gentleman would join with him and support him, I cannot conjecture or divine. Be he who he may, I will venture to say thus much: He is some gentleman who expects to be sent upon a mission himself, and, with great forecast and prudence, he was calculating to throw upon the present administration beforehand all the odium of the increase of the salary which he hoped to finger. I am disposed to be more just to the gentleman and to the administration, because I believe that he will get full as much as he may deserve; and they have full as much weight as they can carry, without adding to it another feather.

I am afraid that I may be charged with some want of continuity, but what I have to say is at least as relevant; ay, and as pertinent too to the subject before the House as the handbill which the gentleman read, till *his* delicacy would permit him to read no farther, though I must confess I thought that he had already gone so far that there was no *ultima Thule* beyond. Sir, the gentleman might have spared himself this last exertion of his delicacy, and even have read to the end. There could be nothing more gross behind than what we had already heard, and were to hear, in the case of the ill-fated Queen of France. The gentleman, with much gravity, with some dexterity, and with great plausibility, but against certain principles which I have held in this House, *ab ovo,* and which I shall continue to hold, *usque ad mala,* till I leave the feast, spoke of the headlong commencement of the opposition before the administration could give reasonable cause of discontent. I have now no *palinodia* to sing or to chant upon that subject. I drew from that fountain, which never failed an observing and sagacious man, and which even the simple and inexperienced (and I among the rest) may drink at—it is nature and human life. I saw distinctly, from the beginning, that if we permitted this administration— if we listened to those who cried to us, "Wait, wait, there is a lion in the path" (and, sir, there always is a lion in the path to the sluggard and the dastard), and which cry was seconded no doubt by many who wished to know how the land lay before they ran for a port—on which side victory would incline before they sounded *their* horn of triumph. If we had thus waited, the situation of the country would have been very different from what it is now. Sir, there was a great race to be run—if you will permit me to draw an illustration from a sport to which I have been much addicted—one in which all the gentlemen in Virginia, when we had gentlemen in Virginia, delighted, and of which I am yet very fond—I mean from the turf—and it must be lost or won, as the greatest race in this country was won—I mean the race on Long Island, which I saw, and that was by running every inch of the ground—by going off at score—by following the policy of Purdy. Purdy, sir, was a man of sound sense and practical knowledge—a man of common sense I mean, and worth a thousand of your old and practised statesmen and "premature" gentlemen who never arrive at maturity—and who, meaning to side with the next administration in case of our success, were, nevertheless, resolved to get all they could in the meantime out of this. Sir, to one of these trimming gentry, it is worse than death to force him to take sides before a clear indication of victory; and hence the cry of its being "premature," to stir the question of the next Presidential election. If we had set off one session later, we should not have had ground enough left to run upon, to overtake, and pass, and beat them, before they would have passed the winning post and pocketed the stakes. Such would have been the effect if we had delayed our push, and I know no one who would have enjoyed the result and chuckled at our folly with more hearty glee than one of these same old and practised statesmen. [Here something was said which our reporter did not hear, and to which Mr. Everett was understood to reply, that he had not stated it as his sentiment, but as a fact.] I beg the gentleman's pardon: I never was misrepresented by him, and I never will misrepresent him unless I misunderstand him. But I wonder it never occurred to the gentleman from Massachusetts what could be the cause why such a hue and cry should be raised against an administration so very able (permit me in this, however, to differ from the gentleman—*de gustibus non est*); what, I say, could have been the cause why Actæon and all his hounds, or, rather, why the dogs of war were let slip against this wise and able and virtuous and loving administration; these patterns of political friendship and consistency; and have continued to pursue them, till they lie panting and gasping for breath on the highway—until they realize the beautiful fable of the hare and many friends. The cause of all this is to be found in the manner in which they came into power—the cause of this "premature" opposition lies there, and there mainly. I would defy all the public presses in the world to have brought them to this pass, had there not been a taint of original sin in their body politic, and which cleaves to them even as the sin of our first parents taints our fallen nature and cleaveth to us all. The gentleman refers to those who compose the party called the opposition, and says it is formed of very discordant materials. True, sir; but what are the materials of the party which upholds the administration; nay, of the administration itself? Are they perfectly homogeneous? I know one of them, who has been raised to a higher station than most men in this country. Was that because he opposed, or because he espoused, the election of the present chief magistrate?

Let me ask the gentleman from Massachusetts what could cause the old Republican party in New England—the worthy successors of John Langdon *—to be now found acting with us? They know—but perhaps some in this House do not know—they know that the southern interest is as much their ally in protecting them against an overweening oligarchy at home, as England is the natural ally of Portugal against the power of Spain and France; and though they left us for a time, yet now apprehending danger, and seeing through the artifices of their betrayer, they have returned to us their old, natural, and approved allies. Have not the administration as well as the opposition ways and means and funds in their hands to obtain influence and buy success? Have they not the whole of the great mass of patronage in their hands? But the gentleman says, that so far from taking care of their adherents, they have been too liberal in bestowing this upon their enemies. But it is easy to account for this. An ancient apophthegm tells us that it is better to judge between two of your

---

* See Appendix—Note G.

enemies than between two of your friends. In the one case you are almost sure by your decision to make a friend, and in the other to lose one. Now, sir, our able and practised statesmen know that by giving a loaf and a fish to an enemy they make a friend, when by giving them to one of their friends they might disoblige another, who might think his claims disparaged—and that, sir, is the whole secret of their neglecting their friends.

Permit me, sir, again to ask, how comes it that this administration are brought into their present very curious and unprecedented predicament? How happens it that they alone, of all the administrations which have been in this country, find themselves in the minority in each House of Congress—"*palsied by the will of their constituents*"—when the very worst of their predecessors kept a majority till midnight on the third or fourth of March, whichever you please to call it? Ay, sir, under the administration to which I allude, there were none of these compunctious visitings of nature at the attacks made on private character. We had no chapter of lamentations then on the ravaging and desolating war on the fair fame of all the wise and virtuous and good of our land. The notorious Peter Porcupine, since even better known as William Cobbet, was the especial protegè of that administration. I heard them say, I do not mean the head of that administration, but one of its leaders, that he was the greatest man in the world; and I do not know that, in point of sheer natural endowment, he was so very far wrong. Yes, sir, it was that very Cobbet, who, if the late publications may be trusted, now says that Mr. Adams has fifteen hundred slaves in Virginia. Was there any slander too vile, too base for that man to fabricate? I remember well the nicknames under which we passed—yes, sir, I can proudly say *we*, although the humblest in the ranks: Mr. Gallatin was CITOYEN GUILLOTINE, with *le petit fenetre national* at his back. The caricature then, as well as now, constituted no small part of the munitions of political war. The pencil and the graver (they had no want of *tools* of any sort) lent their aid to the pen and the ballad and the military band of music. "Down with the French!" (that is, the best men of our country,) was the cry. My excellent and able colleague, Mr. Nicholas—one of the purest and most pious of men, who afterwards removed to the State of New York, and was a model of Republican virtue and simplicity, that might have adorned the best days of Sparta or of Rome—he, sir, having the misfortune to lose an eye, was held up to ridicule as *Polyphemus?* * You are shocked at this, sir; but let me tell you that it was only a little innocent, harmless, Federal wit—and the author was the especial protegé of "government" and its adherents. All chuckled over the Porcupine. To that party the present incumbent then belonged—and another member of this pure administration; and these two Sedition Laws, black-cockade heroes, are recommended by the "ANTI-JACKSON Convention" to Virginia for her President and Vice President! They have not even the merit of an early conversion. They are true Swiss of State—*point d' argent, point de Suisse*. My venerable friend from North Carolina was Monsieur Maçon, with a *cedilla* under the ç, to mark him the more for a Frenchman. I forget the cognomen of the learned gentleman from Louisiana (Mr. Livingston): I know that he was never spared. I remember well my own: I wish, sir, it was applicable now, for I was then a *boy*. Every sanctuary was then invaded. As to Mr. Jefferson, every epithet of vituperation was exhausted upon him. He was an atheist, a Frenchman; we were all atheists and traitors; our names and cause associated with the cannibals and the cannibalism of the revolutionary tribunal, and with all the atrocities, the most atrocious and revolting of which has this day been presented to the House by the chaste imagination of the gentleman from Massachusetts. Yes, sir, then, as now, a group of horrors was pressed upon the public imagination, to prop the sinking cause of a desperate administration. Religion and order were to be subverted, the national debt to be sponged, and the country to be drenched in its best blood by Mr. Jefferson and his Jacobin adherents. Even good men, and not unwise men, were brought to believe this. Mr. Jefferson was elected; and we know what followed. But this, it may

---

* He also was described as CITIZEN NICOLAI. General Sumpter, of South Carolina, a veteran of the Revolution, covered with honorable wounds and scars, was, by some of the myrmidons of the administration, forced from his seat in the CIRCUS, compelled to stand up, his hat taken from his head, and his hands forcibly made to clap, when Mr. Adams entered the theatre, and "HAIL COLUMBIA!" was struck up by the band. This stern old Republican was thus involuntarily compelled to join in the incense to the idol of the day. He yet lives to read I hope this mention of him by an old friend.

My venerable friend, Mr. Macon, told me, within twenty-four hours past, that the only time in his life that he ever drew a knife was in the play-house, when our party (myself especially) was insulted by the military.

They used to play the Rogue's March under the windows of the house where he and Nicholas and Gallatin lodged! So much for THE REIGN OF TERROR! as it was justly styled by the Republicans of that day.

be said, was not done by our own people; it was done by foreign hirelings, mercenaries. Sir, it is not only of this description of persons that I speak. It was done in the glorious days of the Sedition Law and the black cockade, when we found in General Shee and his legion protection against the Prætorian bands of the administration. These brave fellows were many of them Irish or German, and most of them of Irish or German parentage, chiefly from the Northern Liberties, then the stronghold of Republicanism; and therefore branded with the opprobrious name of the Fauxboug St. Antoine, the most Jacobin quarter of Paris.

At the very time that the act noted by the gentleman from Massachusetts was passed (May, 1800), when Professor Cooper was escorted to jail, a victim of the Sedition Law, the New York election then, as of late, rung the knell of the departing administration. Sir, when the gentleman favored us with his opinion of the present stupendous administration, I imagine he drew it from a comparison with some of the administrations which preceded it. In comparison with some of these, even this administration is great: for we have seen the least of all possible things—the poorest of all poor creatures that ever was manufactured into a head of a department (and that's a bold word), a member of a former administration—almost a satire on the name. This personage, as I have very lately learned, in imitation of another great man from the same State, took some liberties in public with my name, when he had the Atlantic for a barrier, the Summer before last. Like his great friend, his courage shows itself three thousand miles off. It is in the ratio of the square of the distance of his adversary. Sir, I should like to have seen how he would have looked, if, on finishing his harangue, he had found me at his elbow. I think I can conceive how he would have *felt*.*

Sir, I have much to say, which neither my own weakness, nor my regard to the politeness of this House, will permit me now to say. As I have exonerated the principal of that weighty affair of the billiard table, I also exonerate him and his lieutenant from every charge of collusion—*in the first instance;* and, if it is in order, I will state the reasons for my opinion. When the first alliance was patched up between the two great leaders of the East and West, neither of the high contracting parties had the promotion of the present incumbent at all in view. Sir, I speak

---

* " Mr. C. very humorously, and it is said very closely, mimicked Mr. Randolph in quoting some parts of Mr. R.'s speech."—*Salem Observer.* " O rare Ben !"

knowingly as to one of these parties, and with the highest degree of moral probability of the other.* Can it be necessary that I prove this? The thing proves itself. The object was to bring in one of the parties to the compact, whom the constitution subsequently excluded, and, of course, to provide for the other. A gentleman, then of this House, was a candidate, who, to the last hour, cast many a longing, although not lingering, look, with outstretched neck, towards Louisiana—*jugulo quæsita negatur*—to discover whether or not he should be one upon the list. Sir, it is impossible that he could, in the first instance, have looked to the elevation of another, or have designed to promote the views of any man, but in subserviency to his own. Common sense forbids it. But all these calculations, however skilful, and Demoivre could not have made better, utterly failed. The partners had two strings to their bow—Mr. Crawford's death, or Mr. Clay's being ahead of Mr. Crawford, by getting the vote of Louisiana, or those votes in New York which were so strangely, and at the time unaccountably, given to Mr. Crawford. They took the field with a double percussion gun, and banged away, right and left; but, good marksmen as they were, both barrels missed. Louisiana refused to vote as obstinately as Mr. Crawford refused to die; and so the gentleman was excluded. It was then that Mr. Adams was first taken up, as a *pis aller*, which we planters of the south translate, *a hand plant*.

Sir, I have a right to know; I had a long while before an interview with the very great man; but not on that subject: no, Sir,—It was about business of this house—and he so far descended, or I should rather say of so very great a man, condescended, as to electioneer even with me. He said to me, among other things, "if you of the South will give us of the West any other man than John Quincy Adams for President, we will support him." Let any man deny this who dare—but remember, he then expected to be a candidate before the House himself. "If you will give us any other man!" Sir, the gentleman in question can have no disposition to deny it. It was at a time when he and the present incumbent were publicly pitted against each other, and Mr. Adams crowed defiance and clapped his wings against the Cock of Kentucky. Sir, I know this to be a strong mode of expression. I did not take it literally. I thought I understood the meaning to be that Virginia, by her strenuous support of Mr. Crawford, would further the success of Mr. Adams. "Any

---

* See Appendix—Note B.

other man, sir, besides John Quincy Adams." Now, as neither Mr. Crawford nor General Jackson in the end proved to be "any other man," it follows clearly who any other man was, viz: *one* other man—*id est*, myself (as a gentleman once said in this House), "we will support him." But, sir, as soon as this *egomet* was out of the question, we of the South lost all our influence, and "we of the West" gave us of the South this very John Quincy Adams for President, and received from him the very office, which being held by him, we of the West assigned as the cause of our support, considering it to be a sort of reversionary interest in the presidency. (See the letter to Mr. F. Brooke.) It was, indeed, "ratsbane in our mouth," but we swallowed the arsenic.*

Sir, a powerful party of New England was equally opposed to Mr. Adams, the high Federal party, or the Essex junto, so-called—all the successors of the George Cabots, and Caleb Strongs, and Stephen Higginsons—I should rather say their representatives, and all their surviving coadjutors—were against him, with one exception, and that was an honest man, of whom it was said in this House that he ought to desire no other epitaph but that which might truly be inscribed to his tomb: "Here lies the man who was honored by the friendship of Washington, and the enmity of his successor." Sir, who persecuted the name of Hamilton while living, and followed him beyond the grave? The father and the son. Who were the persecutors of Fisher Ames, whose very grave was haunted as if by vampyres? Both father and son. Who attempted to libel the present chief justice, and procure his impeachment—making the seat of John Smith, of Ohio, the peg to hang the impeachment on? The

---

* It has been suggested to me since the above was spoken, by one who ought to know a good deal of New York politics, and to whom it occurred while I was making this development, and in consequence of it, that Mr. Adams, who could not be blind to the game that was playing between Mr. C. and Mr. W., caused the vote which Mr. Crawford got in New York to be given to him, then no longer the most formidable opponent, for the express purpose of excluding Mr. Clay, from whom the greatest danger was to be apprehended from the House, by ensuring Mr. Crawford's return. Thus the *biters were bit*, and Messrs. C. and W. had to make terms with Mr. A. who, in requital for the vote of Mr. C. and his friends, graciously received them into favor. Yes, the allies completely circumvented by this manœuvre on the part of Mr. A., had no other alternative than to go over to him, who, no doubt, nothing loth, met them full half way.

Reader! Is there anything in Moliere or Congreve surpassing this? Can Scapin or Maskwell beat this?

son. I, as one of the grand jury, and my colleague, Mr. Garnett,* were
called upon by the chairman of the committee of the Senate in Smith's
case (Mr. Adams) to testify in that case. Sir, do you remember a committee, raised at the same time in this House, to inquire whether the failure
of Burr's prosecution grew out of "the evidence, the law, or the administration of the law?" For my sins I suppose I was put upon that committee. The plain object was the impeachment of the judge who presided
on the trial. This was one of the early oblations (the first was the writ of
habeas corpus) of the present incumbent on the altar of his new political
church. Who accused his former Federal associates in New England of
a traitorous conspiracy with the British authorities in Canada to dismem-
ber the Union? The present incumbent. Yet all is forgiven him—
Hamilton, Ames, Marshall, themselves accused of treason—all is forgiven; and these men, with one exception, now support him; and for
what?

Sir, I will take the letter to the President of the Court of Appeals in
Virginia, and on that letter, and on facts which are notorious as the sun at
noonday, it must be established that there was a collusion, and a corrupt
collusion, between the principals in this affair. I do not say the agreement was a written or even a verbal one—I know that the language of
the poet is true—that men who "meet to do a damned deed" cannot bring
even themselves to speak of it in distinct terms—they cannot call a spade
a spade—but eke out their unholy purpose with dark hints, and inuen-
does, and signs, and shrugs, where more is meant than meets the ear. Sir,
this person was willing to take any man who would secure the end that he
had in view. He takes office under Mr. Adams, and that very office too
which had been declared to be in the line of safe precedents—that very
office which decided his preference of Mr. Adams. Sir, are we children?
Are we babies? Can't we make out apple-pie, without spelling and put-

---

*James M. Garnett, Esq., of the county of Essex, Virginia, a member of the grand jury, and also of Congress during Mr. Jefferson's administration. Our friendship com- menced soon after he took his seat in Congress, and has continued uninterrupted by a single moment of coolness or alienation during three-and-twenty years, and very trying times, political and otherwise. I take a pride in naming this gentleman among my steady, uniform and unwavering friends. In Congress he never said an unwise thing, or gave a bad vote. He has kept the faith from 1799, when he supported the doctrines of Madison's famous report made at the session of the Virginia Assembly, of which he was a member. He came into Congress in 1805, and left it March 4, 1809.

ting the letters together—a-p, ap, p-l-e, ple, ap-ple, p-i-e, pie, apple-pie? Sir, the fact can never be got over, and it is this fact which alone could make this administration to rock and totter to its base in spite of the indiscretion (to say no worse), in spite of all the indiscretions of its adversaries. For, sir, there never was a man who had so much cause as General Jackson has had to say, "'Save me from my friends and I will take care of my enemies." Yes, sir, he could take care of his enemies—from them he never feared danger; but not of his friends—at least of some, whose vanity has prompted them to couple their obscure names with his—and it is because he did take care of his enemies, who were his country's enemies, and for other reasons which I could state, that his cause is now espoused by that grateful country. "But General Jackson is no statesman." Sir, I deny that there is any instance on record in history of a man not having military capacity being at the head of any government with advantage to that government, and with credit to himself. There is a great mistake on this subject. It is not those talents which enable a man to write books and make speeches that qualify him to preside over a government. The wittiest of poets has told us, that

"All a Rhetorician's rules,
Teach only how to name his tools."

We have seen Professors of Rhetoric who could no doubt descant fluently upon the use of these said tools; yet sharpen them to so wiry an edge as to cut their own fingers with these implements of their trade. Thomas à Becket was as brave a man as Henry the Second, and, indeed, a braver man—less infirm of purpose. And who were the Hildebrands and the rest of the Papal freebooters who achieved victory after victory over the proudest monarchs and states of christendom? These men were brought up in a cloister perhaps, but they were endowed with that highest of all the gifts of heaven, the capacity to lead men, whether in the Senate or the field. Sir, it is one and the same faculty, and its successful display has always received, and ever will receive, the highest honors that man can bestow; and this will be the case do what you will, cant what you may, about military chieftains and military domination. So long as man is man, the victorious defender of his country will, and ought, to receive that country's suffrage for all that the forms of her government allow her to give.

A friend said to me, not long since, "Why General Jackson can't write"—"admitted." (Pray, sir, can you tell me of any one that can write? for I protest I know nobody that can.) Then turning to my friend I said, "It is most true that General Jackson cannot write" (not that he can't write his name, or a letter, &c.), "because he has never been taught; but his competitor cannot write, because he was not teachable;" for he has had every advantage of education and study. Sir, the Duke of Marlborough, the greatest captain and negotiator of his age—which was the age of Louis XIV—and who may rank with the greatest men of any age; whose irresistible manners and address triumphed over every obstacle in council, as his military prowess and conduct did in the field—this great man could not even spell, and was notoriously ignorant of all that an under graduate must know, but which it is not necessary for a man at the head of affairs to know at all. Would you have superseded him by some Scotch schoolmaster? Gentlemen forget that it is an able helmsman we want for the ship of State, and not a Professor of Navigation or Astronomy.

Sir, among the vulgar errors that ought to go into Sir Thomas Brown's book this ought not to be omitted: that learning and wisdom are not synonymous, or at all equivalent. Knowledge and wisdom, as one of our most delightful poets sings—

> "Knowledge and wisdom, far from being one,
> Have oft times no connexion—knowledge dwells
> In heads replete with thoughts of other men;
> Wisdom, in minds attentive to their own.
> Knowledge is proud that he has learned so much;
> Wisdom is humble that he knows no more.
> Books are not seldom talismans and spells,
> By which the magic art of shrewder wits
> Holds the unthinking multitude enchained."

And not books only, sir—speeches are not less deceptive. I not only consider the want of what is called learning not to be a disqualification for the command in chief in civil or military life, but I do consider the possession of too much learning to be of most mischievous consequence to such a character; who is to draw from the cabinet of his own sagacious mind, and to make the learning of others, or whatever other qualities they may possess, subservient to his more enlarged and vigorous views. Such a man was Cromwell—such a man was Washington.* Not learned, but wise.

---

* Washington had a plain English education, and mathematics enough to qualify him for a land surveyor.

Their understandings were not clouded or cramped, but had fair play. Their errors were the errors of men, not of school boys and pedants. So far from the want of what is called education being a very strong objection to a man at the head of affairs, over-education constitutes a still stronger objection. [In the case of a lady it is fatal. Heaven defend me from an over-educated, accomplished lady. Yes, accomplished indeed, for she is *finished* for all the duties of a wife, or mother, or mistress of a family.] We hear much of military usurpation—of military despotism—of the sword of a conqueror—of Cæsar, and Cromwell, and Bonaparte. What little I know of Roman history has been gathered chiefly from the surviving letters of the great men of that day—of Cicero especially—and I freely confess that, if I had then lived, and had been compelled to take sides, I must, though very reluctantly, have sided with Cæsar, rather than have taken Pompey for my master. It was the interest of the house of Stuart—and they were long enough in power to do it—to blacken the character of Cromwell—that great, and, I must add, bad man. But, sir, the devil himself is not so black as he is sometimes painted. And who would not rather have obeyed Cromwell than that self-styled Parliament, which obtained a title too indecent for me to name, but by which it is familiarly known and mentioned in all the historians from that day to this. Cromwell fell under a temptation, perhaps too strong for the nature of man to resist—but he was an angel of light to either of the Stuarts—the one whom he brought to the block, or his son, a yet worse man, the blackest and foulest of miscreants that ever polluted a throne. It has been the policy of the house of Stuart and their successors—it is the policy of kings to vilify and blacken the memory and character of Cromwell. But the cloud is rolling away. We no longer consider Hume as deserving of the slightest credit. Cromwell was "guiltless of his country's blood." His was a bloodless usurpation. To doubt his sincerity at the outset, from his subsequent fall, would be madness—religious fervor was the prevailing temper and fashion of the times. Cromwell was no more of a fanatic than Charles the First, and not so much of a hypocrite. It was not in his nature to have signed the attainder of such a friend as Lord Strafford, whom Charles meanly and selfishly and basely and cruelly and cowardly repaid for his loyalty to him by an ignominious death—a death deserved, indeed, by Strafford, for his treason to his country, but not at the hands of his faithless, perfidious master. Cromwell was an usurper, 'tis granted; but he had scarcely any choice left him. His sway was every way preferable to that miserable corpse of a Parliament that he turned out, as a gentleman would turn off a drunken butler and his fellows; or the pensioned tyrant that succeeded him—a dissolute, depraved bigot and hypocrite, who was outwardly a Protestant, and at heart a Papist. He lived and died one, while pretending to be a son of the church of England; ay, and swore to it, and died a perjured man. If I must have a master, give me one whom I can respect, rather than a knot of knavish attorneys. Bonaparte was a bad man; but I would rather have had Bonaparte than such a set of corrupt, intriguing, public plunderers as he turned adrift.* The Senate of Rome—the Parliament of England—"the councils of elders and of youngsters"—the Legislature of France—all made themselves first odious and then contemptible; and then comes an usurper; and this is the natural end of a corrupt civil government.

There is a class of men who possess great learning, combined with inveterate professional habits, and who are *ipso facto*, or perhaps I should rather say *ipsis factis*, for I must speak accurately, as I speak before a professor, disqualified for any but secondary parts anywhere—even in the cabinet. Cardinal Richelieu was what? A priest. Yes, but what a priest! Oxenstiern was a chancellor. He it was who sent his son abroad to see—*quam parva sapientia regitur mundus*—with how little wisdom this world is governed. This administration seemed to have thought that even less than that little would do for us. The gentleman called it a strong, an able cabinet—second to none but Washington's first cabinet. I could hardly look at him for blushing. What! Sir, is Gallatin at the head of the treasury?—Madison in the department of State? The mind of an accomplished and acute dialectician, of an able lawyer, or, if you please, of a great physician, may, by the long continuance of one pursuit—of one train of ideas—have its habits so inveterately fixed, as effectually to disqualify the possessor for the command of the councils of a country. He may, nevertheless, make an admirable chief of a bureau—an excellent man of details—which the chief ought never to be. A man may be capable of making an able and ingenious argument on any subject within the sphere of his knowledge; but every now and then the master

---

* The Directory and the Councils (the first especially), we are told by high authority, were known familiarly in Paris by the appellation of "*Les Gueux plumés.*" It was then and there probably that a late President of the United States acquired the first rudiments of his taste for *etiquette* and *costume*, which has since displayed itself so pitiably.

sophist will start, as I have seen him start, at the monstrous conclusions to which his own artificial reasoning had brought himself. But this was a man of more than ordinary natural candor and fairness of mind. Sir, by words and figures you may prove just what you please; but it often and most generally is the fact, that in proportion as a proposition is logically or mathematically true, so is it politically and commonsensically (or rather nonsensically) false. The talent which enables a man to write a book or make a speech, has no more relation to the leading of an army or a Senate than it has to the dressing of a dinner. The talent which fits a man for either office is the talent for the management of men—a mere dialectician never had, and never will have it; each requires the same degree of courage, though of different kinds. The very highest degree of moral courage is required for the duties of government. I have been amused when I have seen some dialecticians, after asserting their words—"the counters of wise men, the money of fools"—after they had laid down their premises, and drawn, step by step, their deductions,* sit down, completely satisfied, as if the conclusions to which they had brought themselves were really the truth—as if it were irrefragably true. But wait until another cause is called, or till another court sits—till the bystanders and jury have had time to forget both argument and conclusion, and they will make you just as good an argument on the other side, and arrive with the same complacency at a directly opposite conclusion, and triumphantly demand your assent to this new truth. Sir, it is their business—I do not blame them. I only say that such a habit of mind unfits men for action, for decision. They want a client to decide for them which side to take; and the really great man performs that office. This habit unfits them for government in the first degree. The talent for government lies in these two things—sagacity to perceive, and decision to act. Genuine statesmen were never made such by mere training—*nascuntur non fiunt*—education will form good business men. The maxim (*nascitur non fit*) is as true of statesmen as it is of poets. Let a house be on fire, you will soon see in that confusion who has the talent to command. Let a ship be in danger at sea, and ordinary subordination destroyed, and you will immediately make the same discovery. The ascendancy of mind and of character exists and rises as naturally and as inevitably, where there is free play for it, as material bodies find their level by gravitation. Thus a great logi-

---

* See Appendix—Note C.

cian, like a certain animal, oscillating between the hay on different sides of him, wants some power from without, before he can decide from which bundle to make a trial. Who believes that Washington could write as good a book or report as Jefferson, or make as able a speech as Hamilton? Who is there that believes that Cromwell would have made as good a judge as Lord Hale? No, sir; these learned and accomplished men find their proper place under those who are fitted to command, and to command them among the rest. Such a man as Washington will say to a Jefferson, do you become my Secretary of State; to Hamilton, do you take charge of my purse, or that of the nation, which is the same thing; and to Knox, do you be my master of the horse. All history shows this; but great logicians and great scholars are for that very reason unfit to be rulers. Would Hannibal have crossed the Alps when there were no roads—with elephants—in the face of the warlike and hardy mountaineers—and have carried terror to the very gates of Rome if his youth had been spent in poring over books? Would he have been able to maintain himself on the resources of his own genius for sixteen years in Italy, in spite of faction and treachery in the Senate of Carthage, if he had been deep in conic sections and fluxions, and the differential calculus—to say nothing of botany, and mineralogy, and chemistry? "Are you not ashamed," said a philosopher, to one who was born to rule; "are you not ashamed to play so well upon the flute?" Sir, it was well put. There is much which it becomes a secondary man to know—much that it is necessary for him to know that a first rate man ought to be ashamed to know. No head was ever clear and sound that was stuffed with book learning. You might as well attempt to fatten and strengthen a man by stuffing him with every variety and the greatest quantity of food. After all, the chief must draw upon his subalterns for much that he does not know, and cannot perform himself. My friend, William R. Johnson, has many a groom that can clean and dress a race horse, and ride him too, better than he can. But what of that? Sir, we are, in the European sense of the term, not a military people. We have no business for an army—it hangs as a dead weight upon the nation—officers and all. All that we hear of it is through pamphlets, indicating a spirit that, if I was at the head of affairs, I should very speedily put down. A state of things that never could have grown up under a man of decision of character at the head of the State or the department—a man possessing *the spirit of command*—that truest of all tests of a chief, whether military or civil. Who rescued Braddock when he was fighting—*secundum artem*—and his men were dropping around him on every side? It was a Virginia militia major. He asserted in that crisis the place which properly belonged to him, and which he afterwards filled in the manner we all know.

Sir, I may, without any mock modesty, acknowledge what I feel, that I have made an unsuccessful reply to the gentleman from Massachusetts. There are some subjects which I could have wished to have touched upon before I sit down now and forever. I had the materials in my possession when I came to the House this morning, but I am disabled by physical weakness from the most advantageous use of them.

What shall we say to a gentleman, in this House or out of it, occupying a prominent station, and filling a large space in the eye of his native State, who should, with all the adroitness of a practised advocate, gloss over the acknowledged encroachments of the men in power upon the fair construction of the constitution, and then present the appalling picture, glaring and flaming, in his deepest colors, of a bloody military tyrant—a raw-head and bloody-bones—so that we cannot sleep in our beds; who should conjure up all the images that can scare children, or frighten old women—I mean very old women, sir—and who offers this wretched caricature—this vile daub, where brick-dust stands for blood, like Peter Porcupine's BLOODY BUOY, as a reason for his and our support in Virginia, of a man in whom he has no confidence, whom he *damns with faint praise*—and who, moreover—tell it not in Gath! had zealously and elaborately (I cannot say ably) justified every one of these very atrocious and bloody deeds? Yes, sir, on paper—not in the heat of debate, in the transports of a speech, but—as the author of the Richmond Anathema full well knew—and knew that we, too, knew—deliberately and officially. Who instituted the festival of Santa Victoria on the 8th of January in honor of General Jackson, and of Mrs. Jackson too? The present incumbent, when Mr. Crawford was the great object of dread. If we did not know that lawyers never see but one side of a case—that on which they are retained, and that they fondly hope that the jury will see with their eyes—what should we say of such a man? His client having no character, he attacks defendant's character upon a string of charges, in every one of which (supposing them to be true) his client was self avowed *particeps criminis*—having defended, adopted, and made each and every one of them his own. Sir, such a man may be a great lawyer (although this is but a poor specimen of his skill in that line), or a great mathematician, or chemist; but of a man guilty of such glaring absurdity it may be fearlessly pronounced that, in the management of his own concerns and in the affairs of men, he has not "right good common sense." And here, sir, we come to that great and all-important distinction which the profane vulgar—whether they be the great vulgar or the small—too often overlook; and which I have lamely, I fear, endeavored to press upon the House—I mean the distinction between knowledge and learning on the one hand, and sense and judgment on the other. And there lies the great defect of the gentleman in question. I have heard it said of him, by those who know, and love him well, "that "he can argue either side of a question, whether of law, of policy, or of "constitutional construction, with great ingenuity and force; but he wants "that sagacity in political affairs, which first discerns the proper *end*, and "then adopts the most appropriate *means:* and he is deficient in that know- "ledge of mankind, which would enable another (much his inferior) to "perceive that his honest disinterestedness is played upon by those who "are conscious that he prides himself upon it. *It is the lever by which he "is on all occasions to be moved.* It is his pride—an honest and honorable "pride, which makes him delight to throw himself into minorities, because "he enjoys more self-gratification from manifesting his independence of "popular opinion—than he could derive from anything in the gift of the "people. His late production—the Adams Convention manifesto, is the "feeblest production of the day. The reason is, *his head and heart did "not go together."* *

This picture is drawn by the hand of a friend. As we have had billiard tables and chess boards introduced into this debate, I hope I may be allowed to borrow an illustration from this last game. One of these arguing machines reminds me of the bishop at chess. The black or white bishop (I use the term not in reference to the color of the piece, but of that of the square he stands upon) is a serviceable piece enough in his way; but he labors under this defect; that, moving in the diagonal only, he can never get off his original color. His clerical character is indelible. † He can scour away all over *just one-half* of the board; but his adversary may be on the next square, and perfectly safe from his attack. To be safe from the bishop, you have only to move upon any one of the thirty-two squares that are forbidden ground to him. But not so the irregular knight, who, at successive leaps, can cover every square upon the board, to whose *check*

. * See Appendix—Note D.   † As Horne Tooke found to his cost.

the king can interpose no guard, but must move or die. Even the poor pawn has a privilege which the bishop has not; for he can elude his mitred adversary by moving from a white square to a black one, or from a black square to a white one, and finally reach the highest honors of the game. So even a poor peasant of sense may instruct the philosopher, as the shepherd did, in that beautiful introduction, the finest of Mr. Gay's fables but one, who drew all his notions of men and things from nature. It is in vain to turn over musty folios, and to double down dog's ears; it does very well in its place—in a lawyer's office or a *bureau*—I am forced to use the word for want of a better; but it will not supply the place of that which books never gave, and never can give—of sagacity, judgment and experience. Who would make the better leader in a period of great public emergency—old Roger Sherman, or a certain very learned gentleman from New York, whom we once had here, who knew everything in the world for which man has no occasion, and nothing in the world for which man has occasion? The people, who are always unsophisticated—and though they may occasionally be misled, are always right in their feelings, and always judge correctly in the long run—have taken up this thing. It is a notorious fact that in Virginia, in the county courts, where men are admitted to sit as judges, who are not of the legal profession—plain planters, who have no pretensions to be considered as lawyers—the decisions are much seldomer reversed than in those courts where a barrister presides—his reasons may be more plausible, but his decisions will be oftener wrong. Yes, sir, the people have decided upon this thing.

On my return home last March I passed by Prince Edward Court-house. It was court day. I had been abroad during the recess of Congress, and I had not seen my constituents for two years. They crowded around me, and many of them said, "Now we expect that you will explain to us how it is that we are to vote for General Jackson." They, as well as myself, had had objections to General Jackson, although I always said in regard to him, "*that I could put my finger upon his public services*—that he had strong claims upon his country, while his competitors, and the predecessor of the successful one, had never rendered any for which they had not been amply paid, and some of them greatly overpaid." My objections to General Jackson were greatly diminished by a personal acquaintance with him when he was last in the Senate. But to my constituents. Singling out one of them, a steady old planter, and staunch Republican friend, I asked him, "When you have had a faithless, worthless overseer, in whom you could place no confidence, and have resolved to dismiss him, did you ever change your mind, because, for no matter what reason, you could not get the man that you preferred to every other? or have you been satisfied to turn him off, and employ the best man that you could get?" Sir, a word to the wise is enough. They were entirely satisfied, and in a few weeks we were, as we are, unanimous for Jackson.

I will suppose a case: I will suppose that the late convulsive struggles of the administration may so far succeed as they shall be able to renew their lease for another four years. Now if a majority of this House can't get along with such a minority hanging on their rear, cutting off supplies, and beating up their quarters, what will be the situation of the administration then? Sir, what is it now? "*Palsied by the will of their constituents.*" Did anybody ever hear of a victory obtained by the Executive power while a decided majority of the Legislature was against it? I know of no such victory, but one—and that was the parricidal victory of the younger Pitt over the constitution of England; and he gained that only by the impenetrable obstinacy of the king, which then gave indications of the disease that was lurking in his constitution, and afterwards so unhappily became manifest.

The king was an honest man, and a much abler man than he ever had credit for. But he was incurably obstinate. He had just lost the colonies. No matter—he would risk the Crown of England itself, and retire to his hereditary States in Germany rather than yield; and, but for a barefaced coalition, he would have so retired, and have supplied a most important defect in the act of settlement—the separation of Hanover from England. But the corrupt bargain of Lord North and Mr. Fox, to share office between them, disgusted the people—they took side even against their own liberties. But here the coalition is not on the side of the people's rights, but against them. Mr. Pitt (the Crown rather) triumphed. Knaves cried Hosanna; fools repeated the cry. England recovered by that elasticity which belongs to free institutions, and Mr. Pitt attained a degree of power that enabled him to plunge her into the mad vortex of war with Revolutionary France. Nine hundred millions of debt; taxes, in amount, in degree, in mode, unheard of; pauperism, misery, in all possible forms of wretchedness; attest the greatness of the heaven-born minister, who did not weather the storm, but was whelmed beneath it, leaving his country to that Providence whom it pleased to rescue her in her utmost need, by inflicting madness on her great unrelenting enemy, and sending this modern Nebuchadnezzar to grass. Mr. Pitt is as strong an instance for my purpose as I could have wanted. He was a rhetorician, a speech maker; a man of words, and good words too, at will; a dexterous debater; and if he had continued to ride the Western circuit, he might have been an eminent wrangler at the bar, and, in due time, a Chief Justice or Lord Chancellor. But, for the sins of England, he was made Prime Minister, and at five-and-twenty, too. Mr. Pitt no more saw what was ahead of him, than the pauper in the parish work-house. He no more dreamed, when the war began, to what point he would be able to push his system, if system it may be called, than any clerk in his office. He did not even foresee the stoppage of the Bank, which he was compelled to resort to in the fourth year of the war. If he had foreseen it, the war would never have been made. Indeed, Mr. Pitt did not foresee even the war—for in the preceding year, I think, he held out the promise of a long peace to the faithful Commons.

The productive powers of a people like the English, where property is perfectly secure and left free to act, and where the industrious classes are shut out from almost any participation in public affairs, is incredible, is almost without a limit. Two individuals discovered each a mine, more precious and productive than Guanaxuato or Potosi, that furnished the means for his prodigality, that astonished even Mr. Pitt. These were Sir Richard Arkwright and Mr. Watt—the spinning machine and the steam engine. And this imbecile and blundering Minister has been complimented with what is due to the unrivalled ingenuity and industry of his countrymen.* So, sir, in like manner this young Hercules of America, who if we can keep him from being strangled in the cradle by the serpents of corruption, must grow to gigantic strength and stature; every improvement which he makes, in spite of the misrule of his governors, these very modestly arrogate to themselves.

We have been told, officially, that the President wished the great question to have been referred back to the people, if, by the forms of the constitution, this could be done. If I were the friend, as I am the undisguised enemy of this administration, I would say to them, you may be innocent, your intentions may be upright, but you have brought the country to that pass that you can't carry on the government. As gentlemen, possessing the least self-respect, you ought to retire—leave it—try another venue—

---

* See Appendix, Note E.

you can't carry on the government without us, any more than we can act while everything in the Executive Government is against us. Sir, there are cases in which suspicion is equivalent to proof; and not only equal to it, but more than equal to the most damning proof. There is not a husband here who will not ratify this declaration—there may be suspicion so agonizing that it makes the wretch cry out for certainty as a relief from the most damning tortures. Such is the picture which the great master of the human heart presents to us in the person of the noble Moor—and Shakspeare seems to have known the heart of man as if himself had made it. Such suspicions, resting on no false suggestions of an Iago, but supported by a cloud of witnesses and a long array of facts and circumstances that no sophistry can shake, are entertained with respect to these gentlemen; and although they are making a convulsive effort to roll back the tide of public opinion, they cant allay the feeling; the suspicion rests upon the facts; and, do what they may, facts will not bend at their bidding. Admit it to be suspicion, it is equally fatal as regards them and the public service with the reality. Mr. R. would not go in pursuit of the *alibis* and *aliasses* of the accused—of the tubs, whether with false bottoms or double bottoms, thrown out to amuse the public. The whole conduct of the accused had displayed nothing of the calm dignity of innocence, but all the restlessness of conscious guilt. Every word of Mr. Clay's late pamphlet might be true, and yet the accused be guilty notwithstanding. Mr. R. would not now examine his inconsistent declarations to different persons and at different times and occasions. The secretary was not the first witness who had proved too much. "He who pleads his own cause," says the proverb, "generally has a fool for his client." *

The gentleman from Massachusetts warned us, that if the individual we seek to elevate shall succeed, he will in his turn become the object of public pursuit, and that the same pack will be unkennelled at his heels that have run his rival down. It may be so. I have no hesitation to say, that if his conduct shall deserve it, and I live, I shall be one of that *pack;* because I maintain the interests of stockholders against presidents, directors and cashiers. And here, sir, I beg leave to notice an objection urged, as I have heard, against me by the gentleman from Ohio (Mr. Vance). He says that I have been opposed to all Administrations. Sir, I deny it to be fact. I did oppose the elder Adams, because he attacked the liberty of

---

* See Appendix—Note F.

the press and of the subject, because his opinions were at war with the genius of our institutions. He avowed them openly; and I liked him the better for his frankness. But I supported for more than five years the administration of his successor. I did for it what I could—little enough, God knows. The first case in which I differed from that administration was the ease of the Yazoo claims, which I thought a case of flagrant corruption! I do not mean, and I never did believe, that there was corruption in the president or his two secretaries; and it did not cause me to separate myself from them. I separated from that administration three years afterwards, with pain and sorrow, and not without some anger too; for I have no idea of that extreme of candor and meekness which denounces the measures of a government, as Bottom says in the play, "and will roar you as gently as any suckling dove." It is not my nature to do so; and it would be criminal and ridiculous in me, because it would be hypocrisy to affect it. When the former restrictive system was first commenced, I thought I saw what I now know I did then see—the fatal and ruinous consequences that would grow out of it. I told Mr. Jefferson, candidly and frankly, that if he expected support in a certain quarter and did not find it, he must not impute want of candor to me. I will not repeat what he told me on that occasion; it is unnecessary to say that his language and conduct was that of a gentleman. I frankly laid before him the facts and reasons which rendered such an event inevitable. I will not repeat what he said: but he deplored it.

Sir, I know that he deplored it—for he told me so. And when some of the *ear-wigs*, that infest all great men, sought to curry favor with him by relating, after their manner, the hard and sharp things which I was said to have uttered on the floor of this House on that occasion, he coldly replied, that, to do Mr. R. justice, he had been full as explicit as severe in his presence.* But permit me to reimnd you, sir—for you were then too young to know much of these matters—that previously, but nearly at the time of my leaving that administration, a certain wise man from the East joined it, who soon after went off to Canada, under strong suspicion of felony; and this was soon followed by a certain gentleman's giving in his adhesion, who had before been violently opposed to it, and to all its

---

* How unlike the existing system of delators, and spies, and runners, from the Senate Chamber or Hall of the Representatives to the Secretary of State's office or house during a debate, in which that great man does not choose to be present in person.

best measures. Sir, I have not the least objection to its being said of me, that I separated myself from Mr. Jefferson, when Barnabas Bidwell and John Quincy Adams joined him.*

---

*Never was an administration more brilliant than that of Mr. Jefferson's up to this period. We were indeed in the "full tide of successful experiment." Taxes repealed, the public debt amply provided for—both principal and interest—sinecures abolished—Louisiana acquired—public confidence unbounded. We had all, and we wanted more than all. We played for eleven and lost the game, when we held ten in hand. From the junction of Bidwell and Adams, we may date that embargo of fifteen months that eclipsed the sun of our glory, and disastrous twilight shed on more than half the nation. Mr. Madison removed this *incubus*, of which we were tired, but ashamed to rid ourselves. The arrangement with Erskine followed. At the May session of 1809 the House of Representatives evaded a motion expressive of their approbation of the promptitude and frankness with which the President had concluded this arrangement. It was soon after disavowed by England.

Mr. Madison's first message to Congress was sent on Tuesday, May 23, 1809, announcing the arrangement with Erskine, and the consequent restoration of our intercourse with England from and "after the 10th day of June next." "On Friday, the 26th, a motion was made by Mr. Randolph, and seconded, that the House do come to the following resolution:

"*Resolved*, That the promptitude and frankness with which the President of the United States has met the overtures of the government of Great Britain towards a restoration of harmony and a free commercial intercourse between the two nations, receives the approbation of this House." Reports Journal, 1 Sess. 11 Congress, page 35.

[Here is, I presume, another proof of Mr. Randolph's opposition to all administration, right or wrong.]

Mr. Ezekiel Bacon, of Massachusetts, moved to amend (in order to defeat it), and Mr. John G. Jackson, of Virginia, moved the indefinite postponement of both the resolution and amendment. It is curious to pursue the fate of this resolution through pages 39, when the House refused to resume the consideration of the unfinished business (which was Mr. Randolph's resolution)—pages 44, 45, 46—when the consideration of the resolution was carried by yeas 66, against nays 61 (a lean majority!)—all the decided friends of the administration voting in the minority, among them connexions of Mr. Madison himself—*e. g.* John G. Jackson, Richard Cutts, who were nearly connected with him by marriage. See further, pages 48, 49, 54, when the motion for indefinite postponement being withdrawn by Mr. Jackson, was renewed by another member—pages 62, 63—when (May 31st) the resolution received the *go-by* by an adjournment.

When Mr. Randolph was asked by the late Mr. Bayard and some other friend "What he thought of the state of things?" He replied that "we must have war with England." "With France you mean," said they. (For then our interdict—taken off England—was in force against France.) "No, with England. The vote of the House of Representatives, on the motion to approve the conduct of the President, assures me of that fact." And accordingly he wrote to his correspondent in Virginia to the same effect.

The embargo struck the first staggering blow on our agriculture, and *scuttled* our ships.

APPENDIX.

Some allusion has been made to the discordant materials of the present opposition. They are somewhat discordant—at least they have been so. But are they more so than the adherents of the present administration, or the materials of the administration itself? I well remember almost the first propitiation (the first was the writ of *habeas corpus*) which he who is now the President of the United States made to Mr. Jefferson and his party. It was an attempt to run down the present chief justice. The right of John Smith to a seat in the Senate was made the peg to hang it on. I will tell the gentleman the whole reason why I have opposed the administration since that time, and may again, if, according to my judgment, they shall not consult the good of the country. It is, Sir, simply because I am for the interests of the stockholders—of whom I am one—as opposed to those of the President, Directors, and Cashiers; and I have the right of speaking my opinion, and shall exercise it, though it happen to be against the greatest and proudest names.

Sir, I am no judge of human motives: that is the attribute of the name which I will not take in vain—the attribute of Him who rules in heaven, or who becomes incarnate upon earth: motives free from alloy belonged to that Divine incarnation, and to Him only, of all that have borne the form of man. Mere man can claim no such exemption.

I do not pretend that my own motives do not partake of their full share of the infirmity of our common nature—but, of those infirmities, neither avarice nor ambition form one iota in the composition of my present motives. Sir, what can the country do for me? Poor as I am—for I am

---

The landed and navigating interests have never recovered from it. It is the *nidus* * of the manufacturing system and policy—fostered since by the war by double duties and by tariffs. What bounty on manufactures does the Harrisburg Convention propose that is equal to a total prohibition of exports?

* The hot-bed rather, and the *fomes* too. Virginia may thank herself. She is the author of her own undoing. Mercantile clamor induced her in an evil hour to commence the restrictive system. She laid embargoes, and at length made war for "Free Trade and Sailors' Rights." *Cui bono?* The Hartford nation, as Mr. J., their greatest, although unintentional benefactor, denominated them. *We* took the *credit, they* the *cash*. "Which had the better bargain?" "Honest Congreve is a man after my own heart." The Hartford nation may sing now to an old tune—

"*Populus me sibilat at mihi plaudo
Ipse domi, simul ac nummos contemplor in arca.*"

General reflections are always unjust, and therefore unwise. Mr. Randolph greatly respects many New England men, and many points in the New England character. He regrets the change at home, as well as there, from the original distinctive marks of the cavalier and the covenanter. New England has no longer her Samuel Adamses and her Roger Shermans. Virginia also seeks in vain for her Washingtons, and Randolphs, and Blands, and Lees, and Nelsons, and Henrys. But, at the worst, the character of a miser is far preferable to that of a spendthrift. Even the cheat is not more contemptible than the bubble.

much poorer than I have been—impoverished by unwise legislation—I still have nearly as much as I know how to use—more certainly than I have at all times made a good use of—and as for power what charm can it have for one like me? If power had been my object, I must have been less sagacious than my worst enemies have represented me to be (unless, indeed, those who would have kindly shut me up in bedlam) if I had not obtained it. I may appeal to all my friends to say whether "there have "not been times when I stood in such favor in the closet that there must "have been something very extravagant and unreasonable in my wishes if "they might not *all* have been gratified." Was it office? What, sir, to drudge in your laboratories in the departments, or be at the tail of the corps diplomatique in Europe? Alas! sir, in my condition a cup of cold water would be more acceptable. What can the country give me that I do not possess in the confidence of such constituents as no man ever had before? I can retire to my old patrimonial trees, where I may see the sun rise and set in peace. Sir, as I was returning the other evening from the capitol, I saw—what has been a rare sight here this winter—the sun dipping his broad disk among the trees behind those Virginia hills, not allaying his glowing axle in the steep Atlantic stream; and I asked myself if, with this Book of Nature unrolled before me,[*] I was not the most foolish of men to be struggling and scuffling here in this heated and impure atmosphere, where the play is not worth the candle? But then the truth rushed upon my mind that I was vainly perhaps, but honestly, striving to uphold the liberties of the people who sent me here—yes, sir, for can those liberties coëxist with corruption? At the very worst the question recurs,—Which will the more effectually destroy them?—collusion, bargain and corruption here, or a military despotism? When can that be established over us? Never, till the Congress has become odious and contemptible in the eyes of the people. I have learned, from the highest

---

[*] " O how canst thou renounce the boundless store
 Of charms which Nature to her votary yields!
 The warbling woodland, the resounding shore,
 The pomp of groves and garniture of fields,
 All that the genial ray of Morning gilds,
 And all that echoes to the song of Even,
 All that the mountain's sheltering bosom shields,
 And all the dread magnificence of heaven,
 O how canst thou renounce and hope to be forgiven?"

of all authority, that the first step towards putting on incorruption is the putting off corruption. That recollection nerves me in the present conflict, for I know, that if we are successful, I shall hold over the head of those who shall succeed the present incumbent a rod which they will not dare, even if they had the inclination, to disobey. They will tremble at the punishment of their predecessors. Sir, if we succeed, we shall restore the constitution—we shall redress the injury done to the people—we shall regenerate the country. If the administration which ensues shall be as bad as the character of the opposing candidate [General Jackson] is represented by his bitterest foes to be, still I had rather it were in the seat of power than the present dynasty, because it will have been fairly elected. The fountain of its authority will not be poisoned at the source. But if we perish under the spasmodic struggles of those now in power to reïnstate themselves on the throne, our fate will be a sacred one—and who would wish to survive it? There will be nothing left in the country worth any man's possession. If after such an appeal has been made to the people, and a majority has been brought into this and the other House of Congress, this administration shall be able to triumph, it will prove that there is a rottenness in our institutions which ought to render them unworthy of any man's regard. Sir, my "*church-yard cough*" gives me the solemn warning, that whatever part I shall take in the chase I may fail of being in at the death. I should think myself the basest and the meanest of men—I care not what the opinion of the world might be—I should know myself to be a scoundrel, and should not care who else knew it—if I could permit any motive, connected with division of the spoil, to mingle in this matter with my poor but best exertions for the welfare of my country. If gentlemen suppose that I am giving pledges they are mistaken—I give none—they are entitled to none—and I give none. I shall retire upon my resources—I will go back to the bosom of my constituents—to such constituents as man never had before, and never will have again—and I shall receive from them the only reward that I ever looked for, but the highest that man can receive—the universal expression of their approbation—of their thanks. I shall read it in their beaming faces—I shall feel it in their gratulating hands. The very children will climb around my knees to welcome me. And shall I give up them and this? And for what? For the heartless amusements and vapid pleasures and tarnished honors of this abode of splendid misery, of shabby splendor, for a clerkship in the War Office, or a foreign missson, to dance attendance abroad instead of at home, or even for a department itself? Sir, thirty years make sad changes in man. When I first was honored with their confidence I was a very young man, and my constituents stood almost in parental relation to me, and I received from them the indulgence of a beloved son. But the old patriarchs of that day have been gathered to their fathers; some adults remain, whom I look upon as my brethren: but the far greater part were children—little children—or have come into the world since my public life began. I know among them grandfathers, and men muster-free, who were boys at school when I first took my seat in Congress. Time, the mighty reformer and innovator, has silently and slowly, but surely, changed the relation between us; and I now stand to them *in loco parentis*—in the place of a father—and receive from them a truly filial reverence and regard. Yes, sir, they are my children—who resent, with the quick love of children, all my wrongs, real or supposed. Shall I not invoke the blessings of a common Father upon them? Shall I deem any sacrifice too great for them? To them I shall return, if we are defeated, for all the consolation that awaits me on this side of the grave. I feel that I hang to existence but by a single hair—that the sword of Damocles is suspended over me.

If we succeed, we shall have given a new lease to the life of the constitution. But should we fail, I warn gentlemen not to pour out their regrets on General Jackson. He will be the first to disdain them. The object of our cause has been, not so much to raise Andrew Jackson to the Presidency—be his merits what they may—as the signal and condign punishment of those public servants on whom, if they be not guilty, the strongest suspicion of guilt must ever justly rest.

NOTES.

NOTE A, PAGE 279.—It would be matter of curious inquiry to ascertain how it has come to pass that in proportion as we in Virginia have proscribed or abandoned the cheerful exercises and amusements of our fathers, we have become less amiable and moral as a people. When I was a young man, no gentleman was ashamed of playing a game of billiards or of cards. There was much less gaming then than now. Men then drank and played in public, from a spirit of society, as well as the love for both inherent in human nature. Publicity is the great restraint upon individuals as well as government. The "*hells*" of London and the styes of Capreæ and the *Parc aux Cerfs* attest this. Publicity represses excess, until the man is sunk in the beast and every restraint of shame thrown off. Formerly, friends had it in their power to restrain the votaries of chance or of the bottle; but now their incurable ruin, in mind, body and estate, gives the first notice of their devotion to play or drink. Solitary intoxication on ardent spirits is the substitute for the wine table; and in some den of thieves, some cellar or some garret, the unhappy youth is stripped of his property, with no witness of the fairness of the game but his desperate and profligate undoers.

In Virginia we are, and I trust shall ever be, alive to States rights. But have the people no rights as against the Assembly? All oppression commences under specious pretexts. I have wondered that no rural, or rather rustic, Hampden has been found to withstand the petty tyranny which has as good a right to take away his wife's looking-glass or frying pan as his billiard table. By what authority is this thing done? Under color of law, I know, but a law in the teeth of all the principles of free government.

The principle of what is called the dueling law—it ought to be called the perjury law—is yet more detestable. I am no advocate of dueling; but it may be put down by something worse. Bad as it is, it is better than dirking and gouging; and they are hardly worse than calling names and bandying insults, if so bad. The oath prescribed by the dueling law is in the teeth of every principle of free government, of the act for establishing religious freedom, and would justify any test, religious or political, even an oath of belief in transubstatiation.

We were a merry-making, kind-hearted, hospitable people, fond of "*junketting*" (as the old President of the Court of Appeals used to say); and no one, as the men of Caroline county and Essex can testify, liked "junketting" ("*soberly*," as Lady Grace says,) better than Edmund Pendleton. Yes, the Mansfield of Virginia, whom he resembled in the polished suavity of his manners, his unrivalled professional learning and abilities, and the retention of his faculties unimpaired to a very advanced old age. There is another splendid example of the same rare qualities in the first judicial officer of the United States. Who is fonder of a game of billiards, or any other innocent amusement, than the Chief Justice? Yes, I regret, nay, deplore, the change from our old and innocent pastimes and holidays to the present state of listless *ennui* or prowling rapacity. In proportion as we have approached puritanical preciseness and gloomy austerity, so have we retrograded in morals.

I do not indeed carry the matter quite so far as an acquaintance of mine, who has a knack of "hitching into rhyme," and who, among other good advice, says:

* * * * * * *

"Hence, if you have a son, I would advise,
(Lest his fair prospects you, perchance, may spoil)
If you would wish him in the State to rise,
Instead of GROTIUS, let him study HOYLE.
And if his native genius should betray
A turn for petty tricks, indulge the bent;
It may do service at some future day;
A dextrous CUT may rule a great event,
And a stock'd PACK may make a President."

NOTE B, PAGE 287.—After my arrival in Europe, I saw in the newspapers Mr. Webster's toast, given, if I forget not, on the fourth of July— " Henry Clay, the orator of the West," &c., &c. I quote from memory. N. B.—Mr. Clay was then the rival and declared enemy of Mr. Adams. Mr. Clay, in the debate on the Greek motion of Mr. Webster, and in the affair of Mr. Ichabod Bartlett (a name of omen), was ostentatious in his declarations of friendship and connection with Mr. Webster, whom he gratuitously assumed to have been assailed by the said Ichabod! that he might manifest his devotion to his new friend. I then looked upon Mr. Clay as laying an anchor to windward and eastward, and in fact offering his blandishment to New England in the person of Mr. Webster, while at the same time he proclaimed his strength in that quarter as the ally of Mr. Webster and the powerful party of which he is the leader and mouthpiece. If the maxim be true, *ars est celare artem*, then there lives not a less artful man upon earth than Mr. Clay. His system consists in soothing by flattery, or bullying—these constitute his whole stock in trade—and very often he applies both to the same person. The man of delicacy, to whom his coarse adulation is fulsome, and the man of unshaken firmness, when these two characteristics unite in the same person, cannot be operated on by him.

Mr. Webster and the rival of Chilly McIntosh were put on the A. B. Committee to run down Mr. Crawford. I too, though in Baltimore when Mr. Floyd (my colleague) moved to raise that committee, was put upon it. I was not then the *political* friend or supporter of Mr. Crawford. His political principles, on the United States Bank and some other questions, were to mine nearly, although not quite, as obnoxious as those of his competitors. I never took sides with him until he was persecuted. Mr. Macon and Mr. Floyd both know that, on my arrival from Baltimore, I peremptorily declared that I would not serve on that committee. I believed it to be (as it was) a snare for me—a snare from which I providentially escaped. Mr. Webster's true character first developed itself to me then, as at the time I told Mr. Tazewell. At the earnest persuasion of Mr. Macon and entreaty of Mr. Floyd, I reluctantly agreed to serve. Mr. Floyd being taken violently ill and confined to his bed, I abandoned my seat in the committee and went abroad for health.

NOTE C, PAGE 294.—A caterpillar comes to a fence; he crawls to the bottom of the ditch and over the fence, some of his hundred feet always in contact with the subject upon which he moves. A gallant horseman at a flying leap clears both ditch and fence. "Stop!" says the caterpillar, "you are too flighty, you want connection and continuity: it took me an hour to get over; you can't be as sure as I am, who have never quitted the subject, that you have overcome the difficulty and are fairly over the fence." "Thou miserable reptile," replies our fox-hunter, "if, like you, I crawled over the earth slowly and painfully, should I ever catch a fox, or be anything more than a wretched caterpillar?" N. B.—He did not say, "of the law."

NOTE D, PAGE 297.—Some of the members of the Richmond Adams Convention (I like to call things by their right names) have had, I am told, the modesty to say that "it was the most august body that had assembled since the Congress that declared independence!" The same declaration, in the very same words, was made in the Senate, concerning another "august body"—the Hartford Convention—by Mr. Otis, a member of said "august body."

This moderate hyperbole, I suspect, must have come from some wiseacre south of Appomattox, or of Roanoke, who was at once his own constituent body and representative. I know many very worthy and respectable members of the "august body"—two of them, in particular, excellent and sensible men, my own good friends and constituents, whose names, I own, surprised me when appended to such a manifesto. Others, no doubt, are equally respectable. But what shall we say—not to the Secretary—no, it is needless to say anything of him. His name, associated with that of Chapman Johnson, must be grateful to that distinguished luminary of the bar and of Virginia. In our part of the country we still retain the old-fashioned prejudice against the three degrees of borrowing, begging and stealing. We still believe, in Charlotte and Prince Edward, that every honest man pays his just debts. If I were to go to Oakland (where I hope soon to be), and were to steal one of my friend William R. Johnson's plough horses, value perhaps sixty dollars, I should subject myself to the penitentiary. But would he not rather be robbed of a work horse than that any man should buy MEDLEY or SALLY WALKER of him for some thousands of dollars and never pay him. *Suum cuique tribuito* is still held in respect with us; and we pay small deference to the opinions of judges, even in the last resort, whose creditors cry aloud in vain for justice against the dispensers of justice—a judge who finally and conclusively determines between *meum* and *tuum*, who possesses nothing *suum*. If we do have a convention, I trust that the corrective will be applied to *this* and some other abuses of the only privileged class among us.

"Some are born great, some achieve greatness, and some have greatness thrust 'upon them?" and this last has been the good luck of our political Malvolio. Like Moliere's Mock Doctor, the Virginia Assembly (who make towns without houses) have made him a judge in spite of himself— *Malgrè lui*.

His worthy elder brother stumbled upon his office, as Falstaff says Worcester did upon rebellion: "It lay in his way, and he found it."

Some men should bear in mind the advice of Junius to Sir William Draper, and not attract the public attention to a character which will only pass without censure when it passes without observation. *Quædam causæ modestiam desiderunt.* And this is true of the persons of certain would-be leaders in the cause of Coalition, as it is of the cause itself. What business have these "most forcible Feebles" in the van of election battles? Who gave them the right or the power to call conventions, forsooth, and excommunicate and anathematize their betters, in every point of view that gives value to the character of man. Let them stick to their dull, heavy, yet light, long-winded opinions in the Court of Appeals, where to our sorrow and to our cost they may play "Sir Oracle"—where, when they ope their lips no dog must bark—but what they say must be received as law in the last resort—without appeal. No bill of exceptions can be tendered to their honors. Yes, let them keep to their privileged sanctuary.— For if these men, who are great by title and office only, shall attempt to interfere between men at arms, let me tell them that their judicial astrology will stand them in little stead: "There is no Royal road to the Mathematics:" and these *ex officio* champions will fare like the delicate patrician troops of Pompey at the battle of Pharsalia. The Tenth Legion will aim at their faces—and our fair-weather knights must expect to meet with cracked crowns and bloody noses, and to staunch them as they may.

"But have you no respect for the ermine?" Yes, as I have for the lion's skin, but none at all for the ass beneath it. I was bred in a respect for the ermine, for I lived when Pendleton, Blair and Wythe composed the "High Court of Chancery" in Virginia. Yes, I respect the *pure* ermine of justice, when it is worn as it ought to be—and as it is by the illustrious judge who presides in the Supreme Court of the United States, with modest dignity and unpretending grace. I was bred in a respect for it approaching to religious reverence. But it is the unpolluted ermine that I was taught to venerate. Daggled in the vile mire of an election—reeking in the fumes of whiskey and tobacco—it is an object, not of reverence, but of loathing and disgust. "A parson may not" (say the canons of many churches) "use himself as a layman." And a judge is, so to speak, a lay parson. He should keep himself, emphatically, "unspotted from the world." A judge has political rights as well as a juror. God forbid that I should deny or suppress their exercise. It is the mode of exercise that I object to, as unbecoming, not to say indecent.

We have no faith, on the south side of James river, in the president who called or him who presided over the Richmond Adams convention—the successor, in form, of Pendleton and Spencer Roane. Lichas wielding the club of Hercules. A man who does not endeavor to make up by assiduity and study for the slenderness of his capacity and his utter want of professional learning.

They were so heartily ashamed of their president or secretary, perhaps of both, that their manifesto is sent forth to the world in a pamphlet, unattested by the signature of either. It is without *teste;* and, notwithstanding the caption, may be said to be anonymous. The want of such signatures detracts nothing from its weight or value.

But let us see the honorable means resorted to by these High Priests of Themis, to forward their unholy conspiracy against the South; Virginia in particular. Without paying the ex-Presidents the respect of presuming them to be observant of that reserve imposed upon them by their position, and which, of all our Presidents, one only has violated—Mr. Adams, senior; or of consulting them, the names of Mr. Madison and Mr. Monroe are ostentatiously stuck up at the head of their ticket. They knew that these gentlemen could not, with any sense of propriety or decorum, accept or decline the proffered honor, until officially notified of the proceedings by the president of the Adams convention.

This notification was held back nearly one month by the president of the Adams, *alias* "Anti-Jackson," convention (who, to our misfortune, is also president of the High Court of Errors and Appeals), upon a pretext at once frivolous and *false*. This trick of the highest judicial officer in Virginia, played off to effect public opinion, and the Vermont and New Hampshire elections especially, was worthy of a Newgate solicitor. It was done to affect public opinion, and especially the New Hampshire election. How short-sighted is fraud and falsehood and folly. They did not reflect upon the reaction when the trick could be no longer concealed.

"There is a tide in the affairs of men,
Which, taken at the flood, leads to Fortune."

Mr. C. is as strong an instance of this as Shakspeare himself could have adduced. Hardly a second rate lawyer at the county court bar of Amherst and Buckingham, sheer accident made him governor of Virginia. Happening then to be a member of the Assembly [when a very obnoxious character was held up for the office]—possessing good temper and amiable manners, and most respectable and powerful connections—*the untying of* *a member's shoe* caused him to be pitched upon to keep out the only candidate. With that exception, the office was going a-begging. Conducting himself most unexceptionally and inoffensively as governor, he had a county,* and one of the finest, too, in the State, named after him, and was advanced to the Court of Appeals, of which he bids fair to be president; a court in which, if he had remained at the bar, he most probably would never have obtained a brief.

My venerable friend, Mr. Macon, has more than once observed to me, that, with the exception of North Carolina, no state, not even Virginia, had named a county after or done honor to the president of the first Congress, who, if he had lived, and the day had gone against us, would, with another Virginian, have been singled out as the ringleaders of the REBELLION, and made examples of, accordingly, *in terrorem* of all future offenders.

I have seen the Lord Chief Justice of the court of Common Pleas, Sir William Draper Best and Sir John Bayley (both very infirm men) sit, day after day, the one at *Nisi Prius*, and the other on the Crown side, from nine in the morning until five in the afternoon, and despatch more business in one day, than any of our courts in Virginia transact in a week. I have seen a judge in Guildhall sitting in court with his teapot and bread and butter before him, taking his breakfast while counsel were pleading, that business might not be delayed. The judges in England (there are but thirteen for that great kingdom, where each of three counties that I could name contain more white people, and incomparably more wealth, than our poor Old Dominion) work harder and are worse paid than any other officers of that government.

How is it with us in Virginia? We find men anxious enough to get the appointment—but are they (in the general) as anxious to discharge the duties—to earn the salary as to draw it? There are, no doubt, and to my personal knowledge, honorable exceptions; but are there not too many instances in which very insufficient causes are laid hold on to excuse the judge from holding his court, and for breaking it up and going home, to the delay of justice and the harassment and expense of counsel, suitors and witnesses? Is not this a crying evil? And if the tenure by which judges hold in Virginia be changed, will it not be owing to their own neg-

---

* If it had been called after his uncle, old Colonel Will. Cabell, of Union Hill, all would have cried, Well done! Posterity, it is to be hoped, will know no better.

ligence and misconduct? In England, where two counties of the northern circuit (York and Lancaster) contain more than two millions of inhabitants, and vastly more wealth than the kingdom of Prussia, such neglect of duty as occurs every day in Virginia would not be tolerated for one half year. "*To delay justice to no one,*" and "*to be unwilling to change the laws of England;*" these are the oath and declaration of the ancient Kings and Barons of England.* But we seem to be guided by maxims the very reverse of these.

As to the laws, they are so often chopped and changed that we never have time to find out what the existing law is—much less to have it settled in the only way that it can be settled—by adjudication. Much of this evil has proceeded from the Senate, at the instance of the author of the Richmond Adams manifesto. I have seen Sir John Bayley try some six or eight criminals in one day, that here would consume the time allotted for one, or more than one, superior court. It is true there lawyers are only admitted to cross-examine the witnesses, and are not suffered to take up a day in frothy declamation to mislead the jury. But I can conceive of no form of trial more fair than that in England; and the summing up of Sir

---

* It is impossible, even at this day, to read the ancient evidences of our liberties, without a throb of gratitude to those brave men who extorted their acknowledgment not only from such weak and worthless princes as John and Henry the III, but obtained their confirmation by Edward the I, the Justinian of England, a warlike monarch, and perhaps the most sagacious and powerful of all that wondrous race of kings—the Plantagenets.

"*Nullus liber homo capiatur vel imprisonetur aut disseisiatur de libero tenemento suo, vel libertatibus vel liberis consuetudinibus suis, aut utlagetur, aut exulet, aut aliquo modo destruatur, nec super eum ibimus, nec super eum mittemus, nisi per legale judicium parium suorum, vel per legem terre. Nulli vendemus, nulli negabimus aut differemus rectum vel justitiam.*"—MAGNA CHARTA, confirmed 25 EDW. I.

No free man shall be taken or imprisoned, or be disseised of his freehold, or liberties, or free customs, or be outlawed, or exiled, or any otherwise destroyed; nor we will not pass upon him, nor condemn him, but by lawful judgment of his peers, or by the law of the land. We will sell to no man, *we will not deny or defer to any man either justice or right.*

They put the *denial* and *delay* of justice on the same foot.

Well might Lord Chatham, in the greatest of all his incomparable speeches, say of these precious words, couched in "the rude and simple Latin of the times," that they were "worth all the classics!"—"*Nolumus leges Angliæ mutari.*"—"We are unwilling that the laws of England be changed," was the answer of those "Iron Barons" to the Sovereign who wished to introduce the Salic law of the continent in lieu of the English law of descents. This change would have deprived England of two of her most glorious reigns—those of Elizabeth and Anne.

John Bayley (who is, indeed, counsel for the accused) is the most perfect specimen of fairness and clearness and conciseness that I have ever heard or can conceive. He never omits the most minute circumstance that makes for or against the prisoner; and without showing the least bias either way, he never fails to tell the jury that "if, upon the whole, they doubt, the accused is entitled to the benefit of that doubt." I cannot go so far as an Irish gentleman, whom I heard (humorously) say at Norwich assizes, "that it must be a pleasure to be hanged by Sir John Bayley;" but I take a pleasure, and a pride too, in here naming the honor that I received in his acquaintance, and that of Lord Chief Justice Best, and the very kind attentions and hospitality by which I was distinguished by both of them, the last more especially.

The trials that I speak of were ordinary cases, civil and criminal; not cases of libel and treason—of *political* law. In England, as in other countries, not excepting Virginia, I fear that there is always a leaning on the side of the bench to POWER, in whatever hands it may be placed.

NOTE E, PAGE 300.—Mr. Madison (I speak it without the slightest disrespect to that eminent man) is a still stronger case in point than Mr. Pitt. Except Mr. Jefferson and Mr. Jay,* as Secretary of State, he had not perhaps his equal in our country—his superior nowhere—a profound thinker, a powerful reasoner, "with tongue or pen"—a great civilian, reminding one of his prototype, John Selden; to whose "MARE CLAUSUM" no man was better fitted than Mr. Madison to have opposed a MARE LIBERUM. Yet, advanced to the helm of affairs, how consummate his ignorance of men, let his selections for great offices, civil and military, tell. I will enumerate a few just as they occur to me, beginning with his cabinet.

Secretary of State—Robert Smith.

Secretary of the Treasury—George W. Campbell; also Minister to St. Petersburg.

Secretary of War—Dr. Eustis.

Secretary of the Navy—Paul Hamilton and Benjamin W. Crowninshield, the Master Slender—no, the Master Silence of Ministers of State.

---

* As Mr. Jay is mentioned, I cannot omit my poor tribute to the example of consummate dignity which this great and good man has set to every other great man in retirement. He has been withdrawn from public life too long (yet even here his error leans to virtue's side), about thirty years. Who sees, or has seen, his name in a newspaper? *O si sic omnes!*

Shakspeare himself could go no lower. It is the thorough base of human nature. He seems to us to have drawn Robert Shallow, Esquire, and his cousin Slender, as the comparative and superlative degree of fatuity; and when we believe that he has sounded his lowest note, as if reveling in the exuberance of his power, he produces Silence as the *ne plus ultra* of inanity and imbecility. Mr. Madison has, in this one instance, outdone Shakspeare himself—he gives us the real man whom the bard only drew.

Attorney General—Richard Rush; not being fit for Comptroller, he is selected to preside over the treasury! and by the Richmond Adams Convention for Vice President!

Commander in the Northwest—William Hull.

Commander in the Northeast—James Wilkinson and Wade Hampton.

Commander at Bladensburg—William Winder! assisted by "The Flying Cabinent," as Wilkinson had the insolence to designate them in his diagram of that famous rout. In this memorable *disengagement* the GRAND ROLE was played by Mr. Attorney General, "for that time only," *without his hat.* We have no "Master of the Rolls" in our country; but, like the witty authors of the Rolliad, for Sir Lloyd Kenyon, we might take as a motto for Mr. Rush, " *Jouez bien votre role.*" And, verily, never did political adventurer make more of his *parts* than this solemn gentleman has done. Never were abilities so much below mediocrity so well rewarded; no, not when Caligula's *Horse* was made Consul.

A few days ago I stumbled upon the following stanza of an unfinished poem on the Glories and Worthies of our Administration:

> "And as for R., his early locks of snow,
> Betray the frozen region that's below.
> Though Jove upon the race bestow'd some fire,
> The gift was all exhausted by the sire.
> A sage consnm'd what thousands well might share,
> And ASHES! only, fell upon the heir!"

These lines are the only article of the growth, produce or manufacture of the country north of Patapsco, that I have knowingly used since the Tariff bill passed. They are by a witty son of a witty sire—as Burns sings, "a true gude fellow's get."

NOTE F, PAGE 301.—Mr. Clay took his seat in the House of Representatives in December, 1811; his first stride was from the door to the chair, where he commenced to play the dictator: he fixed his eyes on the presidency, and I, who had been twelve years in Congress, fixed mine upon him, and have kept them there ever since. Sylla said that he saw many a Marius in Cæsar. So I, who had heard Mr. Clay for the first time in the Senate the year before, on the renewal of the charter of the Bank of the United States, was persuaded that he would not keep the faith. Without affecting an inferiority that I do not feel, I may be allowed to say, that my position as the guardian of the constitution and country, against the assaults of a man goaded and blinded by his ambition, would have placed a dwarf on a level with a giant. He went to Europe, and returned a changed man.

And not Mr. Clay only. Mr. Monroe, the stern Mr. Monroe, for whom General Washington's administration was not Republican enough, comes back after four years spent in Paris, Madrid, and London, to settle points of *etiquette and invent coat patterns* for our foreign ministers, because, forsooth, they are not Franklin's. (See Mr. Sergeant's speech.) So that, like the king's fool, our envoys must have a party-colored coat to make up for their want of sense and dignity.—" *Motley is your only wear.*"

NOTE G, PAGE 283.—With this venerable friend and sterling patriot, Mr. Randolph believes that "the great body of the people of New England are genuine Republicans, of steady and virtuous habits, unsurpassed by any other people upon earth. But they are too often hoodwinked by the priesthood and the press in the interest of the aristocracy.

POSTSCRIPT, IN LIEU OF A PREFACE.

It is unnecessary perhaps, but candor demands the avowal, to apprize "the courteous reader" that there is much in the foregoing speech that was not spoken on the floor of the House of Representatives. There are some things too, for example, page 281, lines 32 to 38, reported not as the speaker said them; but, at the distance of a fortnight, under the pressure of other avocations, he could not correct such parts of the report. Not recollecting what he did say, he was fain to let it stand, although he was conscious that he had not said what is there set down. To his friends he is indebted for the restoration of many passages which their memory had preserved and recalled to Mr. Randolph's recollections. Of these he will here indicate but two relating to Mr. Jefferson, in pages 402 and 303, and the page preceding, referring to Othello.

This date speaks volumes to the old, tried, consistent Republicans. This day, seven and twenty years ago, not two hours after its commencement, the elder Adams* took his flight from the capitol, shrouding himself in darkness from the intolerable light of day and the public gaze. What should we have said that morning if it had been predicted that the son, without the recantation of a single principle, with no other recommendation but that which has been held anything but a recommendation elsewhere, with no other recommendation but that of an approver or states' evidence should, in four and twenty years, succeed that father? Ay, and that an "August Convention" in Virginia should recommend and support that son for this high office against an uniform, unwavering, tried Republican, who had fought in the war of our Revolution, and shed his stripling blood for his country, and who, in the second war with England had crowned himself and her with imperishable renown—laurels that

---

* On reaching an inn beyond Baltimore, 'tis said that Mr. Adams, walking up to a portrait of Washington, and placing his finger on his lips, exclaimed, "If I had kept my lips as close as that man, I should now be the President of the United States."

can never fade, that will flourish and grow green in history and in song, while Mississippi shall pay his tribute to the sea!

Men of the South! matrons and maids of Louisiana! How say you? Do you find against your defender? Republicans of every state and clime! How say *you?* Do you find for the Sedition Law and its advocates against a tried Republican in the Reign of Terror?

"Remember March! The Ides of March remember!"
"Shall Rome ———? Speak, strike, redress!"

MARCH 4, 1828.

www.ingramcontent.com/pod-product-compliance
Lightning Source LLC
Chambersburg PA
CBHW021206230426
43667CB00006B/583